Jean M. Baker, PhD

How Homophobia Hurts Children

Nurturing Diversity at Home, at School, and in the Community

Pre-publication
REVIEWS,
COMMENTARIES,
EVALUATIONS . . .

"In *How Homophobia Hurts Children,* Jean Baker provides a readily accessible resource for parents and many school professionals while simultaneously giving beginning and intermediate college students a valuable supplementary text for understanding the multiple psychosocial issues, and resilience, of gay, lesbian, bisexual, and transgender youth. Dr. Baker supports her perspectives with research that she explains thoroughly and clearly enough for the lay reader; she also engages us with personal experiences from her own life with two gay sons. On one hand, *How Homophobia Hurts Children* enumerates the real and serious challenges facing gay youth in the United States today, but on the other it also offers hope through concrete means of creating change and fostering health in our communities and our homes.

This is a book for all allies to youth—required reading for parents, extended family, school personnel, and anyone in relationship with young people who identify as gay or with youth who are questioning their sexual orientation. Students of cultural diversity, human development, educational psychology, and secondary education will also want to read *How Homophobia Hurts Children.* Dr. Baker provides the reader with practical suggestions that anyone can follow to enhance the lives of young people who will grow up to be gay."

Gary Hollander, PhD
Administrator, Center
for Urban Population Health,
University of Wisconsin
Medical School,
Milwaukee

More pre-publication
REVIEWS, COMMENTARIES, EVALUATIONS . . .

"**D**r. Baker has written a thoughtful, factual account of what gay, lesbian, bisexual, and transgender youth suffer in our public schools and in their personal lives. The survey and research data cannot be refuted. The quotations by students and teachers must be listened to. This is a book that all educators—counselors, teachers, administrators—as well as mental health professionals should read, and then take action to end the harassment and victimization that GLBT youth suffer. Of particular interest are the chapters on transgender, since so little is known and understood about this community.

This book should be used at the university level as part of every teacher-preparation program as well as in graduate programs in education and counseling. It should be absolutely required reading for these professionals."

Alan L. Storm, PhD
Chair-elect of the
Committee on Lesbian,
Gay, Bisexual Concerns
(CLGBC), American
Psychological Association;
Assistant Superintendent
for Student Services,
Sunnyside Unified
School District,
Tucson, Arizona

"**W**ho better to instruct us in *How Homophobia Hurts Children* than Jean Baker who, in her first book, *Family Secrets,* bravely confronted her own homophobia and the devastating impact it had on her and on those she was closest to—her two gay sons. Now she has gone beyond the personal to the universal, helping others to recognize in themselves what she had difficulty recognizing in herself.

This book offers a passionate argument for parents, for schools, and for communities to take the lead in shattering the silence around homosexuality, a silence that gay and lesbian youth cannot break all by themselves. It is a plainly written, step-by-step call to arms for making the world a safer place for those who are 'different' and for all of us together.

In words simple and direct, these brave young people have now spoken for themselves. Is anyone out there listening? Jean Baker is."

Andrew R. Gottlieb, PhD
Author,
*Out of the Twilight:
Fathers of Gay Men Speak*

"**H**ow *Homophobia Hurts Children* offers a comprehensive look at the overwhelming challenges facing GLBT youth and offers concrete steps on how to make our homes, schools, and communities safer for all children. Dr. Baker presents successful practices and policies that have made a difference and can be implemented in communities nationwide. *How Homophobia Hurts Children* will help people in all areas of society understand the problems, the pain, and the needs of GLBT youth. Indeed, the lives and well-being of the next generation depend on it."

Kirsten Kingdon
Executive Director,
Parents, Families,
and Friends of Lesbians
and Gays (PFLAG)

How Homophobia Hurts Children
Nurturing Diversity at Home, at School, and in the Community

HAWORTH Gay & Lesbian Studies
John P. De Cecco, PhD
Editor in Chief

How Homophobia Hurts Children
Nurturing Diversity at Home, at School, and in the Community

Jean M. Baker, PhD

Harrington Park Press®
An Imprint of The Haworth Press, Inc.
New York • London • Oxford

Published by

Harrington Park Press®, an imprint of The Haworth Press, Inc., 10 Alice Street, Binghamton, NY 13904–1580

PUBLISHER'S NOTE
Interviewee names and circumstances have been changed to protect confidentiality.

Cover design by Jennifer M. Gaska.

Library of Congress Cataloging-in-Publication Data

Baker, Jean M.
    How homophobia hurts children : nuturing diversity at home, at school, and in the community / Jean M. Baker.
        p. cm.
    Includes bibliographical references and index.
    ISBN 1-56023-163-7 (alk. paper)—ISBN 1-56023-164-5 (alk. paper)
    1. Homophobia—United States. 2. Gay youth—United States—Psychology. 3. Gay students— United States—Psychology. 4. Sexual harassment in education—United States. 5. Coming out (Sexual orientation)—United States. I. Title.

HQ76.45.U5 B34 2001
306.76'6—dc21
                                                                                2001045682

To the memory of my son
Gary Thomas Baker,
and to my son
Andrew Jackson Baker

ABOUT THE AUTHOR

Jean M. Baker, PhD, is a clinical psychologist who has had a private practice in Tucson, Arizona, since 1970, the year she received her doctorate from the University of Arizona. She has been a consultant on child abuse and neglect to the State of Arizona Child Protective Services since 1980.

Dr. Baker is a past President of the Arizona Psychological Association and currently serves as Chair of its Gay/Lesbian/Bisexual Issues Committee. She is also a member of the American Psychological Association, the Southern Arizona Psychological Association, PFLAG (Parents, Families, and Friends of Lesbians and Gays), and GLSEN, the Gay, Lesbian, Straight Education Network. She is also a member of Wingspan, Tucson's Gay, Lesbian, Bisexual, and Transgender Community Center, and serves as Co-Chair of its Youth Services Committee.

Dr. Baker is the author of *Family Secrets: Gay Sons, A Mother's Story* (Haworth, 1998). She has written articles and book chapters on child custody and child development. She has presented papers at professional conferences, including the APA, on gay/lesbian and AIDS-related issues. She has received awards from the Arizona Psychological Association for Outstanding Contributions to the Practice of Psychology (1999), the Southern Arizona Psychological Association for Outstanding Contributions to Psychology (1997), and the Godat Award from Wingspan for Outstanding Contribution to the Gay, Lesbian, Bisexual, and Transgender Community in Tucson, Arizona (1999).

CONTENTS

Acknowledgments

This book was made possible by the inspiration of my sons and by the contributions of many other people. I am especially grateful to the young students who were willing to share their stories about what high school was like for them as sexual minority youth and to the four transsexual adults, Michael, Alexander, Mark, and Jeffrey, who described the traumas involved in having an inner sense of gender identity that does not conform to one's physical body.

I owe a great deal to three people who read the manuscript or part of it and gave valuable feedback on the content and the organization. Amelia Craig Cramer read the chapter on legal issues and gave me invaluable feedback based on her legal expertise and broad knowledge of GLBT issues. Richard Muszynski, a clinical psychologist with expertise in GLBT issues and a dear friend, read the entire manuscript verifying accuracy and improving clarity. My son Andrew is a great editor and made many helpful suggestions to improve the organization and flow of several of the chapters.

I am most grateful also to the two teachers, Gayle Brickert-Albrecht and Guy Velgos; the school nurse Tam DeWitt; and the school librarian Sally Hansen, all of whom have been GSA (Gay/Straight Alliance) sponsors at their respective schools and who were willing to take the time to submit to lengthy interviews with me and share their experiences. Thanks also to teacher Barb Mathers for her very moving and insightful coming-out story.

In addition, thanks to all the wonderful and helpful people at The Haworth Press: Bill Palmer, Jennifer Gaska, Rebecca Browne, Lisa Welch, Dawn Krisko, and lastly Peg Marr, who did a monumental job of editing a far less than perfect manuscript. Thanks also to editor Dr. John De Cecco for believing in this and my previous Haworth book.

Introduction

Gay children and adolescents are moving silently and secretly through our lives—through our homes, our schools, and our communities. Very often nothing distinguishes these children from other children and so no one knows they are growing up to be gay. Long before they have any real understanding of what the word means, gay children have already been instilled with the belief that to be gay is something terribly unnatural and shameful. When a child finally figures out that maybe he or she is one of these people, one of these "homosexuals," the child is struck with the realization that all those disparaging comments heard throughout childhood apply to himself or herself. Those casual, degrading remarks about homosexuals based on false stereotypes and used in unthinking or joking ways can stamp themselves on the minds of children who are trying to figure out how they fit into a world that sometimes seems not meant for them.

As a clinical psychologist who has worked with children for over thirty years, and as a mother of two gay sons, I have developed a compelling interest in the ways in which gay children experience the prejudice around them, a prejudice that may be as strong in their own families as it is in society at large. The secrecy and the stigma surrounding the experience of growing up gay can keep these children from reaching out to their families, their friends, or their teachers. Most of them are forced to cope totally alone with the growing knowledge that they are part of a disdained group, a group that their parents and friends seldom belong to.

Through examining my own experiences as a mother of gay children, interviewing youth who have been participants in gay/straight alliances (a commonly used term for gay support groups or clubs in high schools), interviewing gay adults remembering their childhoods, studying the research documenting the experiences of gay children in their homes and schools, and applying my training and experience as a psychologist, I have identified some ways in which we can bring about significant and positive differences in the lives of gay children.

In this book you will read about the experiences of these children, in their own words; what it is like for them as they gradually discover they are different from most other children in this one particular way: their sexual orientation. Adults involved with children—as teachers, parents, coaches, school principals, counselors, physicians, and Sunday School teachers—are bound to come in contact with these children though they are seldom obviously different from their peers. If you are an adult in a role that touches the lives of children you will have an impact, whether intentionally or not, on how children struggling with their sexual identity come to view themselves. There is nothing you can do to prevent children from growing up to be gay, but there are many things you can do and say to help them keep their hopes and dreams alive and to help them grow up to lead happy, fulfilling lives.

Many of the suggestions I make in this book involve simple steps that any individual can take which can enhance the lives of children who will grow up to be gay. These are changes in behavior and language requiring little effort other than awareness and willingness. I also suggest additional steps that are somewhat more complex and might require more demanding personal changes in behavior and attitude. Finally, I present ideas about more radical changes in education, in legislation, in social policies, and in the way we think about parenting.

Homosexuality, in and of itself, is not the problem facing gay children. The problem is the reaction of families and of society. We do not need to change gay people. We do not need to "cure" them. What we do need to cure is homophobia.

Chapter 1

Shame Can Shatter Their Dreams

> I was around thirteen when I realized what I was and the more I found out, the more scared I became, how it was in society and the family. (Eighteen-year-old girl)

Though many believe that there are no gay children, these children do exist and their minds and souls are shaped as they gradually grow in the awareness that they belong to a group disdained by many, sometimes even by the people closest to them. It is during their childhoods, before they are aware of sexual orientation and what it means, that these children begin to understand how our society views homosexuality. If children growing up to be gay hear little information to the contrary, their imaginations may be indelibly stamped with a sense of inferiority. They may come to believe that certain doors will be forever closed to them. Too many even come to feel that suicide is the only alternative to life as a homosexual.

Somehow, in the midst of the antigay rhetoric, a very simple fact gets lost: the fact that in every society there are and will always be individuals who fall in love with persons of their same gender. Another fact that gets lost in the clamor, one that is more difficult to acknowledge for those who believe homosexuality is a shameful or sinful condition, is that there will always be children who are growing up to be gay or lesbian. Denying that gay children exist allows the antigay movement to avoid placing itself in the ugly position of accusing children of being immoral or evil and further suggests that if we were only able to rid the world of gay adults, then there certainly would be no gay children. This perspective may come about as a result of one of the more damaging myths concerning homosexuality: that children would never grow up to become gay or lesbian unless some "perverted" gay adult had first molested, converted, or corrupted them. But elimination of adult homosexuals from the world or keep-

2

HOW HOMOPHOBIA HURTS CHILDREN

ing children away from any contact with homosexuals would not eliminate a new generation of gays and lesbians. Children growing up to be gay or lesbian will not disappear because of social disapproval. No vaccine can prevent homosexuality in children. No parenting methods or religious admonitions can do so. There will always be children who will grow up to be gay.

We now know that, despite the social ostracism and the pressures to be heterosexual, homosexuals constitute a small part of every society. We also know that sexual orientation, whatever its origin, is often established at an early age and is not readily susceptible to change.

HOMOPHOBIA: A RESPECTABLE PREJUDICE

Peter J. Gomes, professor of divinity at Harvard University, has referred to homophobia as "the last respected prejudice of the century." Gomes' words help explain why so many gay children and adolescents grow up afraid of what their lives are going to be, afraid that they will face harassment and ridicule if their secret identity becomes known. Gomes' words also help explain why even people who would never make racist or anti-Semitic remarks feel free to express disdain for "queers," and why we still have laws in states and communities across our nation that explicitly deprive homosexuals of basic civil liberties. Abuse and humiliation of homosexuals has long been actively allowed and even condoned by our society. And it is the social acceptability of this prejudice that contributed to keeping gays and lesbians silent for so long, fearful of asking for equal treatment. After all, if almost everyone seems to agree that antigay prejudice is justified, that there is something intrinsically wrong with being homosexual, then why should gays expect equality?

THE GAY RIGHTS MOVEMENT

As the civil rights movement of the sixties gained momentum, it gradually expanded to include sexual minorities, empowering some gays and lesbians to believe that they too had civil rights. Public protests against mistreatment of homosexuals were slower to erupt than among other minorities, but erupt they eventually did.

One of the early protests, and certainly the most highly publicized, happened spontaneously on a June night in 1969 at a popular gay bar, the Stonewall Inn, in the Greenwich Village area of New York City. The Stonewall had long been a site for police raids, a place where customers were routinely arrested and hauled off to police stations for nothing other than their sexual-minority status. On that night, the long-passive bar customers resisted arrest and fought back against the astonished policemen.

Though not the first protest of the gay liberation movement, Stonewall became its symbol and its driving force. Once started, the rebellion was irrevocable and increasing numbers of gays and lesbians began to come out of hiding and join in the demand for equal rights. The fight continues to this day and progress has been made. Public attitudes toward gays have become more positive and certain court rulings and laws have ensured rights that were not previously granted. More details about these legal issues, about progress in the gay rights movement, and about what is still needed will be discussed in later chapters.

THE HOMOSEXUAL DEBATE: PATHOLOGY OR NORMAL VARIATION?

Homosexuality was for so long a hidden issue, something not discussed openly except perhaps in clinical or criminal terms. But one major effect of the gay rights movement has been to force homosexuality into the realm of public discourse, to force an open discussion on a topic many would prefer to ignore. The inflammatory debate provoked by the gay rights movement raised questions around the nature and origin of homosexuality. In other words what is it, what causes it, and why does it exist? On one side of the debate, homosexuality has been defined as a crime, a sin, a sickness, an irresponsible choice, a sexual perversion, a dangerous threat to family values, and even a destroyer of morale in the armed services. On the other side, it is viewed not as any of these, but as a natural variation of human sexuality that occurs in every society. People with widely diverging viewpoints about sexuality, morality, and equality and inequality take opposing positions. The antihomosexual advocates claim that family values are threatened while gay supporters argue for their human rights and assert their own definitions of family values.

GROWING UP IN A HOMOPHOBIC CULTURE

Although significant progress toward acceptance of homosexuals has been achieved by the gay rights movement, antagonism and disrespect toward gays is still evident to anyone who reads a daily newspaper or watches TV news. The famous as well as the unknown feel free to vilify homosexuals and proclaim them undeserving of equal treatment. The implicit superiority of heterosexuality is the subtext underlying homophobia. Following, however, are some examples of explicit public messages about homosexuals that gay children and adolescents have grown up with. It is not difficult to imagine how these public messages, added to the implicit and explicit antigay messages they already hear from peers and adults in their private lives, must make them feel about themselves.

- General Colin Powell, former chairman of the Joint U.S. Chiefs of Staff, in the early 1990s repeatedly stated that allowing openly gay individuals to serve in the armed services would be demoralizing and would jeopardize the effectiveness of the military. General Powell's view helped define the current hypocritical policy of "don't ask, don't tell." (In other words, it's OK to be gay as long as you keep it a secret.)
- In 1992, the state of Colorado passed a constitutional amendment stating that no laws or statues could be enacted anywhere in the state or in any of its agencies or subdivisions entitling any person to claim discrimination on the basis of sexual orientation. Fortunately, in 1996, this amendment was overturned as unconstitutional by the U.S. Supreme Court in the *Romer v. Evans* decision. The majority opinion, written by Justice Anthony Kennedy, said, "A state cannot so deem a class of persons a stranger to its laws."
- Religious right groups urged their members to boycott Disneyland and Disney products in the late 1990s because of the Walt Disney Company-owned TV channel airing an episode of the sitcom *Ellen* in which the Ellen DeGeneres character comes out as a lesbian.

- Dr. Laura Schlesinger, a well-known TV commentator and columnist, writing "I see homosexuality as a biological faux pas—that is, an error in proper brain development with respect to potential reproductivity." (Rutenberg and Elliott, 2000, p. A-22)
- The Boy Scouts of America banned gays and atheists from membership in its organization and expelled an Eagle Scout assistant scoutmaster in 1990, when it was revealed in a newspaper article that he was gay. On June 28, 2000, U. S. Supreme Court Justices, in a five-to-four decision, ruled that expelling a gay scoutmaster was within the organization's constitutional rights.
- Former U. S. Senate Majority Leader Trent Lott declared homosexuality a sin and compared it to alcoholism, sex addiction, and kleptomania. (Lacayo, 1998, p. 34)
- In South Carolina Reverend Stan Y. Craig, pastor of a Baptist church in Greenville, called homosexuality "demonic" and "a stench in the nostrils of God." (Sack, 1998, p. A-12)
- A group of religious organizations including the Christian Coalition and the Family Research Council sponsored newspaper advertisements in major newspapers, including *The Washington Post, The New York Times,* and the *San Francisco Chronicle,* proclaiming that homosexuality is a free and sinful choice and can be cured. (Leland and Miller, 1998)
- A young gay man, Matthew Shepard, was brutally murdered in Wyoming in the fall of 1998 by two other young, presumably heterosexual, men who disliked "fags."
- In Arizona, in 1997, state legislators for the second time introduced legislation that would ban student gay support groups in public schools, claiming that such groups would be "part support group, part recruitment."
- Also in Arizona, one state legislator declared publicly that she finds homosexuality "disgustingly disturbing" while another said, "Gays want to sodomize and I don't want them recruiting for that."
- The U.S. Senate blocked the presidential nomination of a gay man, James Hormel, as Ambassador to Luxembourg because senators were disturbed by his sexual orientation.
- The Southern Baptists, at their annual meeting in 1999, voted to denounce President Clinton for his order proclaiming June as Gay and Lesbian Pride Month.

- The Army Reserve, in 1999, began an investigation of a twenty-seven-year-old Republican State Representative in Arizona because he publicly admitted that he loves another man. Another fall-out from the faulty "don't ask, don't tell" policy.
- A 1999 study found that 45 percent of military officers agreed with the statement that homosexuals should be barred from teaching in the public schools.

Messages denigrating homosexuals are not limited to those reported in the mass media but are repeated daily in homes and neighborhoods where gay children live and play and in the schools they attend. These messages can profoundly affect how gay children come to view themselves.

How Homophobia Affects Gay Children

Extremist antigay attitudes and practices inevitably harm homosexual youth, making them feel that something must be fundamentally wrong with who they are. Children are not born, of course, knowing they are gay or straight. They only gradually figure out the true nature of their sexual feelings and attractions. But before they are even aware of sexual feelings, those children who are growing up to be gay may start to catch on that they are different from other children and that this difference is shameful in some mysterious and poorly understood way. As they gradually become more aware of their sexual attractions they become frightened about what these feelings will mean in their lives. They may even come to hate that part of themselves that others seem to hate, a process that has been called "internalized homophobia." This is a process of incorporating into one's own self-image the negative feelings associated with the label "homosexual," and it can cripple hopes and dreams for a productive future. Internalized homophobia may also help explain why gay youth are believed to attempt suicide at rates that are much higher than the rates among their heterosexual peers (Gibson, 1989; Goodenow and Hack, 1998; Remafedi, Farrow, and Deisher, 1991; and Roesler and Deisher, 1972).

How Homophobia Affects Nongay Children

Heterosexual children also are influenced by the homophobia in society. When they hear adults infer that gays are inferior and do not deserve respect, this attitude influences how they will treat their peers whom they perceive to be gay. The mistreatment of gay children by other children is a direct result of the attitudes that children have learned from the adults in their lives. When respected adults express contempt for homosexuals, how can heterosexual children help but conclude that it is permissible to harass other children whom they believe to be gay? Even gay children themselves, in desperate attempts to fit in and avoid being identified, may participate in the harassment of those children who have been targeted. Prejudiced adults send a powerful message to children that intolerance toward gays and lesbians is acceptable and that this group of people differs in such a unique way from others that their mistreatment is justified. We can see then that just as homophobic remarks made by adults hurt gay children directly, they also hurt them indirectly through their impact on nongay children who learn that it is OK to make fun of other children just because they appear to be gay.

WHAT IS IT LIKE TO GROW UP GAY?

Gay children often grow up with no one recognizing or accepting who they really are. As they become aware of their sexual feelings they also become aware of the stigma of homosexuality. They are afraid to tell anyone. They worry about their futures. They are sometimes very young when they begin to feel that somehow they are not like other children. Maria, an eighteen-year-old high school student, recalled that as early as first or second grade she started feeling different from other children and began to sense that she didn't really fit in.

> I noticed that the little girls were avoiding the boys and the boys were hitting the girls. I noticed the girls more, but I was more comfortable with the guys. I was definitely a tomboy. When I was about twelve, I understood what the term gay meant. It finally clicked. That's what it is. I now knew what I was. The bad thing was that everybody said it was immoral—my grandmother, my family. I felt ugly, horrible; I wanted to change. That was my goal. If I couldn't change I would still have to try to lead a straight life.

Rich, thirty-seven years old at the time of our interview, in recalling his childhood experiences also remembered the feeling that he didn't fit in with other children, that he was different somehow. He remembered his struggle trying to figure out what that difference meant.

> I had an awareness of being different at age six or seven and of the difference being shameful. I liked kickball, basketball, and so forth, but the girl games also felt natural. Playing the girl games quickly got you labeled as "homo" or "sissy." In fourth or fifth grade I connected together what homo or sissy meant and I knew it applied to me, but I couldn't quite articulate it. Awareness grew by high school when I had the cognitive ability to understand what homosexual men were. But I purposely tried not to acknowledge this in myself because of internalized homophobia. I allowed myself to think I was bisexual. I would think that I can't allow myself to be gay. I have to marry and I can't give expression to these feelings.

Ivy, a seventeen-year-old girl, said that she realized she was different by middle school, around age ten or eleven, but she had no idea what it meant.

> I would bond with my girlfriends and get really close. I thought everybody was that way. I had never met anybody gay. But in my freshman year in high school I started thinking, maybe that's what I am. I was very uncomfortable about it. I was raised that it was wrong and I thought it was wrong.

These memories of what it is like to grow up gay were similar to the thoughts that emerged in many of my interviews with students who were members of gay/straight alliances and support groups in high school. These young people talked about what it is like to go through each day of their lives worried about how they are going to be treated by other people and how they are going to deal with their sexual identity.

> The hardest thing in high school is the name calling, the physical and mental abuse. To be tormented day in and day out. It still goes on. (Eighteen-year-old girl)

I felt shame to begin with and I have had to overcome it. I'm still ashamed in dealing with my family members. I've tried to deny my sexuality. (Sixteen-year-old boy)

Waking up every morning and not knowing what to expect. Having to face another day, the prejudice. Dealing with what other people think about you. (Eighteen-year-old girl)

It's how some people treat you. Some people are so skeptical, unbelieving that we can be human. We get asked prying questions about what we do in bed. We wouldn't ask straights what they do in bed. It's like prying. Very uncomfortable. (Seventeen-year-old girl)

I got tormented my freshman year. Name calling, people throwing things at me. (Seventeen-year-old girl)

What's hard in high school is not being able to be open. It's your teen years and you want to be accepted. Straight couples can hold hands, but we don't because we're afraid. (Sixteen-year-old girl)

When I was thirteen, I went into a deep depression. I thought there was only one way out. Suicide. I just wanted to end it. (Eighteen-year-old girl)

If you're in the closet you have to put on a face and build walls, but if you let others know they put you in a category, their own conceptions or stereotypes. (Eighteen-year-old girl)

The hardest thing is trying to get out of the mind-set of intolerance that other kids have. Also feeling paranoid about what people may do. You are conditioned to watch your back twenty-four hours a day. (Eighteen-year-old boy)

People talking behind your back, starting rumors, making fun of you, whispering. People who don't respect those who are not "perfect." So they will humiliate you. Making you feel all queasy. (Eighteen-year-old girl)

ADULT ATTITUDES

What do parents, teachers, politicians, clergy, and therapists say? How does what they say affect gay children? Most parents do not allow even the glimmer of a thought that they themselves might have a gay or lesbian child. And schools, acting as though they have no gay or lesbian students, are places where teachers hardly mention homosexuality and where children suspected of being gay are taunted and teased while teachers and administrators do not seem to notice. Politicians, catering to certain groups of voters, sponsor legislation to deny gays certain civil rights and claim that "family values" are threatened by homosexuals. Some churches condemn homosexuality as a sin. Certain therapists call it an illness and attempt to "cure" it. So it is that many gay children as they grow up are exposed to antigay sentiments in the broader community, while at the same time in their own homes, in their schools, and in their churches they hear that homosexuality is immoral and sinful.

When gay children hear their parents make demeaning remarks about gays they begin to be afraid that their own parents might stop loving them if their terrible secret were discovered. Or if parents never mention homosexuality, positively or negatively, children may come to believe that their feelings are so incomprehensible that there are no acceptable words for their experience.

If children then attend a school where teachers never utter the word homosexual, they hear another powerful message; that to be a homosexual is such a horrifying possibility that it must not be spoken of. As Ernestine Schlant (1999) pointed out in her book, *The Language of Silence: West German Literature and the Holocaust,* silence is itself a form of speech that conveys its own message.

When children suspected of being gay are harassed and tormented by their peers with minimal reaction from teachers or administrators, the underlying message is that homosexuals deserve to be mistreated. Additionally, if there are no openly gay teachers or administrators in the school, the message is that you should not aspire to a respectable career if you are a homosexual.

Then, finally, the child may attend a church where homosexuality is decried as one of the deadly sins. In fact, children growing up gay may be surrounded by adults in all areas of their lives who teach them, directly or by omission, that they are imperfect in some significant and uncorrectable way.

Why Parents Don't Help

Most parents are uneducated and misinformed about sexual orientation and are themselves persuaded by the messages of sin, crime, and sickness. They do not recognize that their child is gay or they refuse to accept it if they do find out. Unlike the parents of children from other minority groups, the parents of gay children are seldom members of the minority to which their children belong and this lack of common experience can hinder even the most well-intentioned parents from helping their gay children feel OK about who they are and about the way they happen to be different from other children.

Parents, Families and Friends of Lesbians and Gays (PFLAG) is an organization which has responded to the needs of families who learn they have a gay family member. It is dedicated to helping families support their gay children and family members and learn more about sexual orientation. This organization began in 1981 with a small group of parents in one community. PFLAG has grown from that one small group into an organization with a national office, currently based in Washington, DC, and with hundreds of local chapters in communities throughout the United States and Canada and in several foreign countries. Among its many services, PFLAG offers support groups for parents who are trying to cope with their child's homosexuality, educates the public about sexual orientation issues, and advocates for gay rights. PFLAG is especially concerned about mistreatment of gay children in the schools and one of their major goals is expressed in a project called "Safe Schools for All Our Children."

But not every parent of a gay or lesbian child joins PFLAG and those who do join are often already more understanding and supportive than the average parent even before attending their first meeting. Also, and most important for the purpose of this book, in my own experience as a member of PFLAG, the majority of PFLAG members are parents of college-age or adult gays and lesbians. I suspect this is because parents of younger gays and lesbians are seldom aware of their child's sexual orientation. By the time parents discover they have a gay child they may have already added to that child's negative self-image through casual remarks or by silence and simply never having acknowledged in day-to-day conversations with their child that homosexuals exist.

The Role of Churches

Some religious institutions still perpetuate homophobia and contribute to its harmful influence on children. Leadership for gay rights among churches is only beginning to emerge from the religious community. And many gay children, already frightened by the voices of intolerance surrounding them, are taught in their churches that they are sinners because of what they cannot help being. The frequently voiced nostrum, "Love the sinner, but hate the sin," does little to comfort a gay child. The position of some churches in accepting homosexuals and offering them love, compassion, and pastoral support but only if they do not practice homosexual sex is not very comforting advice for an adolescent becoming aware of his or her sexual orientation. An additional fallout from the churches' position that homosexuality is a sin is that it gives credence to individuals who use the power of the church merely to justify their own bigotry.

The drastic effect that an intolerant church had upon one gay child is graphically illustrated in the book, *Prayers for Bobby: A Mother's Coming to Terms with the Suicide of Her Gay Son* (Aarons, 1995). In this book, the mother of a gay son tells the story of how the influence of her church prevented her from accepting her child's homosexuality and led her to pressuring him to try to change. The extent to which Bobby was tormented by the lessons he had been taught in his church and by his family is revealed in quotes from his personal journal, written when he was sixteen years old:

> I can't let anyone find out that I'm not straight. It would be so humiliating. My friends would hate me. They might even want to beat me up. And my family? They've said they hate gays, and even God hates gays, too. Gays are bad, and God sends bad people to hell. It really scares me when they talk that way because now they are talking about me (p. 57).

On the night of August 27, 1983, Bobby Griffith, age twenty years and two months, jumped off a bridge onto a freeway and died instantly when he was hit by a large tractor trailer. His mother came to feel that her efforts to save her son from damnation had helped drive him to suicide.

Why Schools Are Important

For those gay children whose parents are unaware, unable, or unwilling to tolerate the concept of having a gay child, and who may attend churches that denounce gays as sinners, schools become a last resort and a decisive influence in how they will come to view themselves. However, at this point few individual schools in the United States and even fewer school systems openly acknowledge the particular difficulties confronting gay children as they are growing up. And few have established policies and procedures to help make schools safe and accepting places for them. Many if not most schools still pretend that homosexuality does not exist among youth. Or some knowingly choose to ignore the issue as the simplest and safest solution to avoiding the controversy that might erupt were they to openly acknowledge their gay students and take steps to protect them. Silence is the response of many schools to the issue of gay students.

One impressive example to the contrary is Massachusetts, where, in 1992, then-Governor William Weld, disturbed by the data revealing the high frequency of suicide among homosexual youth, appointed a Governor's Commission on Gay and Lesbian Youth. The Commission held public hearings throughout the state, listening to gay and lesbian teenagers as well as to school and community representatives, and then reported to the Governor a broad list of recommendations presented in a manifesto titled *Making Schools Safe for Gay and Lesbian Youth* (Governor's Commission, 1993). These recommendations were later implemented at the Governor's order in school districts throughout the state.

Among the recommendations of the Massachusetts commission were that schools change their policies to protect gay and lesbian students, that teachers and staff have specific training on gay issues, that there be school-based support groups for gay and straight students, that there be information in school libraries for gay and lesbian adolescents, and that the curriculum include gay and lesbian issues. Massachusetts, thanks to Governor Weld and to the commission, has led the nation in its sensitivity to the needs of gay youth in schools.

Antigay prejudice, like other minority group prejudices, contributes to violence and discord in society as well as in the microcosm of the school itself. School playgrounds, hallways, bathrooms, cafeterias, and even classrooms are places where harassment of gay youth is often witnessed and are the places where the need for protection is greatest. Gay children harassed at school, fearful of revealing their secret, often do not tell their parents and neither do the harassers tell their parents, so parents are unable to take steps to protect gay children or to teach straight children that bullying and taunting is wrong. The school is a key player in implementing the changes needed to reduce violence and to protect gay children from the teasing and taunting that may seriously damage their self-esteem and emotional well-being.

Public schools can play a vital role for gay children and adolescents by helping to counteract stubborn societal prejudices and also by reflecting the changes in public opinion about gays that have occurred in recent years. Schools should acknowledge that there are gay students in their midst and making it clear that harassment toward them will be treated in the same way as harassment toward any other group. Schools should stress the importance of the dignity of all students and explicitly include gay and lesbian students. Schools should not allow a small sector of the population that believes homosexuality should not be mentioned in schools to deter them from doing what is right for all their students.

One of the first and most important steps for schools to take, as noted in the Massachusetts recommendations, would be to expand cultural diversity programs and antidiscrimination policies to specifically include sexual minorities. Although cultural diversity programs and antidiscrimination policies have become common in many schools, seldom are gay, lesbian, and bisexual students or faculty explicitly mentioned as minorities in the same manner as are ethnic, racial, and religious minorities. When school boards and administrators take just this single and simple step it gives a reassuring message to gay students that they matter and it informs heterosexual students that antigay harassment won't be tolerated. This is one small but critical step that lets gay students know that it is OK to be gay.

But preventing overt discrimination and harassment, though necessary, is only a first step. Curricula should be modified to incorporate in a serious and scientifically accurate manner issues related to sexual orientation and to set forth the significant contributions to society that homosexuals and bisexuals have made throughout the ages. Sex education at appropriate age levels should include information about homosexual orientation and explicit information about the sexual transmission of AIDS and other sexually transmitted diseases. School administrators and faculties should become leaders in ensuring that gay children are given equal treatment in all aspects of their education. Overall, public opinion toward homosexuals is changing, and schools should be willing to take some flak for doing what is right rather than trying to placate a small vocal group that may disapprove.

Saving Our Gay Children

Let us remember that many children living in our midst are growing up lonely and frightened, struggling to understand why it is that what they are and cannot help being is said to be shameful. A radical transformation of the way society views sexual orientation and major changes in our social structures could protect present and future generations of our gay children from shame and stigma. But even if this transformation does not take place or before it does, those of you reading this book can remind yourselves that there are always going to be children who are growing up to be homosexual and that you can, in small and simple ways, make a difference in their lives. The attitudes you display through your behavior and through your words may deepen the shame these children feel or may lift their spirits in ways you may never know. Our gay children will not disappear. They will always be with us.

Children of Gay Parents

I wish to point out that the effects of antigay prejudice on gay children apply also to children who have gay parents. These children, too, as they hear homophobic remarks and observe the mistreatment of gays and lesbians, can become vicarious victims of prejudice and come to believe that if their parents are thought to be bad so, too, must they themselves be bad. Although this topic deserves more attention than can be given in this particular book, I should at least mention that research to date shows no evidence that the psychological adjustment of children raised by lesbian mothers or gay fathers is significantly different from children reared in heterosexual families. Children from gay families are essentially just as normal as a similar group of children from nongay families (Patterson, 1994, 1996; Steckel, 1987).

Schools, especially, need to become more aware that these families exist and reach out to them in a supportive way. An excellent resource for how to accomplish this can be found in a book chapter titled "Lesbian and Gay Parents Encounter Educators: Initiating Conversations" (Casper and Schultz, 1996). These authors urge lesbian mothers and gay fathers ". . . to move beyond their fears and talk to teachers about their family configurations and their sexual orientation" (p. 326). Only by opening up this issue can there be any hope for change in the way schools and society deal with children from gay families.

Chapter 2

Myths and Fallacies

I thought it was a disease. I thought about suicide all the time. I thought nobody would ever accept it. I could never have a happy life. I thought I should starve myself to death. (Sixteen-year-old boy)

Every child growing up in this country is confronted with the many negative stereotypes and myths about homosexuality. Over time those children who are growing up to be gay or lesbian begin to fear that this name, "homosexual," may apply to themselves and they begin to suspect that this is the reason for their vague feeling that they are different from other children. The age at which this realization occurs varies widely, but in recent years generally seems to be occurring earlier than previously. How frightening and confusing it must be for a child to face the fact that he or she may be one of these people, these "homosexuals" that everyone says are abnormal or sick. Secretiveness is very common at first. These children often have no idea where to find out what it means to be gay or lesbian. They are usually afraid to confide even in their parents or closest friends about the feelings troubling them. Their anxiety becomes more acute as they reach adolescence, the exact time when they most need peer acceptance and approval and also the time when they become even more aware of their difference from their peers. The self-esteem of children or adolescents who suspect they are gay or lesbian can be seriously undermined by the many myths they hear about gays, by their sense of the disapproval of society and the family, and by the fear that they will be denied the possibility of a happy and successful future.

MYTH: HOMOSEXUALITY IS A MENTAL ILLNESS

This is one of the more common stereotypes about homosexuality. The sickness label was for many years perpetuated by psychiatrists, psychologists, and other mental health professionals who were taught during their training that homosexuality was a psychiatric disorder. While I, myself, was in training as a clinical psychologist in the 1960s, scientific research had already discounted the mental illness theory but the results had not yet reached practitioners nor the clinical training programs. I knew nothing about the research until years after I left the classroom.

Psychologist Dr. Evelyn Hooker (1957) conducted the landmark study which laid to rest the theory that homosexuality is a sickness. She compared gay men and heterosexual men on a battery of psychological tests. When the results of these tests were scored and interpreted by eminent psychologists, unaware of which test results were those of gay men and which of heterosexual men, the psychologists were unable to differentiate between the two groups. The homosexuals showed no higher level of psychological disturbance than the heterosexuals. The finding confounded the professionals. How could this be, when so many eminent psychiatrists and psychologists had known with such certainty that homosexuality was a serious psychiatric disorder? Perhaps it was the threat to the egos of the mental health professionals, so certain in their imperfect knowledge, that explains why so much time elapsed before this research was incorporated into training programs and professional practice. Or perhaps it was merely because most of the homosexuals seen by psychiatrists and psychologists were those who did have serious psychiatric problems.

The many subsequent replications of Hooker's now-famous study all reached similar conclusions as noted in reviews by Gonsiorek (1982, 1991). Gay men and lesbians are *not* mentally ill, at least no more so than heterosexual men and women. But it was not until 1973, sixteen years after Hooker's findings had first been reported, that the American Psychiatric Association voted to remove homosexual orientation per se as a disorder from the *Diagnostic and Statistical Manual of Mental Disorders* (DSM). "Ego-dystonic homosexuality" was the new diagnosis used to replace homosexuality in the manual. This meant that a psychiatric diagnosis was used only for those persons whose psychological disturbance came not because they were homo-sexual but because they did not want to be homosexual or were un-happy about being homosexual. If an individual was happy as a gay man or a lesbian, he or she was no longer considered to be mentally ill just because of sexual orientation. In later versions of the manual all references to homosexuality were removed. In 1975, the American Psychological Association supported the decision of the American Psychiatric Association by issuing a policy statement urging psy-chologists to take the lead in removing the stigma of mental illness that had for so long been associated with homosexuality.

This does not mean that there are no psychologically unstable ho-mosexuals. Just as there are psychologically disturbed heterosexuals, there are psychologically disturbed gays and lesbians. But homosex-uality per se is no longer considered a mental illness. Indeed it is amazing that so many homosexuals, despite the discrimination they experience as they grow up, somehow survive and become produc-tive, creative adults.

The conclusion of those professionals who have been willing to consider the facts about sexual orientation through studying the sci-entific research is that homosexuality is not an illness, is not a sexual deviance, and is merely a fairly common variation of human sexual-ity, nothing to be afraid of, nothing to hate and despise, nothing to be ashamed of.

MYTH: HOMOSEXUALITY CAN BE CURED

Despite all the evidence that homosexuality is not a disease, some mental health professionals and therapists claim that sexual attraction between individuals of the same gender is a sickness that can be cured if only those so "afflicted" would seek treatment to help them change their orientation. Some of these professionals claim success in their efforts to cure. No valid evidence exists to support these claims of cures, only anecdotal reports, testimonials, and case examples. Douglas Haldeman (1991) reviewed the reports of these so-called "conversion therapies" or "reparative therapies" and concluded that there is no credible scientific evidence to support the theory that sexual orienta-tion can be changed.

Many health and mental health professional organizations, including the American Academy of Pediatrics, the American Counseling Association, the American Psychiatric Association, and the American Psychological Association, have adopted policies making it clear that they do not support reparative therapy to change people's sexual orientation. The policies of these organizations point out that reparative therapy has the potential to be harmful.

Information about this issue has been summarized in a brochure, *Just the Facts About Sexual Orientation and Youth* (American Psychological Association, 1999), which was distributed to all school superintendents in the United States and supported by the organizations just mentioned as well as a number of other major mental health and educational associations. *Just the Facts* attempts to make schools aware that the major mental health organizations in the country have joined in making clear the position that homosexuality is not an illness that needs to be cured and urges them not to yield to pressure to promote reparative therapy or "transformational ministry" (the use of religion to eliminate homosexual feelings) in their schools. Kevin Jennings, executive director of the Gay, Lesbian, and Straight Education Network (GLSEN), a group working to end antigay prejudice in schools, had the following to say about this document in a *New York Times* interview, "The entire mainstream education and mental health establishment has said that it isn't lesbian, gay and bisexual students who need to change, it is the conditions in our schools that need to change" (Goode, 1999).

It is certainly possible for someone to quit engaging in homosexual sex and begin having heterosexual sex. But behavior is not orientation. Most homosexuals are capable of performing sexually with the opposite sex; it is simply that their predominant sexual and romantic desires are toward their own sex. John Money, author of *Gay, Straight, and In-Between* (1988), has made this issue clear when he writes about the difference between sexual acts and falling in love. One is homosexual not because he or she has engaged in sex with someone of the same gender but because he or she can fall in love with someone of the same gender. Homosexual desires and attractions are just as strong as heterosexual desires and attractions and are unlikely to be eliminated by therapy. In the attempt to become "normal" through therapy, the individual may form heterosexual relationships, may avoid homosexual behavior, and may even marry and have children, but these behavioral changes do not mean the person has now become heterosexual. Not surprisingly, none of the "reparative" therapists have ever attempted to change heterosexuals into homosexuals and would likely say that such an attempt would be irrational. The success rate would, no doubt, be equally dismal.

Many mental health professionals now believe it unethical to attempt to change such a basic component of a person's identity and believe that the primary reason many homosexuals have even sought such treatment is the stigma associated with their orientation. Martin Duberman (1991) wrote a book titled *Cures: A Gay Man's Odyssey,* in which he describes his agonizing years of going from one therapist to another in an unsuccessful attempt to rid himself of his homosexuality.

During this time period, primarily the 1950s and 1960s, therapists still maintained the position that homosexuality was a mental illness and held out the hope of a cure to troubled people who believed they had an affliction. Therapy reinforced Duberman's sense of deviance but did not reduce his homosexual feelings in the slightest. His years of therapy were emotionally devastating as well as being totally unsuccessful in changing his orientation. Many gays and lesbians have had similar tragic experiences, sometimes seeking therapy at the urging of their families and sometimes just as part of their own usually futile efforts to conform to societal expectations.

Homosexuals may, of course, need psychotherapy for many different reasons just as do heterosexuals, not the least of which may be the need for help in coping with the feelings caused by an unaccepting and hostile environment. The homosexual patient whose self-image has been damaged by homophobia may need help in adjusting to and accepting his or her sexual orientation. What these people definitely do not need is to be made to feel guilty because they are gay or to be encouraged to try to become heterosexual.

This issue is particularly important for adolescents. Even the best-intentioned parents may make the dangerous mistake of sending their children to therapists to try to rid them of their homosexuality. Reputable therapists, however, should not agree to treat an adolescent with the specific goal of attempting to change his or her sexual orientation. Such treatment merely reinforces what may already be an undeserved sense of deviance on the part of the adolescent.

A seventeen-year-old girl describes her experiences of being in the hands of mental health professionals who apparently focused on her sexual orientation as the problem. "I was hospitalized three times and they kept saying 'you're suicidal because you're bisexual.' They didn't work on what my issues really were. What makes people suicidal is being afraid to come out, feeling that they have to hide."

MYTH: HOMOSEXUALITY IS A CHOICE

Another myth about homosexuality is that it is a choice. This is an argument frequently used to deny societal acceptance to gays and lesbians. But for the majority of homosexuals there is little question of a choice to be gay. Just as one doesn't choose to be heterosexual, one seldom chooses to be homosexual. If you are heterosexual are you able to even imagine that somehow this was something you decided to be? That you just woke up one day and said to yourself, "Oh, I think I'll become a heterosexual when I grow up"? Sexual orientation is better thought of as a discovery rather than as a choice, a discovery beginning in childhood and gradually developing over time throughout adolescence and early adulthood.

> Ever since I was six years old I knew I was gay, but I didn't know what it was until 6th grade. (Sixteen-year-old boy)

> I came out to myself when I was around fifteen. I felt in a way that I had always known, but I started to face it. I wasn't afraid except about what people might say. I was confused. (Sixteen-year-old girl)

> I think I was first aware of the feelings when I was twelve or thirteen. But I actually came out to myself when I was fifteen. I wasn't sure. I thought there might be something wrong with me. (Seventeen-year-old girl)

> I questioned early on when other little kids around nine or ten have a girlfriend or a boyfriend. I wasn't certain until eighth grade when I was thirteen or fourteen. Then it happened very fast. (Sixteen-year-old girl)

> By the middle of high school I had figured it out. I had plans for self-guided therapy to change. (Forty-year-old man remembering his adolescence)

If Homosexuality Is Not a Choice, What Causes It?

The stigma attached to homosexual orientation has been one factor leading to the questioning of its causation. Heterosexuality is not questioned, as it is assumed to be the natural and highly preferable state of human beings. When, as the mother of two gay sons, I was occasionally asked, "Why do you think both of your children turned out to be gay?" I had the feeling that the questioner might be implying that something had really gone wrong with my children. Although I do understand that perhaps having more than one gay child could seem unusual, the implication of such a question to a parent is that he or she must have done something really wrong, more wrong even than if he or she had only one gay child.

But the cause of homosexuality is still poorly understood. As with most complex human characteristics, sexual orientation is unlikely to result from a single cause such as a particular gene, a certain sort of family dysfunction, or a specific hormonal difference. Sexual orientation more likely results from an intricate and complex interaction among many different variables—prenatal or postnatal hormonal influences, biological differences in brain structure and function, genetics, early socialization, temperament, and possibly other, unknown factors.

Family Influences

Some psychoanalytic therapists, particularly those who believe homosexuality to be pathological, have attributed causation to certain family dynamics. The overly involved mother and the distant, uninvolved father have been cited as a family scenario that might lead to male homosexuality. These therapists sometimes claim that the homosexual male is seeking through sex with other males the love he did not receive from a positive father figure. The evidence for such simple familial influences is minimal, and Richard Isay (1989), a therapist who has treated many homosexual men, suggests that it is the gay child who influences the parents rather than vice versa. Isay writes that, although many of his gay male patients describe a close bond with their mothers and a more distant relationship with their fathers, this phenomenon may be the result of the son's sexual orientation, not the cause. Isay believes that there is a biological predisposition for homosexuality and that the father of the prehomosexual boy senses that his son is somehow different from other boys, becomes anxious in the father-son relationship, and tends to withdraw from his son.

In general, there is little scientific evidence for any particular family variables being strongly related to sexual orientation (Bell, Weinberg, and Hammersmith, 1981). This is not to say that it is inconceivable that complex family variables may somehow be a factor in the development of sexual orientation. But even if this were true, the variables are probably not the single, simplistic ones that have been examined so far. As all developmental psychologists know, children with different temperaments and personalities evoke different parental reactions and so determine to some extent their own family environments. The factors involved in the development of sexual orientation have so far and may always elude those who seek to find them.

Biological Influences

A number of studies do suggest possible genetic or other biological influences, although not necessarily direct causation, on the development of sexual orientation. For example, Simon LeVay reports in his book *The Sexual Brain* (1994) the discovery of physical differences in the hypothalamic area of the brain when he compared homosexual to heterosexual men. In other studies Allen (1991) and Allen and Gorski (1992) discovered that a certain area of the brain, the anterior commissure, was larger in a population of homosexual males than in heterosexual males.

Nevertheless, even if biological differences between the brains of gays and straights were to be definitively established, such a finding would not necessarily lead to the conclusion that sexual orientation is completely inborn or predetermined. We know that environmental factors, both prenatally and after birth, can alter both brain structure and function. From conception on, heredity and environment interact to influence human development. Neither has been able to be separated to account for sexual orientation or for many other complex human characteristics.

Genetic Influences. Among the studies suggesting an inherited or genetic influence on sexual orientation is one by Bailey and Pillard (1991), who researched sexual orientation in identical and nonidentical twins. They found that for 52 percent of identical twins, when one was gay, the other was also. For nonidentical twins, if one was gay, in 22 percent of the cases the second twin was also gay. These findings support the theory that there may be a genetic component to sexual orientation, since nonidentical twins share only 50 percent of their genes while identical twins share 100 percent. The higher frequency of shared sexual orientation in the identical twins compared to the nonidentical thus suggests a genetic component. However, if genetics alone were responsible, all or almost all, rather than just a little more than half, of identical twins should have the same sexual orientation, whether it be homosexual or heterosexual.

Other evidence for a genetic component to sexual orientation has been reported by researchers (Hamer et al., 1993; Hamer and Copeland, 1994) who discovered that some homosexual brothers share certain sequences of DNA on the X chromosome. Since a male child inherits his only X chromosome from the mother, this research suggests that a predisposition to male homosexuality might be inherited through the maternal genes. But a genetic predisposition to a particular sexual orientation is one thing, a completely genetic explanation is another, and probably unlikely to totally account for homosexuality.

Exotic Becomes Erotic

A highly novel theory has been proposed by Daryl Bem of Cornell University. Dr. Bem (1996) describes his theory in an article titled "Exotic Becomes Erotic: A Developmental Theory of Sexual Orientation." Bem believes that there may be biological predispositions involved in sexual orientation, but he does not believe that these predispositions lead directly to homosexuality. Rather, Bem suggests that a child's inborn temperament predisposes him or her to enjoy some childhood activities more than others and to prefer to play with peers who share these activity preferences. And it is those children who tend to prefer gender atypical activities who are more likely to develop homosexual orientation. Thus, a boy who is less inclined toward active, rough and tumble play and team sports will seek out as playmates children who prefer more passive, perhaps intellectual and artistic activities, and these are often girls. He tends to feel alienated from the more active, boisterous, assertive boys and feels psychologically estranged from them. Bem theorizes that this very sense of estrangement from other males leads the prehomosexual boy to eroticize them; thus, the "exotic," that which is unknown and mysterious, becomes the "erotic." Perhaps the most convincing aspect of Bem's theory may be that it could also account for heterosexuality, in that nongay boys who enjoy boy's activities and the companionship of other boys will have less contact with the girls, perceive them as "exotic" and mysterious, and thus as "erotic." On the other hand, this theory would not account for those gay boys who are very stereotypically masculine in their interests and who prefer the company of other boys during their growing up years. Nor would the theory account for those girls who, during their childhood, are very stereotypically feminine in their interests and prefer the company of girls and yet grow up to be lesbian.

Gender Nonconformity

A good deal of evidence supports that adult gay men and lesbians are more likely to remember gender-nonconforming or gender atypical behaviors and interests in childhood than are heterosexual men and women (Bell, Weinberg, and Hammersmith,1981; Bailey and Zucker, 1995). Gender role behaviors are usually measured by preferences for playing with same-sex or opposite-sex peers, rough and tumble play, toy preferences, imaginary role-playing, interest in competitive athletics, and dress-up play. In the Bell, Weinberg, and Hammersmith study, 89 percent of homosexual men compared to 55 percent of heterosexual men reported that they had avoided physical fights in childhood; avoidance of baseball was reported by 84 percent of homosexuals and only 38 percent of heterosexuals; and a preference for girls as playmates was reported by 33 percent of homosexuals but only 10 percent of heterosexuals. Similar findings, though not as strong, were reported by lesbians, who were more likely to describe themselves as tomboyish during their childhoods than were heterosexual women.

Childhood gender nonconformity for both male and female homosexuals was also found by Bailey and Zucker (1995) in their review and a metaanalysis of forty-eight studies. The total number of participants in these combined studies was impressive, with 11,298 heterosexual men, 5,734 gay men, 8,963 heterosexual women, and 1,729 lesbians being involved. The studies consistently showed that gay men recalled significantly more so-called feminine interests and activities during childhood than did heterosexual men on at least some of the measures. In reviewing studies of women, they found that lesbian and bisexual women recalled more typically masculine play preferences during childhood than did heterosexual women. However, these study results suggested that cross-gender type behavior in childhood is less predictive of homosexuality in girls than in boys. In other words, girls who exhibit tomboyish behavior in childhood are not as likely to grow up to be homosexual as are boys who exhibit effeminate behavior. It should be noted that the Bailey and Zucker reviews and the Bell, Weinberg, and Hammersmith study are all retrospective, meaning that they depended on adult recall of childhood experiences and are, thus, subject to the distortions that often occur in memory.

There are a few prospective studies (Green, 1987; Zucker, 1990) wherein boys were identified in early childhood as extremely gender nonconforming and were studied again years later when they became adolescents or young adults. In Green's study he identified a group of sixty-six extremely feminine boys, whom he referred to as "sissy boys," and a control group of nonfeminine boys. In the effeminate group 70 percent of the boys cross-dressed frequently, 50 percent played with dolls frequently, and over 40 percent occasionally expressed the wish to be girls. In the comparison group none of the boys cross-dressed, fewer than 5 percent played with dolls frequently, and fewer than 5 percent expressed the desire to be girls.

Green reinterviewed the boys when they were adolescents or young adults. He found that about three-fourths of the boys in the effeminate group reported that they had had homosexual fantasies and/or experiences while none of the control group reported homosexual fantasies or thoughts and only one reported having had homosexual experience. One of the boys in the effeminate group said that he was transsexual as an adult and planned to obtain sex-change surgery.

Zucker (1990) reviewed several prospective studies of boys who had displayed significant cross-gender behavior during childhood. Ninety-nine of these boys were followed to young adulthood or adolescence. At the time of the follow-up studies, fifty-nine had homosexual or bisexual orientation, twenty-six had heterosexual orientation, and fourteen could not be determined. It is important to realize that all of these prospective studies involved boys who exhibited marked gender nonconformity. Such extreme effeminate behavior is not typical of the majority of boys who grow up to be gay. There have been no prospective or follow-up studies of tomboyish girls.

The point I wish to make again is that gender atypicality is certainly not the sole path to homosexuality nor is it likely to be a sole explanation of its origin, unless perhaps in the sense that Bem described. Think of the gay male athletes, the highly masculine jocks who are homosexual, and the extremely feminine lesbians. As with any of the other single explanations for homosexuality—the biological, the genetic, the hormonal, family dynamics, or early socialization—none has so far been able to alone account for the vast range of gay men and lesbian women in their infinite variety.

Just as heterosexuals differ widely from one another, so too do homosexuals, and their sexual orientation is only a part of who they are, only a piece of their identity. Andrew Sullivan (1998) has suggested that, despite any gender atypicality in homosexuals, the differences between males and females are still far greater than the differences between heterosexuals and homosexuals.

MYTH:
HOMOSEXUALS ARE SEXUAL MOLESTERS

One of the more damaging and baseless myths about homosexuals, one that is used to argue that they are too dangerous to be around children, is that they are sexual molesters who prey on children. There is no evidence to support this belief. In fact, the studies that have been done (Burgess et al., 1978; Groth and Birnbaum, 1978; Jenny, Roesler, and Poyer, 1992, 1994) suggest that homosexuals may be less likely than heterosexuals to molest children. The Jenny study, for example, reviewed the records of 269 cases of sexual molestation of children examined at the Colorado Health Sciences Center and Children's Hospital and found that in only two of the cases were the perpetrators homosexuals. Dr. Jenny, in a reference to her study, has stated, "A child is 100 times more likely to be molested by a heterosexual partner of a relative than by a homosexual" (Scripps Howard News Service, 1993, pp. 4-10).

When young boys are molested by men, this is often taken as evidence that the molester is homosexual. However, many molesters are pedophiles, individuals who are sexually fixated on children. Sometimes the fixation is on male children, sometimes on female, and sometimes on both. Pedophiles often do not develop mature sexual relationships with adults and some have never had an adult sexual relationship, either homosexual or heterosexual. Sexual attraction to children is unrelated to sexual orientation and pedophilia should not be equated with homosexuality.

The experiences of Tiger, a sixteen-year-old boy, show the damaging effects of the stereotype of homosexuals as sexual molesters: He was falsely accused of sexually molesting a neighbor's son when the mother came to his house and told him that she knew that gay people like him recruited other little boys and she warned him to stay away from her child.

The argument that adult homosexuals such as teachers or Boy Scout leaders are likely to molest children is fallacious. The majority of homosexuals, like the majority of heterosexuals, are horrified at the notion of encouraging, coercing, or forcing children to have sexual contact with adults. Though there are individuals who do infringe upon the rights of others, including children, in their sexual practices, this has nothing to do with sexual orientation per se.

MYTH:
HOMOSEXUALS WILL CONVERT
CHILDREN TO HOMOSEXUALITY

Similar to the fear that homosexuals will molest children is the fear that they will try to "convert" young people to homosexuality. Such a fear is again unfounded. Sexual orientation is not the outcome of teaching or conversion. Such a theory goes against what is known about the development of sexual orientation. If homosexuality developed that way, there would be few or no homosexuals, since the messages and influences from society that children see and hear from a very early age, teach them to be heterosexual, not homosexual. And even if it were possible to persuade a child to be homosexual, homosexuals would have no reason or desire to try to influence children to become gay or lesbian.

MYTHS AND STEREOTYPES PERPETUATE PREJUDICE

These myths and most stereotypes about homosexuality remain merely that. They have little basis in reality and are responsible, at least in part, for the perpetuation of prejudice toward a group of people who are merely different in a particular way from the majority of the population. This group is not different in a way that is innately harmful to others or to themselves. If children who are growing up to be homosexual are freed from the influence of the myths that they are sinful, perverted, or sick, if they are treated as different but normal, they can grow up without the fear and self-loathing that homophobia often imposes upon them. They can have hopes and dreams for their futures just the same as their heterosexual peers.

Chapter 3

Identity Development

> I first had a crush on a female teacher when I was in second grade and I always felt I was different. But I was about twelve or so when I first heard the word gay, but I wasn't sure that's why I felt different. (Eighteen-year-old girl)

> I don't look gay. I'm the typical femme girl. But I don't think anyone would choose to be gay. There's so much negativity. (Eighteen-year-old girl)

Gay and lesbian children go through the same general stages of development as heterosexual children, but their sexual orientation presents unique hurdles centering around their perceptions of being different—different from their peers, different from their parents. How gay children deal with their differentness and how the families and communities in which they grow up react to this differentness influences how accepting they will eventually be of their homosexual identity and of themselves as people. Homophobia and antigay prejudice may interfere with the developmental process at each stage of a child's development and may impose barriers to a healthy adolescent and adult identity. These barriers can be overcome if we change the social and family environments in which gay children grow up and if we change the ways the adults and peers in their lives react to them.

Two researchers who have studied gay/lesbian youth extensively, Richard C. Savin-Williams (1998) and Anthony R. D'Augelli (1998b), have both pointed out that the problems these youth experience throughout their developmental years are much more likely to be due to damaging social contexts and institutions rather than to specific characteristics associated with their sexual orientation per se. D'Augelli clearly states that the problems lie not in the youth but in the community, the family, and the school. He went even further to say that *"home and school are high risk settings for gay/lesbian youth"* (emphasis mine). And Savin-Williams warned of the dangers of assuming that gay youth will develop emotional problems just because they are gay. He suggested that the majority of them will not necessarily be at high risk of serious adjustment problems if certain risk factors are not present in their lives. We will discuss in this chapter what some of these risk factors are at each stage of a child's development.

ERIK ERIKSON'S STAGES OF CHILD
AND ADOLESCENT DEVELOPMENT

Along these lines I wish to refer to Erik Erikson's (1950) theory of child and adolescent development and discuss how the family, the schools, and the neighborhood in which a child grows up may either promote or interfere with healthy development. Erikson proposed a series of psychological stages that children go through as they grow to adulthood and suggested that at each stage children must accomplish a specific developmental task if they are to develop normally. Erikson, while writing one of the classic works on human development, never referred to homosexuality as a normal variation in the development of adolescent and adult identity. In fact, his minimal references to homosexuality were in negative and pathological terms. This was a significant, but totally understandable viewpoint given the era in which Erikson produced his theories.

Nevertheless, I believe Erikson's principles offer a framework to better understand the unique developmental struggles of gay children and adolescents as they grow up. These struggles are the result of the negative attitudes about homosexuality, attitudes that have often been absorbed by the adults and peers in the child's life. In describing the Eriksonian theory I will discuss how these antigay attitudes and stereotypes about male and female roles may interfere with healthy development at each stage of a child's life.

Stage 1—Infancy: Basic Trust versus Mistrust

This stage, according to Erikson, lasts from birth until approximately eighteen months of age. Establishing a sense of trust in others is the major developmental task during these first months of life. The infant learns to trust when his physical and emotional needs are met in a loving way by an attentive parent who is sensitive to the infant's particular temperament and personality. Even during these very early months a child's individual temperament may be evident, with some children being extremely active and demanding while others are more placid and easygoing. Some are slow to adapt to change while others readily do so and may even seem to crave change and stimulation. Some are easily frightened while others seem almost fearless. Some need more physical contact and soothing than others, while a few may even resist physical contact at times.

Parents who are sensitive to a child's individual personality and temperament will be flexible in the way they care for their child and will realize that there is no "one size fits all" approach to being a parent. Parents responsive to the individuality of their child are more likely to recognize the little clues that will help them figure out how to make this particular child feel safe and loved. Whether the child will grow up to be gay or straight, parents who try to adjust their caretaking to their child's cues and temperament will set the stage for him or her to form emotional attachments to others throughout life. John Bowlby (1969, 1973), the famous British psychiatrist well known for his work on early infant development and attachment, reminds us that infants who have not become securely attached to a loving adult during this period of development may have lifelong difficulty in establishing satisfying relationships.

Even during this very early stage of development certain attitudes about gender and sexuality may affect the way parents treat their infant. A parent with rigid ideas about gender roles, for example, may expect that boys, even as infants, need to learn not to be "cry babies," not to be fearful, and not to be overly dependent. Rigid ideas about gender, about what is appropriate behavior for boys and what is appropriate for girls, underlie homophobic attitudes in some people and some parents. Richard Isay, in his book *Being Homosexual* (1989), has suggested that the fear and hatred of femininity in men is a major source of homophobia. J. M. Bailey (1996) has made a similar observation and invented the term "femiphobia," to refer to the fear that men, even gay men, have of being seen as effeminate.

These common fears can lead the parents of a boy who cries "too much," who clings to his mother, who wants to be held a lot, or who is afraid to try new things, to worry that he will grow up to be a "sissy" if they don't correct these "nonmasculine" behaviors. But when parents, for this reason or for any other reason, strive too hard to force their little boy to grow up and be a "man," he may feel pushed into separating emotionally from his mother before he is ready to do so. He may lose his sense of trust if it appears that his parents' love can be withdrawn if he doesn't match their expectations. There is usually less concern on the part of parents about a baby girl who is clingy, shy, or fearful, as such behavior is often considered more acceptable in girls.

Stage 2—Early Childhood: Autonomy versus Shame

This stage begins around the middle of the second year of life and lasts until around three years of age. In Eriksonian theory the child's primary developmental task during this period of life is to develop a sense of independence and control over his or her own body. The child at this age likes to explore and to resist parental authority. The child is often negativistic and rebellious, normal behavior for most children of this age. During this stage children need opportunities to make choices and to feel that they can have an impact on their world. At the same time they need to learn that there are some limits and external controls over their behavior.

However, when parents expect their children to satisfy their own needs, or when they demand instant obedience, the control can be harmful. If children are excessively punished or shamed when they attempt to assert themselves or if they are simply not allowed to express their desires or to make choices, it is more difficult for them to gain that sense of self-control and autonomy. They may, instead, according to Erikson, develop feelings of shame and self-doubt. Throughout this stage of development there is a continuing need for physical affection and closeness; this is just as true for boys as for girls.

As during the infancy stage, children in this stage may be affected by subtle forms of antigay prejudice and homophobia and, indeed, there is more likelihood of this happening now than during the first year or so of life. Children between two and three often have strong preferences for certain activities, clothing, toys, and playmates. Gender stereotypes and parents' fears that a boy may not be masculine enough or a girl not feminine enough can have a negative impact upon the child's psychological development and sense of self. Little girls who refuse to wear dresses or boys who prefer to play with dolls instead of trucks may encounter disapproval and even punishment from their parents.

It is certainly possible that children who make choices not typical of their gender may grow up to be gay. But it also is entirely possible that they will not. Regardless of the child's eventual sexual orientation, however, when the message is conveyed that boys must be "little men," must be tough and independent, and must like the right games and toys, and that girls should be passive and gentle and like little girl playthings, the child may begin to feel that his or her own interests and choices are not OK. These children may even begin to feel that there is something wrong with them. For children growing up to be gay, such experiences may be the beginning of that sense of feeling different, of not really belonging. And for all children, including those who will grow up to be heterosexual, they are being taught that there is something wrong with them if they do not conform to the traditional masculine or feminine ways of behaving.

Many parents do now try to avoid gender stereotyping in raising their children, believing that these stereotypes can stifle the development of their children and limit their ambitions and goals. However, even the most understanding and flexible of parents, those who make no objection when their little girl wants to play with trucks or their little boy to play with dolls and housekeeping toys, may react if their little boy decides he wants to wear a dress to nursery school. Such a choice may be too extreme even for the most tolerant of parents. This is not meant to suggest that I am recommending to parents that they must allow their son to wear a dress to nursery school if he so desires. However, I do believe that, as parents, we need to be aware of how our stereotypes about what is "masculine" and what is "feminine" influence our reactions to our children, sometimes in very hurtful ways.

As I have already mentioned in Chapter 2, many more gay adults than heterosexual adults recall that they had some gender atypical behavior and interests in childhood. And extremely feminine young boys have been found to be much more likely to grow up to be gay or bisexual than boys who have the average range of boyhood interests (Green, 1987). The feelings of a prehomosexual child of being different, of being an outsider, may thus arise, at least in part, from these early onslaughts of disapproval for gender nonconformity. One way of sustaining and supporting these children throughout their development would be for families and communities to become more tolerant of a wide range of interests and behaviors that would be acceptable for both boys and girls. We could lessen the pressures on our children to conform to rigid gender roles and allow all children, not just those who will be gay, the freedom to explore the varied aspects of their natures and to transcend some of the sexual and gender stereotypes.

Stage 3—Play Age: Initiative versus Guilt

This stage starts during the third year and lasts until around six years of age. According to Erikson, the major developmental task for the child during this period is to develop a sense of initiative and a sense of confidence in his or her abilities, abilities that are acted out primarily in play and in physical activity. The child at this age is also developing his or her imagination and may engage in fantasy and in playing out adult roles. Through this kind of unstructured play and fantasy a child develops initiative, creativity, a sense of humor, and perhaps the beginning of a sense of morality. Wise parents encourage these children in their explorations and role playing and allow them to practice their developing skills. An overly protective or punitive parent may stifle the child's curiosity and prevent him or her from developing a sense of confidence.

During these years, antigay prejudice, expressed mainly through disapproval of gender nonconformity, may affect the child even if it has not done so during prior years. The child begins to adopt or not to adopt many gender-specific traits and as a result may receive either praise and reinforcement or disapproval and punishment from parents and other adults. For example, if a four- or five-year-old boy, in his imitating of adult roles, plays with dolls and housekeeping toys, parents, afraid he is not being masculine enough, may show their disappointment in him or may even punish him. And parents with fears about their son's masculinity may disapprove if he cries easily or is more fearful or affection-seeking than they consider normal. In line with Isay's (1989) theory, this may be the time when some fathers begin to withdraw from their effeminate sons.

Though some parents may discourage a daughter's nonfeminine interests, others may be proud of her daring nature and permit or even encourage her tomboyish activities. In general, role expectations for females tend to be more fluid in our society than they are for males, and girls, at least during childhood, are usually less stigmatized when they bend the rules of so-called feminine behavior than boys are for failing to conform to the masculine role.

Sexual exploration between children often occurs at this stage and parents may overreact, whether the sexual play occurs between children of the same gender or the opposite gender. The sense of horror that the parent may express over these usually innocent acts can frighten a child and lead to excessive feelings of guilt about any form of sexuality. This can also occur when the parent reacts excessively to a child's masturbating.

Although parents are significant influences during these early childhood years, at this stage of development the child's peers begin to assume more importance than during earlier stages. Success with their peers is likely to be more difficult to achieve for those boys who do not enjoy the rough and tumble play of other little boys and who prefer more quiet and subdued activities. They may be ignored by their peers or may even be teased and made fun of. This might be especially true of those boys who are extremely effeminate. The tomboyish girls are more likely to be accepted by their peers or even admired.

Judith Rich Harris, in her book *The Nurture Assumption: Why Children Turn Out the Way They Do* (1998), reviewed over 700 scientific papers, articles, and books and she claims, based on her review, that parents have little significant influence on their child's development. Instead, according to Harris, it is peer influence and genetics that primarily determine adult personality. She goes so far as to say, "The world that children share with their peers determines the sort of people they will be when they grow up." Some critics, myself included, have noted that Harris has taken an extreme position. But what Harris has accomplished is to direct attention to the critical influence of peers on child development, an area which has been given relatively little attention by psychological science.

Despite her extreme viewpoint that parental influence on development is minimal, Harris does concede that parents can have an indirect influence on their children's personality and character in that they determine, among other things, the neighborhood in which their children will live, the social class to which their children belong, and the schools their children will attend. Through these influences and others, parents determine the broad range of playmates to whom their children will be exposed and from among whom they will select their friends.

In a recent article in *American Psychologist* (Collins et al., 2000) reviewing a number of studies on parenting, the authors concluded that, although the influence of peer groups has long been under-emphasized by psychologists and other researchers, to turn back the clock and de-emphasize parental influence is not indicated. They suggest that the socialization of children can only be fully understood when parenting practices are studied more carefully in order to un-derstand how these practices mediate other influences. For example, the writers say that peer influence may not be due just to the influence that peers have on one another, but may also be the result of the ten-dency of children and adolescents to select peers like themselves as friends. Thus, parents may have influenced the children in significant ways that have led them to select the particular peers they do choose.

Harris also makes the additional important point that day care teachers and school teachers have significant effects on children's de-velopment that parents do not have. Teachers influence peer group dynamics, which parents usually cannot do. A teacher sets the stan-dards and norms for the behavior of the children in the classroom and on the playground, and models attitudes about gender-role expecta-tions and about acceptance or intolerance of diversity of all types, in-cluding sexual orientation. A teacher's attitudes will strongly influence the peer group norms, whether it be toward tolerance of differences or toward demands for conformity.

Now that many children are in group care starting in infancy and up until entering elementary school, day-care and nursery school teachers are becoming important figures very early in a child's life. As Harris pointed out, this is especially so because of the strong influ-ence these adults have on how the children treat one another. If a nurs-ery school teacher has rigid standards regarding what is appropriate for the girls versus what is appropriate for the boys, or if taunting and teasing of children who are a little different from the norm is toler-ated, certain children may begin to feel like outsiders in the group and begin to doubt their own worth. The child who will grow up to be gay does not, of course, have any idea at this age that his or her feelings of being different from other children are related to sexual orientation. Children at this age are unaware of what sexual orientation means, but they will understand what it is like to be teased because they are different.

Stage 4—School Age: Industry versus Inferiority

This stage of development begins about the time the child enters elementary school and lasts until puberty. The major developmental task for the child is to develop a sense of competence. This is accomplished through the acquisition of skills that go beyond the play, pleasure, and fantasy of Stage 3. The establishment and maintenance of peer relationships is one of the most important of these skills. If the child does not develop competencies and strong peer relationships during this stage the result may be, according to Erikson, a long-lasting sense of inferiority and inadequacy.

Peer influence, of course, becomes increasingly significant as the child grows older. Peer rejection, taunting, and bullying can cause long-lasting psychological damage. Especially for the gender atypical child, particularly male, this can be a very dangerous and frightening period of life. As I have already emphasized, many gay and lesbian children are quite typical for their gender and those who are not vary greatly in the degree to which they are not. But those at the extreme end of the scale often stand out among their peers and may be subject to cruelty and humiliation by other children if adults do not intervene decisively.

During the later years of this stage, many gay children develop an awareness beyond that of being somehow different and become acutely aware of what that difference is. They also become aware that their same-sex feelings are not acceptable to their peers, to their parents, or to their teachers. There is the tendency, therefore, for the youth to deny or suppress the unacceptable feelings. This is a crucial period in the young person's development, one that can make a lifelong difference in terms of adjustment to his or her sexual orientation. Those children who are extremely gender atypical, most especially boys, may be teased and tortured on a daily basis in school and may even be ridiculed and shamed by their parents and siblings. Those children who are beginning to recognize their same-sex attractions but who are not readily identifiable and not gender atypical will, nevertheless, hear the disdainful messages directed toward other children who have been labeled "faggots" or "dykes" and suspect that these messages apply to themselves also. They often suffer vicariously and may be haunted by anxiety for what their future holds.

During this stage of development, children are becoming more cognitively aware and are tuning in more closely to adult conversations and parental opinions. Parents' attitudes about homosexuality are expressed by the things they say as well as the things they do not say. Parents who make demeaning comments about homosexuals convey to the gay child that even home may not be a safe place. When parents say nothing about homosexuality, the child notes the silence and can only wonder what his or her parents would think or do if they were to discover his or her secret. Parents who discuss homosexuality as an acceptable alternative form of sexuality or in some other way convey an accepting attitude will reassure their children that, although they are different, their parents at least will not reject them.

It is during this stage that the school environment becomes even more critical and it can be the place that D'Augelli (1998b) has described as a high-risk setting. Schools seldom acknowledge that sexual orientation is an issue for children. Schools often reinforce gender stereotypes and typically operate as if all students are heterosexual or, even if not, as if heterosexuality were the only satisfactory mode of being. These practices can make schools dangerous places for children who are gay or lesbian. These are the practices that need to be modified if the normal development of gay children is to be supported. I have already mentioned that teachers can play a significant and positive role when they model empathy and acceptance of individual differences and when they establish a classroom atmosphere where bullying, taunting, and teasing of those who are not quite in the mainstream are not tolerated.

Coming out—acknowledging homosexuality to oneself and others— may happen during this stage, although coming out to others is typically postponed until much later. Identifying, even to oneself, as gay or lesbian is a process fraught with anxiety for the child. More will be written about the coming-out process in a later chapter.

Stage 5—Adolescence: Identity versus Confusion

This final developmental stage before reaching adulthood begins with puberty and is a period of rapid physical growth and evolving sexual maturity. The adolescent must develop a sense of personal identity and the developmental risk during this stage is one of confusion about one's role in life, whether it be sexually, vocationally, or socially. Most adolescents are eager to be accepted by their peers and in fact this goal becomes all-important. But those adolescents who are recognizing their homosexual orientation often have trouble establishing close relationships with their peers and may become socially isolated. Since they may feel uncomfortable with heterosexual dating and there is no cultural permission for homosexual dating, they are left out of one of the major socialization experiences for teens. The need for secrecy and the tendencies toward social isolation create what Harry (1982) calls a "social vacuum" and what D'Augelli (1998a) terms "developmental opportunity loss."

Social isolation is increased for the gay male adolescent if he is one of those who does not have an interest in team sports. Also, since adolescents often identify with certain heroes, especially sports heroes, and these heroes are seldom if ever homosexual, at least not openly so, the gay adolescent isn't able to identify with the same role models as the other "guys." Hetrick and Martin (1984) have described this period of life well: "At a time when heterosexual adolescents are learning how to socialize, young gay people are learning how to hide" (p. 6).

It is at this time, if it has not already happened earlier, that the realization by homosexual adolescents of their difference from their peers can become a major stumbling block in the development of a positive adolescent identity. The difficulties were well expressed by a twenty-nine-year-old man in his recall of those years. "When you're gay you have this extra stress on top of all the things a teenager has to deal with. There's the big thing of wanting to belong for a teen and you have no hope of fulfilling that." And an eighteen-year-old girl says that the hardest thing during adolescence is the ". . . feeling that you have to be twice as good as anybody else for them to get past your being gay. They can't get over your being gay. People see you as gay, not as a person. You can't just be average. You have to be superior. You're constantly having to prove yourself. To show that you're as good as or better."

Through these crucial years gay adolescents must cope with the knowledge of their difference and with the even more painful knowledge that this difference is associated with stigma and negative stereotypes. Gay adolescents cope with their different sexual orientation in varying ways. Many struggle against accepting themselves as gay or lesbian. They deny their sexual feelings even to themselves or may convince themselves that the feelings are only temporary. Even those who acknowledge to themselves that they truly are homosexual may still pretend to others that they are heterosexual, a coping mechanism that carries its own particular risks, risks that come from living a life of pretense and being constantly on guard about being discovered.

Those who are openly gay during their high school years are rare, though recently becoming less so. Some high school students are openly gay only because they are so easily identified by their peers and have no choice. Some others who choose to identify openly as gay may be those who are less dependent on approval or those with an unusually strong support system. This is just speculation, as we do not really know how these so-called "early identifiers" differ from other gay and lesbian youths. In general, however, adolescents who come out as gay during high school put themselves at risk of harassment and rejection by their peers and may also face disapproval and even rejection by their parents. Many of these adolescents are understandably afraid to take these risks and try strenuously to conceal their sexual orientation.

A positive sense of personal identity for the adolescent, whether gay or straight, must incorporate one's sexual identity. Heterosexual adolescents have positive role models of adult sexuality, peers with whom they can share their sexual concerns and attractions, societal acceptance of their sexual identity, and parents who are usually also heterosexual and will understand and validate their children's emerging sexuality. Gay adolescents, however, are deprived of all of these supports for healthy sexual development and must struggle in isolation if they wish to conceal their sexual feelings. If his or her sexual orientation is discovered or he or she actively chooses to reveal it, the gay adolescent must often cope with negative consequences, consequences that can range from teasing and taunting to physical assault or even, in extreme cases, being thrown out of his or her own home.

Throughout this developmental period, the school environment is crucial. Does the school offer its gay students a safe refuge, including education about sexual orientation, support of alternative sexual identities, and positive homosexual role models, or is it instead a homophobic, high-risk setting? And what about the athletic teams and the physical education classes? Coaches are sometimes among the most homophobic of school personnel and can make life miserable for the boy who does not fit the masculine stereotype or is unskilled as an athlete.

Despite Judith Rich Harris's theories, I, and most psychologists and mental health professionals, believe that parents, not just peers, continue to exert a significant influence on a child's ability to negotiate this stage of development successfully. If the parents themselves are nonhomophobic and let their possibly gay child know that their love is not conditional upon sexual orientation, they will be helping their child to navigate through adolescence and emerge into adulthood with a strong sense of a positive sexual identity. And unprejudiced parents will teach their nongay children that just because people are different from themselves it doesn't mean there is something wrong with them.

Stage 6—Early Adulthood: Intimacy versus Isolation

Though this is a book primarily about children and adolescents, I wish to include just a few thoughts about early adulthood because the gay or lesbian adolescent who has not negotiated the earlier stages of development successfully and who has failed to overcome the social barriers placed in his or her way, may have serious difficulty with moving into adulthood. The "social vacuum" referred to earlier may leave the gay adolescent with significant social deficits as a result of not having had the normal peer relationships and dating experiences typical for adolescents. Establishing an intimate, long-lasting sexual and romantic relationship, a major goal during early adulthood, is difficult for all of us, but can be especially so for gays and lesbians and this goal may, indeed, be delayed for many years. Rich, at age thirty-seven, described how painful this growing-up process can be for a gay man.

> When you are homosexual you are told at every turn that you cannot love in that intimate way, that you can't love another man in a way that's meaningful. You have to put away all these negative messages in order to find out about the tremendous importance of love in this life and that you can have it just like everyone else.

Chapter 4

Coming Out

I came out to myself when I was 16. I thought I was a nympho. Kids my age would not be constantly thinking about sex or about being in a relationship. I worried about someone finding out, if people had heard about it. (Eighteen-year-old girl)

I was around thirteen when I came out to myself and the more I found out the more scared I became, how it was in society and in the family. (Sixteen-year-old girl)

WHAT IS COMING OUT?

The complex discovery process that children or adolescents go through as they gradually recognize their homosexual identity and acknowledges it to themselves and then to others is often referred to simply as "coming out." This process forces gay children and adolescents, from the time they begin to recognize the source of their feelings of differentness, to think about their sexual orientation on an almost daily basis. This is true whether or not they choose to reveal to anyone else their suspicions about their own homosexuality. Heterosexual children, unlike gay children, do not face a similar roadblock in their development, since their sexual identity or orientation is simply taken for granted from the time of birth and never has to be questioned or analyzed. Heterosexuals, in fact, whether adults or children, seldom give a thought to their sexual orientation. Heterosexuality is such a given that it is not a preeminent issue in their lives or in their minds.

I was struck by a similar phenomenon noted by Patricia Williams in her book, *Seeing a Color-Blind Future: The Paradox of Race* (1998). Williams describes how white people seldom think about race while blacks cannot avoid thinking about it on a daily basis. It is as though blackness, homosexuality, or almost any marginalized status can only be understood in the context of what it is not, that is, for example, not white or not heterosexual. White is normal, heterosexuality is normal. Thus, the child who is growing up to recognize his or her homosexual impulses is forced, often at an early age, to confront the issue of exactly what it is that he or she is not, that is, not heterosexual, just as the black child may have to confront the issue of not being white. White children do not have to think about being white and heterosexual children do not have to think about being heterosexual. Sexual orientation, however, becomes a salient issue in identity formation for gay children and adolescents. And the process of coming out distinguishes the gay child in a unique way from his or her heterosexual peers.

Coming to terms with one's homosexual identity is a developmental task required of the gay child but one for which he or she receives little guidance and for which successful role models are seldom available. It is common for the gay child to move through this singularly difficult process alone and afraid. The experience may strengthen his or her character and personality or may result in serious emotional distress, either short-term or long-term.

EARLY CHILDHOOD EXPERIENCES

As discussed earlier, the first warning of what is to become a central theme in the development of the gay child is a feeling, often emerging early in life, of being different. Trying to figure out why you feel different might even be considered the early beginning of the coming-out process. Certainly there are many heterosexual adults who also felt a sense of difference in childhood, but when questioned in adulthood about whether they felt different from other children as they were growing up, many fewer heterosexuals report having had such feelings than do gay adults. For example, the Bell, Weinberg, and Hammersmith study (1981) referred to earlier surveyed 573 adult homosexual males and 284 heterosexual males. The study found that 72 percent of gay males compared to 39 percent of heterosexual males reported feeling very much or somewhat different from other boys during grade school. Lesbian adults were also more likely than heterosexual women (72 percent versus 54 percent) to have felt dif-

ferent from other girls during grade school, though the difference between the two groups of females was less than that between the two
groups of males.

In these surveys the childhood differences usually reflected a lower
level of interest in activities typical for one's gender. For example,
only 11 percent of adult gay men recalled that they liked football or
baseball very much while they were in grade school, as compared to
70 percent of heterosexual men. Gay men more frequently reported
having liked solitary activities such as reading, drawing, and music.
Lesbian women were much more likely than heterosexual women
(71 percent versus 28 percent) to report enjoying typical boys' activities such as football and baseball during their childhoods. A direct
recognition of sexual orientation as a source for the feelings of
differentness usually came much later.

Maria, an eighteen-year-old girl in one of the school support
groups described the process well.

> I first had a crush on a female teacher when I was in second
> grade and I always felt different. But I was about twelve or so
> when I first heard the word gay. I wasn't sure that's why I felt
> different. In eighth grade I started having recurring dreams
> about my best friend. I was confused. Wasn't sure what my ori-
> entation would be. I was scared of people's reactions, letting
> people down, especially my family. I was in my freshman year
> of high school when I finally admitted to myself.

Richard Isay, who has seen many gay men in his psychiatric practice, wrote on this topic in his book *Being Homosexual* (1989). He
found that many of his male patients described themselves as being
less aggressive during childhood than others their age, as not liking
competitive activities, and as feeling like outsiders

It seems that this sense of differentness, this not fitting into the ste-
reotypical gender role, can evoke these feelings of being an outsider
in one's peer group. Childhood social experiences thus may be quite
different for at least some of the children who are growing up to be
gay as compared to children growing up to be heterosexual. Again, I
would stress that these findings clearly are not universal and many
gay children have skills and interests that are no different from their
nongay peers. However, even those gay adults who describe themselves as having been very similar during childhood to their same-sex

peers in terms of their interests and activities still often report that
they had vague feelings of being somehow different from other kids,
like a foreshadowing of things to come.

Male Socialization and How it Affects
Gay Males in Childhood

The child whose interests and behaviors are unusual for his or her
gender may experience extreme social pressure at home and in school
to conform to the more stereotyped versions of masculinity and femininity. For boys especially, the pressure to conform to the masculine
ideal is extreme and they are often exposed very early to a culture that
values male toughness and dominance. Boys who do not conform
may be labeled "sissy," a term that is associated with being like a girl,
which in turn is associated with being homosexual.

The social pressure to be masculine may make it exceedingly difficult for such a boy to admit his homosexual orientation even to himself, since being a "sissy" is associated with something so negative
for males. This brings to mind again Bailey's (1996) use of the term
"femiphobia" to describe the male fear, especially the gay male fear,
of being thought of as effeminate. The pressure to conform to the
male role sets the stage for the boy to make a valiant effort to fit in, to
be normal, to hide, and to deny his sexual orientation. Boys who are
perceived as being "sissies" but who happen not to be homosexual
may suffer equally from the disdain of their peers and even from
adults such as their parents, teachers, and coaches.

William Pollock, in his book *Real Boys* (1998), wrote of the intense "gender straightjacketing" that takes place in the socialization
of male children. They are taught what he calls the "Boy Code" and
shamed if they display any seemingly feminine feelings or behaviors
or if they allow their emotions to be evident, especially emotions suggesting weakness such as fear, sadness, or despair. Pollock believes
that the "Boy Code" causes emotional damage to all boys, not just
those who are gay. He suggests that it leads boys to repress their deepest emotions and interferes with their being able to emotionally connect with others in adulthood. Pollock goes on to say that encouraging "effeminate" boys to toughen up, to act like men, will not have
any effect on whether they will grow up to be homosexual, but that instead it will make these boys ashamed of who they are and make it

more difficult for them to acknowledge and come to terms with their sexual orientation if they are gay.

Other writers have also referred to the widespread and damaging effects of cultural messages about masculine socialization which demand that males must be tough and not show tender emotional feelings. For example, psychologist James Gabarino, in his book *Lost Boys* (1999), points out that in our society boys are taught to be macho and to ". . . reject as second class everything that is feminine." Gabarino goes on to propose that traditional masculine socialization, the emphasis on toughness and concealment of emotions, contributes to violence in society. He refers to our ". . . socially toxic society that defines manhood in terms of aggression, power and material acquisition" (p. 238). He believes that traditional masculinity leads to disdain and disrespect for women and that the repression of sadness and more tender emotions can turn to anger. Gabarino proposes that we give boys positive experiences in learning how to be men without having to conform to cultural stereotypes of masculinity that reinforce power and toughness. Another writer, Terrence Real, in his book *I Don't Want to Talk About It* (1997), similarly writes of the way our society's rigid notions of masculinity lead boys to ". . . internalize a pattern in which women and womanish things—including half of the boy's own being—are held as inferior" (p. 226).

So-called feminine interests and characteristics in boys tend to bring disapproval from both adults and from other children, especially to those who are most obvious in their failure to conform to the masculine role. They may be mercilessly teased and made to feel like outcasts. The extremely effeminate boy, the one who likes to wear girls' clothes, who openly expresses the desire to be a girl, who engages primarily in girl-typical play, can be subject to the most extreme rejection and ridicule. This child may also be more likely to resist even drastic efforts to persuade him to try to "fit in."

Without an especially understanding home and school environment, these unusually effeminate boys, the so-called "sissy boys," are at very high risk for adjustment problems. This is the type of child who, according to Green's (1987) research, is extremely likely to grow up to be gay or bisexual. This is also the type of child who often cannot avoid being labeled as gay as he moves into later childhood and adolescence since he is so readily identified by his peers as a "sissy," which easily translates into being gay. Remaining closeted in the sense of not identifiable may be almost an impossibility for these boys. They will likely be labeled as gay whether or not they are and whether or not they choose to identify themselves or not. These boys are also believed to be at higher risk for suicide, depression, and other emotional problems. It must be pointed out again that it is not homosexuality per se that puts these youth at risk, but instead it is the prejudice and negativity of society toward them.

Female Socialization and Androgyny

On the other hand, females are generally permitted, at least at younger ages, to be much more fluid in their interests and behaviors and are not as pressured toward femininity as males are toward masculinity. The young girl who loves football and baseball and likes competing with boys seldom receives extreme negative feedback. She may be urged by her mother to wear dresses more often, but the shame inflicted upon the boy who plays with dolls is much less severe for the girl who prefers trucks. On the negative side of this greater flexibility permitted to females in their gender roles comes the nagging thought that, sadly, it may be the lesser value placed upon females in our society that makes it less important for them to conform. Females usually are not perceived as a threat, and lesbians are perhaps more acceptable than gay males because they do not threaten masculine dominance, even though they might exhibit masculine characteristics.

James Gabarino referred to the research of psychologist Emmy Werner (1982), who has reported that in cultures everywhere in the world most successful people, those best able to adapt to their circumstances, are those individuals who are able to incorporate both masculine and feminine characteristics into their personality and behavior. This combining of both masculine and feminine characteristics is referred to by psychologists as androgyny, and Gabarino (1999) proposes that encouragement of androgyny, particularly the encouragement of boys not to be afraid of the feminine side of their natures and to freely express tender emotions and fear, would be a major step in reducing male violence in our society. This concept is obviously applicable to our views about the difficulties faced by young boys who are gay, especially those who do not fit the stereotyped masculine role. In a society in which so-called masculine characteristics were not so highly prized, boys who failed to exhibit some or all of them would not be so likely to be humiliated and harassed.

COMING OUT IN HIGH SCHOOL

Those gay children and adolescents who do not obviously stand out as different from their peers and who are not readily identifiable as being gay are able, if they choose, to delay the process of coming out to others long after they have admitted their orientation to themselves. They may choose not to disclose their homosexuality until after high school or even after college when they have more personal and social resources and are more capable of dealing with the possible negative consequences. Sometimes, though, the process of coming out is not a rational decision based upon a thoughtful consideration of all the pros and cons. Some simple or chance incident may force the individual to suddenly realize that remaining closeted exacts a greater cost than does coming out.

Whether it is desirable for youth to come out to others at an early age, given the stigmatized status of homosexuality, is a debatable point. It has even been suggested that early identification may be one of the strongest risk factors for gay youth and may be associated with a higher rate of suicide and other pathology. The positive aspects of coming out early have not been examined carefully and this is an area of research that will be important as earlier coming out in the younger generation of gays becomes more common.

Why Is It More Difficult for Boys to Come Out in High School?

H. W., one of the boys in a high school support group, was unable to conceal his sexual orientation in high school because it was very obvious. He spoke of what a hassle it was to be out and how he sometimes wished he were "less femme" so he could have stayed closeted. H. W. thought that almost the only gay boys who come out in high school are the feminine ones, which made it hard for him to find a boyfriend since he was only attracted to very masculine boys. H. W. talked of his loneliness and how, since only a few gay boys are out in high school, there isn't a large group to draw on for friendship and dating. He believes that it is easier for girls to come out in high school than it is for boys. Boys are also the ones who do the gay bashing. H. W. described the difference between the situation for boys and girls regarding coming out in high school.

> Males are supposed to be powerful and if a guy is gay he has lost that power. He is bumped down and has little or no respect. You are open to violence if you have no respect. Seeing two girls together, seeing them holding hands, thinking about two women being sexual together is more acceptable than when it is two boys.

H. W. spoke further about how heterosexual male fantasies of women having sex together might help explain the greater tolerance for lesbians than for gay males.

Star, another boy in a school support group, also thought it was much more difficult for boys to come out while they are still in high school. "It's easier for girls. Because males are supposed to have this macho image, be ladies' men. Males get no respect if they are not macho. The stereotypes are more there for males. Expectations for males are more demanding." Tiger also spoke of the difficulties he had in high school, saying, "It's harder for males in high schools than females. Butch women are just seen as tomboys. Feminine gay women, no one even thinks about it. For males, it's cowards, sissies, perverts."

A number of girls also said they thought it was easier for girls to come out in high school. Flaka, for example, said, "It's harder for boys, they're supposed to be buff, manly men. All the jocks are likely to make fun of them and beat up on them. It's society that is harder on males." And Maria agreed, saying:

> It's much harder for males. Society has this standard for males—strong, unemotional, in control. Males who are gay don't fit. People think they're feminine. Society is afraid of that. Women are more open minded, can do more as they please, be more affectionate. Men have the image to live up to. Women can be very feminine or masculine and it's OK. Men can't be feminine. Even straight guys who are a little feminine are thought to be queer.

COMING-OUT MODELS

Various writers (Cass, 1979, 1984; Troiden, 1979, 1988, 1989; Coleman, 1982; Gonsiorek and Rudolph, 1991) have proposed theoretical models attempting to describe the formation of homosexual identity and the coming-out process. These coming-out models are generally based on retrospective recall by gay adults and so are subject to the same distortions of memory and perception affecting any research based upon adult memories of childhood experiences. Nevertheless, given the logistical and financial difficulties of attempting to track experiences of gay individuals beginning in childhood and continuing throughout adulthood, these recollections of adult gays and lesbians are of great value. The various coming-out models generally highlight the social stigma of homosexual orientation and describe how gay youths struggle, often with little outside help, to cope with their gradually emerging recognition of society's contempt for what is such a central part of their identity.

Most of the coming-out models refer to homosexual identification as occurring over an extended period of time and as developing through a series of stages. The stages usually are not viewed as discrete events, but more as a continuum, an ongoing process that evolves over time throughout childhood, adolescence, and into adulthood. Many of the models refer to the tremendous individual variation among gays and lesbians in terms of their experiences in moving through the process of reaching a positive homosexual identity. The process varies in the timing of self-identification, with even more variation in the length of time it takes to proclaim one's orientation to even one other person. That first step of revealing to one other person is typically followed by coming out to close social contacts and beyond that to a wider circle of others. In the case of some famous gays and lesbians, for example, U.S. Representative Barney Frank and actress Ellen DeGeneres, the coming-out process may even extend to the general public at large. And, of course, large generational differences can now be noted with coming out occurring at a relatively early age in many of the current generation of gay youth. The recent phenomenon of earlier coming out corresponds to the rise in gay activism and higher visibility of adult gay role models.

Theoretical models of coming out generally propose that as an individual progresses through the various stages of identity development, he has an increasing recognition and acceptance that the word "homosexual" applies to himself. Self-awareness and self-acknowledgement may evolve through a long and often circuitous route with much questioning, self-doubt, and denial. Acknowledgment to others is usually an even longer and more complex process and still many closeted adult gays live with their secret unacknowledged to their family members or to their colleagues at work. Such self-concealment is more likely among an older generation, many of whom married and lived (and may still live) ostensibly heterosexual lives. The majority who do eventually reveal their homosexual orientation to others may still be selective in choosing with whom they will share the information. Coming out can be an endless process, one which may go on throughout a lifetime.

Troiden's Stages of Coming Out

Troiden (1979, 1988, 1989), one of the more frequently quoted writers in the area of identity development in gays, describes a four-stage model to explain the formation of homosexual identities. He called the first stage *Sensitization,* during which the gay child experiences general feelings or perceptions of being different from his or her peers of the same sex. At this stage, the child's perception of being different has less to do with being sexually different than with having different interests and preferred activities, as already noted previously in references to the Bell, Weinberg, and Hammersmith (1981) studies. Troiden believes that these early childhood feelings are only later given actual sexual significance.

If we apply the Eriksonian model to thinking about this stage of development, the child who is atypical for his or her gender may be more likely to experience negative responses from those around him or her and may begin to experience rejection by peers and disapproval from parents, all of which can exacerbate the feelings that one is different in a way that is wrong or shameful. The resulting feelings of guilt and shame can impede the development of self-confidence and a sense of purpose, in the Eriksonian sense, and perhaps slow the coming-out process.

Troiden's next stage of coming out, *Identity Confusion,* encompasses the experiences of gay youngsters as they move into adolescence, become more aware of sexual feelings and thoughts, and begin to realize that their previous vague and imprecise feelings of difference may mean that they, indeed, fit into that unmentionable category, homosexual. The recognition that "I might be homosexual" may create a sense of panic, given the stereotypes, myths, and secrecy that surround even the word. Fearful of the possible negative consequences of being homosexual, many gay children and early adolescents are secretive about the nature of their emerging sexual attractions, and use many coping defenses and strategies in an attempt to deal with the fear that something is wrong with them. Some of these strategies will be described later in this chapter.

If at this stage their appearance or behavior is such as to lead others to label them as "sissy," "faggot," "gay," "wimp," and so forth, they may suffer severe harassment and victimization. Those who are not readily identifiable may make intensive efforts to fit in, to try to be "normal," to try to present as heterosexual. One of the reasons coming out may be delayed is that, during adolescence, the need for peer relationships and peer acceptance are often more important than the need to assert one's homosexual identity. The resolution of one's sexual identity is a major developmental task of adolescence and one which is made difficult for the gay child because of the barriers society presents.

During Troiden's third stage, *Identity Assumption,* there is a gradual acceptance of one's homosexual identity and a greater willingness to acknowledge one's sexual orientation to other homosexuals. Social contacts with other homosexuals may be sought out and sexual experimentation may begin. Troiden has found that positive initial contacts with other gay individuals help facilitate a positive sexual identity while negative experiences may lead to more denial and feelings of shame and may reinforce internalized homophobia.

Youth who have internalized homophobia are more likely to try to avoid any kind of homosexual activity but will still continue to have homosexual feelings. High school-age adolescents, even though they may have reached the stage of accepting that they truly are homosexual, may still be reluctant to admit to anyone else for fear of what the social consequences may be. Incorporation of one's homosexual identity to the point of coming out as gay to others is often delayed until college or after, although as already noted, during recent years this seems to be changing.

Troiden's fourth stage is *Commitment,* which involves adopting homosexuality as a way of life. Those who have not been unduly traumatized by stigma and prejudice eventually reach the stage of being self-accepting and comfortable with their homosexual identity. Sexual feelings and emotional involvement are now more likely to be combined and seen as positive. The majority of gay youth, at least of high school age, may not have reached this stage, though again the changes taking place in society and the resulting impact on gay youth may throw many of our presumptions about homosexual identity development into disarray.

WHAT DO YOUTH SAY ABOUT COMING OUT?

There has been less information from boys and girls themselves as they are in the process of coming out, primarily because until quite recently there were few youth who openly acknowledged their homosexual orientation or were willing to talk about it to researchers. As openly gay youth increase in numbers and make themselves available to researchers, we may be better able to understand homosexual identity development as it proceeds through childhood and adolescence.

The stories told by gay and lesbian youth I have interviewed reflect vast individual differences in their experiences both in acknowledging their homosexual identity to themselves and acknowledging it to others. Coming out to other people occurred relatively early for most in this particular group of young people, but it should be remembered that these were mostly youth who had already openly identified as gay by becoming involved in a gay support group on a high school campus. They likely are not representative of all gay youth.

> I came out to myself and my family at the same time. I was fourteen. My Mom asked me and I told her I was bisexual. I think everyone is born bisexual. When you're a kid you don't know. Society labels things and then experiences begin to form you. (Seventeen-year-old girl)

> I accepted that I was gay when I was fifteen during National Coming-Out Week, the night after my birthday. But I was homophobic myself. If I knew someone was gay, I didn't want to be around them. I didn't want to admit it to myself. (Sixteen-year-old boy)

I was scared of people's reactions, letting people down, especially my family. They always used to tell gay jokes and I would try to test the waters by saying they shouldn't do that but I wouldn't say why. It was my freshman year of high school when I finally admitted to myself. (Eighteen-year-old girl)

My coming out to other people happened when I was fifteen and I was outed by another gay person in this school. We were boyfriends. He wanted sexual encounters with me. When I wouldn't he was upset and started telling other people. It ruined my reputation. I wasn't ready. I didn't intend to come out until I was an adult. Out of high school. Out of college. I am still angry. I have had to fight to accept what happened. (Sixteen-year-old boy)

I didn't have to come out to other people. People have just always been able to guess. I assumed everyone in my family knew. But then it turned out that when my mother told my grandmother, my grandmother hadn't known. My mother is not so much against my being gay, but she doesn't like the cross dressing. (Seventeen-year-old boy who believes he may be transsexual.)

I knew when I was eight years old. I knew what it meant then. (Seventeen-year-old boy)

Rich Savin-Williams (1996) conducted interviews about early childhood memories with a group of young gay males, ages seventeen to twenty-three, and these interviews also revealed a broad range of differences in the ways the youths dealt with growing up gay. Some in his study, even a majority, seemed to have been aware of their strong feelings toward other males even as very young children, though it was usually not until puberty that they started to place a sexual connotation on the feelings. These youth had strong feelings that their same-sex attractions were natural, were something they were born with and had no choice about. They felt intrigued by masculinity and male bodies.

A smaller group also recalled childhood memories of same-sex attraction and the feeling that these attractions were natural. However, these youth often failed to fit social definitions of masculinity and many were considered effeminate by their peers. They felt more comfortable during childhood and adolescence with girls than with boys and often preferred activities considered more typical for females.

A third small group was much slower to recognize any feelings of same-sex attractions and tended to very actively participate in masculine sports and activities with other boys. They often appeared to have been surprised and unprepared for the emergence of same sex-feelings at puberty.

Very few of the boys in Savin-Williams' study reacted positively to the realization, usually at puberty, that the feelings they had toward males were sexual. Almost all feared rejection or being shamed and they remained secretive about their sexual orientation. Some tried to suppress their attractions or to ignore them and hope they would go away.

How Social Stigma Influences Coming Out

To be confronted as an adolescent with the realization that you are part of a minority group to which neither your parents nor your friends belong and to realize at the same time the present and future ramifications of your sexual feelings is an experience that few heterosexual people can begin to imagine. And perhaps it is this lack of shared experience that prevents so many nongay persons from having even a glimmer of what it must mean to a gay child or adolescent to have to cope alone with knowing that he or she is so different and in such a crucial way from almost everyone else he or she knows.

Unless the child or adolescent has had an unusual upbringing in a home and in schools where homosexuality has been openly and positively spoken of, the awareness that one is different from the average in this very dramatic way is usually so frightening that there is an internal resistance to accepting the idea of being a member of a group so disdained by others. Being young and wanting to fit in and to be normal, these youth may use a number of strategies to manage the dilemma in which they find themselves.

Troiden (1989a, 1989b) has described a group of behaviors he terms *stigma management,* which refers to the various techniques that the emerging young gay or lesbian person uses to deal with the stigma associated with homosexuality. These youth may suppress the feelings and hope they will go away, they may strenuously try to pass as heterosexual, they may withdraw socially and isolate themselves, they may hurl themselves into athletic, academic, or artistic pursuits, or they may become depressed and may despair about the future to the point of becoming suicidal. The excessive use of drugs and alcohol may become an escape for some. Others may experiment with heterosexual behavior. As I have suggested before, the youth may be either damaged or strengthened by a process in which the ordinary nongay adolescent does not have to deal with and cannot even begin to imagine.

Rich, the thirty-seven-year-old gay male mentioned earlier, spoke about the difficulties of coping with the stigma of growing up gay.

> At first I allowed myself to think I was bisexual, but I had no attraction to women. In college I met a girl I liked and I was thinking that I can't allow myself to be gay. I started thinking that I need to fall in love and the gay stuff will go away. I have to marry and I can't give expression to these feelings. The girl wanted to be sexual and I didn't. I became involved with two other women and the same thing happened. I would break up when they wanted to have a sexual relationship. By the time I was twenty-seven, I just couldn't deal with it. I thought I must give up this myth that I can be bisexual. I had tried to do behavior therapy on myself. Then I went to the library and read a book which presented homosexuality in a positive way. I went right home and told my roommate, "I'm gay." That was the first time I ever told anyone.

The Heterosexual Assumption

The assumption of heterosexuality means that no one ever has to announce or tell others that he or she is heterosexual. The gay or lesbian individual on the other hand is continually having to make the decision whether to share their sexual orientation in any given circumstance. The increasing availability of gay role models, the increased positive media attention to gays, and the strength of the gay rights movement have certainly led more gays and lesbians to choose to be open about their orientation to those in their familial, work, and social networks. However, there is still a great variation in the degree of openness in individual lives. Geographic location is important, as is occupation or profession, age, religious affiliation, family circumstances, and the degree of internalized homophobia.

If as a society and in individual families we were to accept homosexuality as a normal sexual variation and were to stop assuming that everybody who is normal will grow up to be heterosexual, the coming-out process for young gays and lesbians would be less complicated, painful, and dangerous. Children could grow up knowing that just as some people grow up to be left-handed instead of right-handed or to have blue eyes instead of brown or to be short instead of tall, some grow up to be homosexual or bisexual instead of heterosexual. When differences in sexual orientation are considered a natural variation, coming out would become much less an issue.

Should Gay Youth Come Out in High School?

In my discussions with gay youth, many say they are reluctant to encourage others to come out while they are still in high school, pointing out the many difficulties that they may face by doing so. When asked the question "Would you advise other gay youth to come out in high school or to wait?" the answers varied but many seemed to recognize that coming out at that age might not be right for everybody, even though most of those who were interviewed had done so themselves. Kate, age seventeen, said, "It depends on the person. If you're really shy, maybe you should only come out at least to one person if you trust them or they're really close." Eighteen-year-old Flaka, though she was glad that she had come out in high school, was cautious in recommending it to others:

> It would depend. If they're strong spiritually, in their head. If they're weak and they'll get crushed by any little remark, then they should wait. If they have ways of pushing all that aside, then they should go ahead. If they're the type that wants everybody to like them or if they have low self-esteem they should wait until later.

Seventeen-year-old Star felt he had benefited from coming out but still warned of the problems that some might have. "It depends. There's so much stress. If they aren't afraid of what people will think, then it's OK. But if you're shy and not ready to accept yourself you should wait. Some are afraid to come out and are not ready to accept the consequences." Sixteen-year-old Tiger, who had been in a support group for some time, was trying to help two other gay teens decide whether to come out and he told them to wait. "I told them that they should wait until they are ready for change and ready for the consequences. Also they should have support before they come out." H. S., an eighteen-year-old boy, spoke of the many factors to consider before making the decision. "It would depend on the kid and what their school is like, and what their support system is. Do they have support from an adult in the school, from peers, or from parents? Will it be a living hell? Be strategic." Tripp, a seventeen-year-old girl, warned those who might be considering coming out while still in high school: "If they do come out, I would say be careful, be prepared for name calling, for physical threats. Kids are mean. You might want to come out but not at school."

Ann, a seventeen-year-old girl, was more positive about the effects of coming out: "I would advise them to come out. If you're shy, find a group of friends first. It gets a weight off your shoulders. It is a good experience. Not having to hide." Andy, a nineteen-year-old girl, also spoke about the positive effects of coming out, saying, "I think they should when they feel comfortable. It can make them stronger, to realize who they are, their identification. They will find someone to talk to, to get advice from, so they can help them." B. H., age fourteen, was one of the few who unequivocally advised everyone to come out. He suggested that gay youth at less-tolerant schools can help start a GSA (gay/straight alliance) or gay support group.

H. W., a seventeen year old, was positive about his own experiences of coming out in high school but suggested caution for others.

> It depends on their situation. But at my high school there's a lot of cultural diversity. It's in the Arts District. We have students with open minds. It's an environment where you can be yourself. In high school you face challenges because of the stereotypes. But I like challenges, like going to school in drag, to be really classy. Some people just stare, but I know I look good. I have to make sure I coordinate everything.

F. F., an eighteen-year-old senior, pointed out that each person is different and coming out should only be when a person feels that it's right. He suggested that college might be a better time to come out when both the individual and the other students are more mature. Eighteen-year-old Judy said that gay students should be sure they are accepting of themselves before coming out to others in high school. She also advised telling parents first, that is, if they are likely to be supportive. She noted that coming out means being honest and until the individual is ready to be honest with himself or herself, he or she can't be honest with others. Carrie, age sixteen, advised caution. Fighting the fear and coming out can be good she said, but warned that the student shouldn't throw himself or herself into danger.

James, a forty-year-old male recalling his own high school years, when there was much less support for gay students than there is in schools now, gave the following advice:

> It's very situation-dependent. You can be in a high school environment supportive of diversity or one that is not. It is also person-dependent. Are you ready to deal with the consequences? And coming out means more than telling people. It means having sex, having relationships. I wasn't ready for that at fifteen or sixteen, especially gay sex.

There is no simple answer to the question about the wisdom of coming out in high school. As noted, coming out early has its own risks as well as its benefits. Each young person faces a set of diverse and often unique circumstances. And sometimes the decision is not a rational, carefully thought out one based on the many factors involved, but is simply a spontaneous one in response to particular situations or events. And some do not have a choice because they are easily identified by others. As one of the students has pointed out, the majority of boys who come out in high school or who are "outed" are those who are somewhat or extremely effeminate. What we do know, however, is that more and more young people are being open about their homosexuality and at younger and younger ages. The youth themselves are changing the schools and society for their own generation and for older generations.

Chapter 5

Parents and Families Coming Out

WHY SHOULD PARENTS COME OUT?

Just as many gays and lesbians are coming out of the closet of secrecy to openly express their sexual identity, some parents and families are making similar choices to come out—that is, to accept and openly acknowledge their son's or daughter's sexual orientation. Some parents may even go beyond mere acceptance and acknowledgement and become involved in gay rights causes and organizations in public support of their gay children.

Coming out as a parent of a gay or lesbian child is not usually an issue until after the child has reached late adolescence or adulthood. Since in early childhood sexual orientation is usually not clear, premature assumptions about eventual sexual orientation should not be made. I have already referred to younger children who may possibly be growing up to be gay and made suggestions to help parents support their children's development whether or not they actually do turn out to be homosexual. But after an adult or an adolescent has recognized his or her sexual identity and informed the parents the situation is quite different.

When parents first learn that their adolescent or adult child may be gay, it usually comes as an enormous shock. At first, at least for many parents, it is almost unbelievable. Many have had no suspicion or hint that their child might be gay. The family may even have been one with very negative attitudes and beliefs about homosexuality. So it is not surprising that when a son or daughter reveals his or her sexual orientation to the parents, many of the parents choose to go into their own closet and do not want anyone to know that one of their children is homosexual.

But some parents will eventually decide to "come out" and tell others they have a gay child. In that process these parents will reshape the identity they present to the world, an identity that will now, at least in some settings, carry a degree of social stigma. You might ask then why should a parent come out? What could the purpose possibly be? Wouldn't it be easier just to go on acting as though your child is like the children of your friends and other family members? Why expose yourself to prejudice and even pity?

It is these very questions that lead many parents to avoid the complications that might arise were they to speak openly about having a gay son or daughter. Secrecy may seem safer and more comfortable for the parents, but it may also diminish the relationship they have with their child. Because gay people face prejudice and discrimination from the broader society, they are in special need of acceptance and support from their families, especially their parents. Parents who decide to give up the comfort of the closet and stop hiding their child's homosexuality give a message of loving acceptance to their child and at the same time they contribute to decreasing the social stigma surrounding homosexuality. Parental acceptance bolsters the esteem and well being of the gay adolescent or adult in a unique and powerful way. Conversely, parental love that is withdrawn, or is perceived to have been withdrawn, after a son's or daughter's homosexuality becomes known can be traumatic. The parent will have confirmed society's negative view of the gay person's identity.

There is another reason I believe it is important for parents of gay adult or adolescent children to be open about their child's homosexuality, a reason most relevant to this book. That is, when parents are open and accepting about their own child's homosexuality they have an influence not just upon other parents but upon other children, not their own, who are growing up suspecting they may be gay. A parent talking lovingly and admiringly about a gay child in front of children and other parents helps to normalize homosexuality and make it a part of everyday life.

HOW DO PARENTS REACT WHEN THEY DISCOVER THEIR CHILD IS GAY?

Certainly families exist in which a gay child will never be accepted, no matter that books such as this one are written, no matter that the family may be smothered with factual information about sexual orientation, and no matter that the family members may even recognize how hurtful their decision is to their child. Some gay adolescents are thrown out of their homes to live on the streets because their parents are so horrified at the very thought of a homosexual child. Some parents of gay adult children, once the discovery has been made, inform their son or daughter that they no longer wish to have anything to do with them and contact is ended, sometimes permanently.

Antigay prejudice has affected families of gays just as deeply as it has gays themselves. Parents often react impulsively based on deeply held beliefs about homosexuality that they have acquired through their lives. However, the majority of parents are bonded enough to their children so that prejudices can be overcome to a greater or lesser degree and some type of relationship can be maintained. The new openness which can result from ending the secrecy may even enhance the relationship between parent and child.

The exact nature of the evolving parent-child relationship varies and many parents cannot bring themselves to openly talk about the fact that they have a gay child. Even fewer will become public advocates for gays and lesbians or join an organization such as PFLAG. Nevertheless such parents may maintain close and affectionate contact with their gay child and accept his or her partner when there is one.

WHAT DOES RESEARCH SHOW?

Some research studies have examined parental reactions to learning that they have a gay or lesbian child. For example, in one study (Muller, 1987), 111 families were interviewed and several patterns of parental reaction were identified. The largest group (48 percent) were in a relationship described as *loving denial,* in which the parents continued to have a positive relationship with the child and even with the child's partner. However, these parents were not open with others about the child's sexual orientation. The next largest group (36 percent) was described as *resentful denial* wherein contact between the child and the parents was limited because of the parents' inability to accept their child's homosexuality. A smaller group (11 percent) were called *loving open* wherein the parents were both accepting of the child and the partner, if the child had one, and were open with others about their child's homosexuality. Only 5 percent were totally nonaccepting and estranged from the child, and this category was termed *hostile recognition.* These results might be different today given the increased social acceptance of gay and lesbian people during recent years.

Another study of parental reaction to their children's homosexuality was conducted by Andrew Gottlieb (2000), who studied fathers of gay sons, a population about which much less has been written than about mothers. Twelve fathers participated in the study, a willing, but not a representative group, as it did not include any who had rejected their sons. Gottlieb broadly distinguished between acknowledgment and acceptance. He defined acknowledgment as merely recognition of sexual orientation; acceptance as involving some degree of positive feeling. One father was barely able to acknowledge his son's homosexuality, hoping and praying that he would eventually change.

Gottlieb then went on to describe the other fathers as falling into three different categories of acceptance. The first category was what he called *resigned acceptance;* seven fathers fit into this category. These men reported that they were not happy with their sons' homosexuality but that they had resigned themselves to the fact that there was nothing they could do to change it. These fathers reported no expectation of change. Another category of acceptance was described as *unconditional acceptance;* three fathers fit into this category. These fathers seemed to have reached the stage of having positive feelings about their sons' homosexuality, with little or no desire or expectation for change. The third category—*narcissistic acceptance*—characterized the response of only one father, a gay man. This category, is ". . . one based on the son filling a narcissistic need and being a narcissistic extension of the parent." (Gottlieb, p. 160).

This study only secondarily examined stages of coming out and so the details of how open these fathers were with others was touched upon, but was not a major focus. Some were quite open; some less so.

STAGES OF PARENTAL COMING OUT

As parents differ considerably in their reactions to learning their child is gay, so do they differ in the degree to which they come out to others. Many researchers and writers have referred to the coming-out process for parents as occurring in stages and over time. Rich Savin-Williams and Eric Dube (1996) and others (e. g., James, 1996) have noted that some writers and theorists have compared the stages of coming out for parents of gays to the well-known Elisabeth Kübler-Ross stages of grief. However, as James noted, death is a disaster and he questioned the wisdom of equating the disclosure of a child's homosexuality with the experience of coping with death. Savin-Williams and Dube (1996) also questioned whether the stages of parental coming out were identical to stages of grief. Their study was designed to examine the stages of parental coming out rather than the type of relationship that evolved after the disclosure of the child's homosexuality. They concluded that the coming-out stages for the parents in their study differed considerably from the well-known stages of grief. They describe the stages as follows:

- *Impact.* This is the initial reaction and it is generally negative. The parents are usually familiar with the stereotypes and myths about homosexuality and worry about their child's future and how difficult and even perilous it may be.
- *Adjustment.* The parent begins to accept the idea that he or she is the parent of a homosexual child but is still struggling. Acceptance gradually increases over time for most. Worry about the child's future continues.
- *Resolution.* The parent begins to reach out, read about homosexuality, and go to support groups such as PFLAG. They still worry about what the future holds for their child. Many parents may not go beyond this stage, and some never reach it.
- *Integration.* Some parents move on to become more fully accepting and proud of their child. They may even become gay activists, particularly if they become involved in groups such as PFLAG.

I wish to point out that a parent can certainly be fully accepting and proud of a gay child and yet still not become an activist or join support organizations such as PFLAG. The activist style simply does not suit all parents, even some of the most loving and accepting. I certainly do not wish to imply that without becoming an activist one's acceptance and love for one's gay child is any less than that of parents who do choose to become gay rights activists.

It should be noted that the parents studied by Savin-Williams and Dube were all members of PFLAG and so were a select group, a group which is probably more likely than the general population to be open and accepting of homosexuality in general. Because of the difficulty of obtaining a representative population of gays and lesbians and their parents, the percentage of parents who are able to move past the initial negative impact and proceed through the various stages of coming out to reach the stage of integration is unknown.

In many ways the process of parental coming out is more similar to the coming-out stages that gay and lesbians go through than it is to the stages of grief. Of course, this is true only if the parents are, indeed, willing to go through the possibly drastic and often painful changes in attitude and belief that may be involved in fully assuming the identity of being a parent of a gay child. Moving to a point of committing oneself to helping change public attitudes and reduce stigma is chosen by some but, as just noted, not a necessary choice for every loving and accepting parent. Numerous books have been written by parents of gays and lesbians that refer to the parental coming-out process (Baker, 1998; Dew, 1994; Fairchild and Hayward, 1989; Griffin, Wirth, and Wirth, 1986). These books usually reflect that the process, though often long and difficult, is ultimately rewarding and enriching.

MY OWN STORY

My own experience as the mother of two gay sons began the night Gary, the younger of my two sons and nineteen years old at the time, told me he thought he might be gay. Though I had never thought of myself as homophobic and had worked as a psychologist with a number of gay and lesbian clients in therapy, I was devastated by the revelation that my own son was gay. It had seemed perfectly acceptable to me for my clients or for anyone else to be homosexual, but when it was my own son, emotion distorted my judgment and made me forget what I knew as a professional psychologist about homosexuality. The suddenness of learning my son was gay took me aback. I had had no time to get used to the idea since I had never had the slightest suspicion he was not growing up to be the ordinary heterosexual male my husband and I had always assumed he would be. The notion of having a gay child was totally foreign to me.

My initial reaction to Gary's announcement was to burst out crying and almost plead with him to tell me he wasn't sure. I think that what I communicated to my young son was that his homosexuality was a tragedy which had befallen us all. At the very least it was obvious I did not view his being gay as desirable. Was the "perfect" son no longer so perfect? Gary later told me how amazed he was at my reaction, thinking that he had never known me to be homophobic and also thinking that since I was a psychologist I would surely be more understanding than most parents. I disappointed him and in retrospect I disappointed myself. Rejection was never a possibility. I loved my son deeply and respected him in all ways. But to have responded to his disclosure with so little understanding and compassion is something I will always regret. I was also forced to recognize my own homophobia, which had existed at some level beyond my awareness. Although it was OK for others to be gay, it was not OK for my own son.

Admitting my own underlying prejudice helped me realize how indoctrinated even those of us who think of ourselves as tolerant are with the antigay attitudes that pervade our society. Most children growing up gay instinctively realize that their parents are not likely to be happy to learn that they are homosexual and often keep it secret for varying lengths of time, sometimes forever. It was not surprising that Gary had not revealed his secret sooner.

Stages of My Coming Out

Avoidance

For months after Gary's coming out I agonized over what was going to happen to my dear son in the future. Would he be humiliated, would he be harassed and made fun of, might he even be physically attacked? Would he experience problems in a career, what would happen to him at school, how were his friends going to react? As for myself, I was, I am ashamed to say, afraid of what other people would think. Self-blaming also came into the picture as I endlessly reviewed my weaknesses and flaws as a parent and as a person, attempting to identify which of them might have been most responsible for my child's homosexuality. It did not seem to help that I knew from scientific research that no particular family characteristics had been found to be related to sexual orientation. Science was one thing; mother-hood was another. Primarily I continued in a state of denial and avoidance, reassuring myself that since Gary was only nineteen years old perhaps his sexual orientation was not fixed and that he might yet turn out to be heterosexual. Wishful thinking and denial were among my dysfunctional coping mechanisms at that time.

Another brief and unsuccessful strategy was to attribute Gary's declaration of his sexual orientation as just another of his youthful rebellions, his desire to be different, to challenge authority and convention. Gary thought this hypothesis was ridiculous, saying he could certainly have found less difficult means of rebelling if that were his goal.

Acceptance

Acceptance began with an intensive study of sexual orientation, reading books by other parents and articles and books by psychologists and researchers in the field. I immersed myself in learning all that I possibly could so that I could understand. I watched my dear son who seemed so happy and well adjusted, doing extremely well in college and having plenty of friends. He was not living as though being gay was a tragedy. He was the same wonderful son I had always known and he was even tolerant of his mother's failure to grasp the fact that his gayness was really such a small part of who he was. He was quite accepting of my flawed reactions, never berating me or demanding more understanding than I was capable of at that moment.

Learning more about sexual orientation was one small step in my own coming-out process, but only when I could quit pretending that Gary might not really be gay and finally say to myself those simple but stark words, "Gary is a homosexual; he is always going to be a homosexual," was I able to accept his homosexuality as a fact and move on to a different level of coming out. This next level meant beginning to tell other people. Once the process of disclosure was begun, it gradually became easier each time I told someone new. Very few people were anything but supportive. I believe most people find it difficult to be critical of a mother who stands up for her child, whatever the reason. However, there were a few who seemed, though supportive, to believe that something unfortunate had happened to Gary and to me, something that we probably wished were different. It sometimes seemed that at least some people thought of his homosexuality as some sort of handicap which both Gary and I would have to learn to bear.

But unforeseen events were looming, events which would propel my coming out to a different level. In May 1987, Gary told his father, his older brother, and me that he had been diagnosed with AIDS. At the time this diagnosis carried a life expectancy of two years or less. Gary, our beautiful son, only twenty-five years old, was facing his death and we were facing life without our beloved child and brother. We were all faced with the stigma associated with AIDS, a stigma most tellingly revealed in the phrases—so common at the time—"innocent victims" and the "gay plague." The first phrase was used to refer to certain groups infected by the virus nonsexually, such as hemophiliacs, anyone infected through blood transfusions, and children of mothers who were infected. The second phrase, "gay plague," implied that those who had acquired the disease through homosexual contact, like my son, were not innocent and thus undeserving of sympathy and compassion. I could do at least one thing for my son and that was to show him unambiguously that his family was just as proud of him as we had always been, that we would never be ashamed of him, of his illness, or of his homosexuality.

I came to believe that parents who "come out" about AIDS and speak publicly about their child's homosexuality and about the illness can play a significant role in reducing the prejudice associated with homosexual orientation and AIDS. It seemed to me that being silent about his illness would have made Gary feel we were ashamed of him. A parent of a child with HIV/AIDS speaking honestly puts an individual face on the epidemic, makes it less easy for others to be indifferent, and helps overcome stigma. This is a socially responsible thing to do. In my own particular case I felt it was a necessary thing to do. In a way, perhaps I could atone for my earlier reactions. My husband and I both wanted our son to know that his family would face his tragedy with him, that we were not ashamed, that we would be beside him at every step of his journey. We wanted him to be able to live openly with his illness and not have the additional worry of having to keep it secret. Facing the fear that my beloved son was going to die finally made me see with absolute clarity how insignificant his sexual orientation was. All I wanted was for Gary to live and for this dreaded illness to be obliterated.

Appreciation

Gary lived for two years and two months after his diagnosis, and those two years were the most intensely lived years of his young life and also of mine. I lived with the certainty that my son would die, yet underneath always yearning to believe that he would not, watching his struggle with both fear and admiration, his valiant attempts to be productive, and to live his life fully even as he knew he was dying. It was during this stage that I realized how much I appreciated Gary's gayness—watching him, admiring him, loving him, I knew he would not be the Gary I knew and loved were he not gay. It was an essential part of his being, part of what made him the miraculous human being that he was.

Gary worked at his job as an editor of *Local Area Network* (LAN), a New York City computer magazine, up until just a few weeks before he died at home with his family and friends around him in Tucson, Arizona, on July 3, 1989, four days before his twenty-eighth birthday. All of our hopes and all of our love had not been able to save him. I would never touch or hold my child again and I will grieve his death until my own.

It was shortly after Gary died when I learned that my older son, Andy, was also gay. Again this was a shock, but my younger child's illness and death had put life in more meaningful perspective. Andy was alive and not infected with HIV. His sexual orientation was irrelevant. I regretted that I had not known sooner, but Andy was the same wonderful son he had always been. Being gay was just a part of who he was and I loved him deeply just as he was and just as I always had. Gary's diagnosis and death and the discovery that both of my sons were gay made me realize how incomplete my coming out had been and how much more needed to be done and could be done by parents like myself. It very possibly would have taken longer for me to reach such a stage under less extreme circumstances.

Advocacy

Grieving Gary's death, I coped with loss and the need for atonement in multiple ways, making a panel for Gary to add to the AIDS Memorial Quilt, becoming a volunteer in AIDS and gay/lesbian organizations, and joining grief groups and support groups, including

PFLAG. I also used any opportunity, both as a psychologist and as a parent, to try to educate others about sexual orientation and, by telling our family story, I have continued to try to help obliterate the stigma surrounding AIDS and homosexuality, to help overcome indifference. These have become missions in my life, the ways in which I keep alive the memory of one son and support the other. I hope I can influence at least some parents to react more positively than I did when I learned I had a gay child. I want parents to know the facts about sexual orientation and to realize when they first hold their newborn infant in their arms that there is always the possibility that this baby may grow up to be gay and there would be nothing wrong if that were to happen. Being the parent of a gay child is as wonderful and rewarding as being the parent of any other child.

I have come to understand how complicated and painful it can be for parents to confront the issue of homosexuality in their children and have come also to realize that those of us who have gone through this experience and learned from it need to share what we have discovered with others. One lesson we learn, perhaps better than most parents, is that we do not have the right nor do we have the power to impose our own expectations, our own hopes and dreams upon our children. All children will create their own hopes and dreams, of course, but when the children are homosexual the discrepancy between the parents' dreams and the children's dreams will probably be more dramatic and more difficult to reconcile than when the children are heterosexual. When we as parents come out, when we say that we are proud of our gay child, we acknowledge that our child isn't going to fit the mold we imagined for him or her; that he or she isn't going to meet certain expectations; but that he or she is going to be him- or herself in all the wonder of what that self is and can be.

Those of us who are parents of gay children are ideally suited to educate others about homosexuality. When we stand up for our children, tell our personal stories, and share the joy and wonder of being the parents of our gay sons and daughters, we have a power that the children themselves sometimes do not have. We should try to use our power wisely to help our own children as well as those children who are to come, children who should not have to grow up feeling ashamed just because they happen to be gay or lesbian.

MARY BORHEK'S STORY

I have read with great admiration a book by another mother (Borhek, 1979) who struggled to overcome the strict teachings of her religion in order to reveal to her church that she had a gay son. Mary Borhek tells of what her coming-out message conveys to other Christians:

> Whenever I say to any pastor or any church member, "I have a gay son," I am saying something important. I am forcing the person to grapple, at least in some small measure, with the fact that homosexuality does happen to people they know, that it does happen to Christians, and that one person at least does not regard it as shameful information to be hidden. (p. 150)

Chapter 6

For All Parents

When parents talk to their children about sexuality, they should mention homosexuality. I didn't understand what was happening to me because it wasn't talked about. (Eighteen-year-old girl)

TO PARENTS WHO DON'T KNOW WHETHER THEIR CHILD IS GAY

Parents can sometimes forget how profound the influences are in childhood of the parents' words, of their holding and hugging and kissing, of all the little things that tell a child that he or she is wanted. But what if those parents who do not forget, who shower their child with affection and attention, also make remarks about gays, about how they are disgusting sinners or perverts, or what if such remarks made by others are tolerated in the home? What if there is a child who is listening and wondering if what is being said applies to him or her? If you are a parent, it is of no use to tell yourself that you could not possibly have a child who is growing up gay or lesbian, because you simply do not know. If you should have a child who is beginning to suspect that he or she actually is one of those people you are demeaning, all those hugs and kisses and loving words will not be a reassurance that you would still love him or her if you knew. Parents need to be aware that a gay child can be emotionally damaged by remarks and behavior heard and observed in the home long before the parents are aware of the child's sexual orientation.

Avoiding demeaning remarks about gays, though necessary, is not sufficient to protect the child from emotional harm. Absolute silence about the topic of homosexuality also conveys a message. Avoiding negative remarks does not teach the child, whether gay or not, anything about tolerance and acceptance. Parents need to go beyond this passive approach and actively influence their children to appreciate differences among people. Parents who fail to teach their children that all people are worthy of respect are failing in a major task of parenting. Children learn prejudice in the home and in the society around them. Children are not born disliking or hating African Americans, Jews, or homosexuals.

However, even parents who are accepting of different races and religions often do not extend that acceptance to homosexuals. Parents of a gay child are seldom gay themselves and, thus, do not identify with nor automatically accept their child's sexual orientation in the way that, for example, an African-American parent will identify with and accept the child who shares his or her race. African American parents are unlikely to express prejudice toward African Americans in front of their child or anywhere else. But the gay child does not have the assurance of a shared sexual identity with his or her parents and when he or she hears his or her heterosexual parents speak with distaste about homosexuals he or she can only wonder if they would still love him or her if they were to find out he or she is gay. The child may live in fear wondering what will happen if his or her orientation is discovered.

Even if parents avoid prejudicial remarks about homosexuals and teach their child to be accepting of those different from themselves, unless they also specifically teach the child that homosexuals exist and that they are normal people, the child will still watch and wonder what her parents really think. I believe that the best approach is a very simple one. Parents should talk to their children about falling in love and how most people, when they grow up, fall in love with someone of the opposite sex, but that some fall in love with someone of the same sex. Children can be told that this happens to a certain number of people everywhere, that this is normal, not shameful. They can tell them that this is just one of the ways some people are different from others. If more parents were to teach this basic lesson, their heterosexual children would be less likely to become homophobic and children who are sensing that they may be different in this way will be reassured that their parents will still love them if they turn out to be gay. This kind of conversation might most easily take place informally while watching a TV show with a gay character, for example, or when someone has made a remark about gays, or when the news carries an article about gays.

Probably not many parents overtly teach their children this lesson, simple though it is. Of course, it is often difficult for parents to discuss any sex-related issues with their children and homosexuality is perhaps even more difficult than other sexual topics. Influenced by more complex issues, by the myths and fallacies that surround homosexuality, and by the fear that a gay child would be a target of discrimination, most parents do not discuss the subject of sexual orientation with their children at all. Parents may also have an even more profound fear than that of discrimination—they may fear that their child might somehow be persuaded to become homosexual if he or she were to hear that it is "normal." Many parents falsely believe that if homosexuality is never mentioned and if their child is kept away from all homosexuals there is no danger that he or she could become a homosexual.

All parents, whether or not they will have a gay child, should have basic information about sexual orientation so that they are not frightened by the myths and fallacies that surround the topic. Parents should be helped to understand that once a child's sexual orientation is fully established it is not likely to change and that there is nothing they can do to prevent a child from growing up to be gay or lesbian. They should know that attempting to change the child's orientation can cause emotional damage. Parents should also realize that if they do have a child who grows up to be gay, it is not because they as parents did something wrong. Most important of all, parents need to realize it is OK to be gay.

As far as is known, tolerant families and societies would not increase the incidence of homosexuality. No evidence supports that the degree of homosexual tolerance in a society has any effect on the number of homosexuals in that society. What is more likely than an increase in the actual incidence of homosexuality is that more gays and lesbians would openly express their sexual identity, making it appear that their numbers had increased. The stigma still associated with homosexuality contributes to secrecy and keeps us from determining with certainty what percentage of the population is homosexual or bisexual.

However, even if a more tolerant society did increase the numbers of homosexuals, why should this be a problem? In a society free from homophobia, gays and lesbians could live openly without fear of condemnation from the society around them. Straight people would realize that they already have friends and family members who are gay and who are just as normal as their heterosexual counterparts. Parents would be more likely to understand that they have nothing to fear if their child grows up to be gay or lesbian.

FAMILY REACTIONS TO GAY CHILDREN COMING OUT

Fear of family reaction is a major factor when a gay child or adolescent is trying to decide whether to come out or to hide his or her sexual orientation. Students who make the decision to join a gay support group in school are taking risks and one risk is that their parents will find out. Many students, knowing their parents' attitudes, are afraid to join a school support group. The following stories are from gay and lesbian students who have decided to come out, at least to the extent of joining one of these groups. Students who suspect that their families would reject, abuse, or humiliate them if they were discovered to be gay will not be likely to make such a decision. Though figures are not available regarding how many gay youths decide to come out while still in high school, it is unlikely that the majority are doing so. Those who do may differ in some very significant ways from the average gay youth. Their families may also differ from the average. Keeping these points in mind, here are some of the stories these particular young people have related about their experiences with their families.

Maria described her family as very bigoted. Maria is half Asian and half Hispanic. On the Hispanic side of the family they made jokes about "Chinks," about gay people, and about black people. She would try to stop the jokes and tell them all that it wasn't right, but she wouldn't say why. Maria said that when she was a child there was no Ellen DeGeneres, no Melissa Etheridge, and she knew her feelings must be wrong. Maria had always been told that she was the perfect one in the family. But learning from her family that homosexuals were immoral and realizing that that was what she was, she felt "ugly, horrible, wrong" and she wanted to change.

Maria began to feel that she would be alone the rest of her life and thought she would never be happy. She began to think that suicide was the only way out. She was thirteen years old at the time and went into a deep depression. She became so depressed and confused in her attempts to keep her secret that she finally told a counselor at school that she wanted to kill herself, although she didn't reveal why. The counselor said she would have to notify her mother and took her to a mental health clinic where the mother met them. To Maria it seemed that it would be worse to have her mother know she was gay than it would be to commit suicide.

Maria was in counseling for a year but never told her counselor that she was a lesbian. It was only later that Maria finally told her mother. Her mother went into the bathroom and cried for a long time. But when she came out she said she loved her. Six or seven months later, Maria told her father. Her parents were divorced and not living together. Maria described her father as a "macho, Mexican male" who was unpredictable. She was afraid he might get violent or hit her. But actually he was not so upset over her being a lesbian as he was that she hadn't told him sooner. He told her that he could never hurt her and that he could not punish her for what she was.

When another young woman, Erica, asked her mother if she could spend the night with her friend and her mother said "I don't want her turning you into a lesbian." Erica was surprised and confused. Though she and the other girl liked each other, they hadn't really figured out what was going on. Then Erica said to herself, "Wow, I like a girl." She decided that she must be bisexual, because that was easier to deal with than thinking she was a lesbian. She was afraid of what her mother's reaction would be if she found out. Erica decided to fake heterosexuality and started following guys around at school to fool the teachers and other kids. She kept thinking she wasn't certain, that maybe she was not gay. Erica's mother was finally told by someone else that her daughter was gay. Erica had just turned sixteen. When Erica's mother asked her if it were true and she said that it was, her mother did not speak to her for two weeks. Erica felt that this was just one more way in which their relationship was troubled. She described her mother as not very open-minded. She said her mother saw her sexual orientation as being just one more problem. Erica's parents are divorced and her mother wants her to tell her Dad. Erica has never initiated the subject with anyone and she thinks it's going to be very hard to tell him.

F. F., whose parents are divorced, has not told his father that he is gay because he thinks his father is not open-minded and he does not trust him. F. F. was fortunate in his mother's reaction; he had just barely hinted to her that he thought he might be gay and his mother said that she had suspected since he was eleven years old. She said that if that was the way he "chose," she would be behind him 100 percent.

Ivy said that when she told her mother she was lesbian, her mother ". . . acted as if I had told her I was going to die." Ivy told her mother right after they had had an argument because she was angry and wanted to hurt her mother. She was sorry she had told her in this way. Ivy's mother told her that homosexuality was against the Bible and then tried not to talk about it too much afterward, although occasionally she would ask Ivy if she were still gay, ". . . like I had the chicken pox." Ivy thinks her mother is finally trying to acknowledge that her daughter is a lesbian and that she needs to accept her as she is.

Tripp said that when her dad found out he disowned her for a short period of time, which hurt a lot. However, they eventually worked it out. Her mom took it somewhat better, but she was always questioning Tripp and didn't really like it. Tripp described her mother as "a hard-core Christian," which made it especially difficult for her to accept that her daughter was a lesbian.

Mary described her mother as distraught, grieving, and self-blaming when she learned her daughter was lesbian. Her mother would tell her that it was just a phase and that Mary should date boys. Her mother has not gone any further toward acceptance. She wants Mary to go to a counselor. Mary thinks her mother is in complete denial and simply will not deal with the issue. Mary spoke of how difficult it is to ". . . feel this pressure to be with a guy, to be what they say is normal."

Carrie was raised by her father after her mother died when she was only three years old. She came out to him as a lesbian when she was fourteen and a freshman in high school. When she told her father he was noncommittal. He wanted to see if it was just a phase. He didn't react negatively but he was worried about society and about her safety.

B. H. told his parents when he was fourteen. His mother was shocked and she cried. However, then she said she had suspected since he was three years old. She wanted to know why and kept him up talking about it long into the night. She wouldn't let him go to sleep. The next day they both felt awkward. B. H. said that his mother doesn't have a problem now except when ". . . I go into my flame mode and act gay." B. H.'s father told him that he already knew because he had read his son's unspoken words. He thinks his father is accepting, although he has been noncommittal.

Bob (a girl) had a very positive experience when her parents learned she was gay. She said that it had been really easy for her, that she had always been accepted and she explained their reaction: "I think it's because my family is really open-minded. My father is not so open-minded as my mother, but he accepts me because I'm his daughter." She said that what had helped her the most was her family accepting it at the beginning. They drilled it into her right from the very first that she was OK. However, she said that for most of the gay kids in her support group their families were not so accepting.

H. W. was confronted with many different reactions in his family. When his mother first learned he was gay it was hard for her and she sought counseling for herself. He was surprised at how difficult it was for her because she is an artist and had always been very open and tolerant. His father is a minister and he has been very "cool" about his son's orientation. A younger uncle, whom H. W. thought would be very accepting, has been hostile and told him that his dead grandfather would never have accepted him. An article about H. W. and the gay support group appeared in the school newspaper. In the article H. W. was quoted as saying that God had made him the way he is. When his grandmother saw the article she called him to say everyone was very proud of him.

One thing that makes H. W. different from the other kids in the support group is that he cross-dresses and has fantasies of being a female. He has been able to cross-dress at his high school without running into too much teasing. He thinks that part of the reason for his not being harassed is that he is so flamboyant about it and carries himself with pride and confidence. He pays a great deal of attention to the details of his outfits and tries to get everything to coordinate. He would probably cross dress every day except that it takes so much more time to get ready, what with plucking his eyebrows, makeup, and finding the right clothes that go together. H. W. thinks that it may be his mission in life to teach tolerance.

When he came out as gay, Star was helped most by his older sister who reassured him and told him not to worry about what people think. His mother was not too accepting at first and kept wanting him to get into counseling. Star and his mother had been very close but his coming out divided them. The relationship has become better over time. Star's dad, on the other hand, just said that he loved him and he wouldn't let his son's homosexuality bother him.

Tiger was never planning to tell his mother, but she heard him talking on the phone to a friend and denying to the friend that he was gay. His mother started asking him about it and he finally admitted that he was. He started crying and telling her he couldn't give her any grandchildren. She was totally shocked and they talked for six hours. Over time, Tiger's mother has come to accept his homosexuality. She is still not too comfortable with it, but he says that at least now he can be more open with her and talk to her about AIDS and about safe sex.

COMMENTS

Most gay children are growing up with parents who are not aware that they have a gay child. These stories help us understand how important it is for all parents to be aware of the possibility of having a gay child and for all parents to consider that the attitudes they convey about homosexuality, both verbally and nonverbally, will have an effect upon their children. If parents are overly rigid about trying to force their little boys to be more masculine or their little girls to be less tomboyish, they are implanting the idea in their children's minds that the children are not acceptable as they are. If it should turn out that one of their children is gay, loving parents do not want to have inadvertently caused emotional damage to their child by saying hurtful things about homosexuals or by criticizing their child for not being masculine or feminine enough.

What gay children want and need are the same things that all children want and need—the love and support of their families. Fearing that they won't have this is what prevents so many children from telling their parents that they are gay. It is a unique and frightening situation for an adolescent to have to tell a parent "I am different from you in this way that you perhaps never even considered, never even thought about." And the child's own difficulty in accepting that he or she is different in this way must be overcome to some extent before he can even begin the conversation with his parents. Once the child gets the courage to tell his or her parents, their reactions, both immediate and long range, can make all the difference in how the child is going to adjust to his or her sexuality and integrate it into a healty personality.

F. F. put it well when he said that parents should try to remember "They're the same kid they always knew." Loving and accepting families can help minimize the difficulties gay children experience while growing up, even when they cannot completely protect them from the emotional damage caused by an unaccepting society.

Chapter 7

What Happens to Gay Children at School?

MEMORIES OF HARASSMENT AND INTIMIDATION

Many gay students hide their orientation at school so successfully that no one ever suspects. But some, even when they try desperately, are unable to keep their secret. What happens in school to openly or obviously gay students or those perceived as gay can range from casual, insulting remarks and can escalate to verbal taunts and shaming, and to actual physical threats and assaults.

Tiger, a student quoted earlier, was outed at his high school by a friend who was also gay. Tiger described the following experience sometime after his homosexuality became known:

> Just about three weeks ago I was physically assaulted. I was running around the track and another student said, "Are you a faggot?" He started running after me. He pushed me and I fell. He said, "Get off the ground you filthy queer." I was so stunned. I just lay there in shock. Two other guys were watching and laughing. The coach and everyone said they didn't see or hear a thing. I was very scared but I went on to the tennis court. He followed me and continued to harass me saying, "I'm going to fuck you up your ass." I went home and told my mother and I came to school the next day and told my counselors. They said I could have him arrested for harassment and physical assault. I felt guilt, shame, and hurting pain. I wrote a poem about it later.

This was not Tiger's only traumatic experience. Another occurred on the athletic field:

Once this year I was verbally assaulted by the whole soccer team when I was walking through the field. They were yelling gay, faggot, butt fucker, bitch. Then twenty-five young men surrounded me, mocking me. I was just alone. I expected to be hit, my shield was shattered, I lost my self-confidence. I felt really hurt. What did I do to deserve this? I felt scared to come to school.

Maria recalled moving to a new high school when she was a sophomore. Another student in the school knew that she was a lesbian and he told everybody, spreading the word that she was a "dyke." Soon after that, two of the football players and another "guy" cornered her and began to taunt her. She has never forgotten the words they used, "We're going to kick your ass. Queers should die. We don't allow queers. You're not welcome here. You're gonna die." Maria was not hit, just humiliated by their taunts, and she just stood there in shock. Then the three harassers disappeared. Maria was later told by school administrators that they wanted to send her to an alternative school because the school atmosphere was dangerous for students known to be gay. The administrators did not believe they could do anything to sufficiently protect her as an openly lesbian student.

As I have already noted, the most victimized and intimidated students are very often those boys who most obviously fail to conform to masculine stereotypes. Names such as "queer" or "faggot" are among the frequently used epithets in schools, one of the more common ways of shaming these atypical boys. Being effeminate is equated with being gay and though many of these boys are gay, some are not. Nevertheless, both groups are victimized by the harassment.

This strict division between boys who fit the masculine stereotypes and those who do not is one of the more obvious measures of social acceptance in junior high and high school. It is often the male athletes, the "jocks," who are at the top tier of the social hierarchy and their influence may permeate the school, encouraging the ridiculing of boys who are unathletic and setting rigid standards about which boys are going to get respect and which are not.

James, a forty-year-old gay man, recalled his experience as a gay male in high school and spoke of the social hierarchy in which males are judged primarily on their physical and athletic abilities. "Physical strength and skill are the epitome for males in high school and it is the lack of those very things that can lead to physical threats. Those likely to be perceived as gay are also those least likely to be able to defend themselves."

Among the students I interviewed, many recalled experiences with harassment, although seldom so severe as Maria's and Tiger's experiences. Star, a male student, recalled mainly verbal harassment.

> A few verbal taunts. . . faggot, queer. I don't let it bother me. There's never been anything physical against me. The hardest thing in high school is the peer pressure from other students. The name-calling because they are homophobic and don't know how to deal with it. The homophobia makes it difficult for kids to come out.

Tripp, a female student, also described verbal harassment, but was helped in dealing with it by one teacher who made a difference.

> It bothers me that teachers mostly don't say anything if people make negative remarks. But I do have one teacher who is very supportive and he said he is going to come and have lunch with our group and if anyone says anything, he will get security and make them do something.

Flaka was also befriended by one supportive teacher but spoke of how even some teachers participate in harassing gay students.

> When I hang out with my friends at lunch, everyone who walks by starts harassing us. But one of the teachers is very supportive. He backs us up and is really helpful. Some teachers don't want anything related to sex talked about in high school. They will make remarks themselves about gays. One teacher even told a dirty, crude joke about gays.

These stories are far from unique. They make us aware of just how frightening it can be for some of the children growing up gay to simply go off to school each day. We all hope that our schools will provide safe and secure environments for our children. Instead our gay children may be entering a "danger zone" (D'Augelli's [1998b] descriptive term), a place where they may have to fend off daily harassment or engage in desperate attempts to hide their sexual identity. From these stories we also hear that even a single compassionate and sensitive teacher can make a significant difference to a gay youth struggling in a hostile school atmosphere. How unfortunate it is, though, when teachers fail to address antigay remarks in their classrooms or even make such remarks themselves.

WHAT DOES RESEARCH SHOW ABOUT HARASSMENT OF GAYS IN SCHOOLS?

Although little research exists that measures the attitudes of children or younger teenagers toward homosexuals, a study (Marsiglio, 1993) questioned fifteen- to nineteen-year-old males, 89 percent of whom said they thought that sex between men was "disgusting." Only 12 percent in the study felt they could befriend a gay person. In another study by D'Augelli and Rose (1990), 75 percent of a group of male college freshman agreed with the statement "Male homosexuals are disgusting." Another study about sexual harassment in high schools by the American Association of University Women (1993) found that students were more upset about being called gay than about any other form of sexual harassment. These studies suggest that a large number of young people, perhaps particularly boys, have very negative attitudes about gay people. These homophobic attitudes underlie much of the harassment of gay students, or those perceived as gay, in school settings. When the harassment is ignored or tolerated by school authorities it is a confirmation for gay students that something is wrong with them.

Growing evidence supports that physical and verbal harassment toward students perceived as gay is common in high school and college settings and even in junior high and elementary schools. For example, Anthony D'Augelli (1996) surveyed 249 lesbian, gay, and bisexual youth and found that 62 percent reported that they had been verbally harassed by other students while in high school and 13 percent reported being hit. Twenty-three percent reported being verbally harassed by teachers and 37 percent lost friends because of their sexual orientation. Only 17 percent of the youths in the study had been mostly or completely open about their sexual orientation while in high school, secrecy easy to understand given the frequency with which gay students are targets of harassment.

In a more recent study, D'Augelli (1999) found that boys were more likely to be victimized in high school than were girls. Further, those boys who were gender atypical, who failed to fit the masculine or "macho" image, were more likely to be victimized than those who appeared more masculine. He also found that those gay students who had been frequently victimized and harassed by their fellow students had a higher rate of mental health symptoms than those who were infrequently or never harassed. His study confirmed the frequently reported high rates of suicidal tendencies among gay youth, finding that in this group of 333 gay and lesbian students, 26 percent of them had felt suicidal sometimes or often during the past year and that 38 percent had felt suicidal at some time during their lifetime.

Another study (Goodenow and Hack, 1998) used the results of The Massachusetts Youth Risk Behavior Survey, a questionnaire that was administered in 1997 to nearly 4000 students in that state's public high schools. This study showed that sexual minority students were significantly more likely than other students to be intimidated in the school setting. Being intimidated was defined as having one's property damaged or stolen at school, being threatened or injured with a weapon at school, or having skipped school because of feeling unsafe. These three measures were combined to form a total called the *school intimidation* score. Students who identified as gay or lesbian or who stated that they had engaged in same-sex behavior scored significantly higher in the extent to which they had been intimidated in school than did students who reported no homosexual inclinations.

The Massachusetts Survey also questioned students about their own violence-related behavior, substance abuse, and suicidal ideation and attempts. Gay students as a group reported higher levels of all of these, with particularly high levels of suicidal plans and attempts. For example, approximately 38 percent of the gay and lesbian students said they had attempted suicide in the past year while only around 8 percent of the other students said they had done so. The researchers suggested that homosexuality, in itself, was not responsible for the higher levels of suicidal tendencies, violence-related behaviors, and substance abuse among gay students, but that instead intimidation at school accounted for the higher frequency of problem behaviors.

A follow-up study (Bontempo, 1999) analyzed the results from the Massachusetts Youth Risk Behavior Survey and a similar survey done in Vermont. Bontempo found that gay students who had been frequently victimized at school had much higher rates of suicide, drug and alcohol use, and truancy because they felt more unsafe than did nongay students who had been equally victimized. Thus, gay and lesbian students appeared to be more adversely affected by intimidation at school than heterosexual students. This study also revealed that gay boys who had been frequently victimized at school were more adversely affected than were lesbians who had been equally victimized.

Bontempo suggested several possible reasons why gay students might have been harmed more by intimidation at school than nongay students. He thought that one reason might be that the victimization of gay youths was more severe than that of nongays. A second reason might be that victimization because of one's sexual identity is more psychologically distressing than other types of victimization. Another possible reason could be that gay youth are less likely to seek help after being victimized. Since parents often don't know they have a gay child, if their child were to come to them about having been harassed at school, the reason for the harassment would likely have to be revealed. The child might be afraid to do that. Children harassed at school for some other reasons might be more likely to seek and receive family support and probably more likely also to report the harassment to school personnel. These are all just hypotheses and the study could not definitively answer the question of why gay youths suffer more severe behavioral effects from victimization at school than nongay youths, but the issue needs further exploration.

Of course, some gay students may have families who know they are gay and would be supportive if told about the harassment. But when school victimization is severe, even a supportive family may not be sufficient to protect against emotional damage. In another study (Hershberger and D'Augelli, 1995) it was found that the mental health of gay boys and girls with high family support was better than for those with low family support. But this was true only for those who had not been subjected to high levels of victimization. Those youth who had been physically attacked, had objects thrown at them, or had been chased or spit on had poorer mental health regardless of whether or not they had family support. So it would appear that the serious harassment that many gay youths experience at school may be so psychologically damaging that even parental support is not a sufficient buffer to protect against serious mental health problems. This finding points out that though parental support for gay youth is certainly important, it is not enough. Equally important is for schools to enact the policies and procedures that will prevent the harassment and victimization these students experience in the school environment.

CULTURAL PERMISSION FOR ANTIGAY HARASSMENT

Karen Franklin (1998) reached the conclusion from her research that a certain level of "cultural permission" exists in our society to denigrate and harass homosexuals. Her research has led her to believe that our culture is so tolerant of "gay bashing" that harassers feel justified in their behavior. In the 1998 study, she surveyed 484 community-college students, asking them whether they had ever harassed or been violent toward a gay male or a lesbian. The male students acknowledged a much higher incidence of such behavior than did females. Thirty-two percent of the males in the study acknowledged that they had verbally assaulted people they thought were gay and 18 percent acknowledged physical assault or making physical threats. Schools and workplaces were the most common sites of the attacks.

Those students who admitted harassing gays justified their behavior by saying that the victim was attempting to sexually proposition them, or that they just wanted to have fun, or that it was a way of proving their heterosexuality and toughness to friends. Common beliefs among the students in the study were that homosexuals are sexual predators or that they are immoral and need to be punished for violating social norms. A large percentage of those who admitted having harassed gays said that homosexuality disgusted them.

Franklin also found that even among those individuals in her study who indicated they had never engaged in acts of physical or verbal harassment against gays, many reported that they refrained because of fear of getting in trouble with authorities or because they were afraid of getting hurt. Franklin concluded that some of those who had never actually harassed gays were not necessarily any more tolerant than were those who admitted being harassers.

Franklin emphasized the point that the people in her study were typical college students, not uneducated people, not people who were criminals or delinquents. Yet many of these typical students appeared to think nothing was wrong with harassing or assaulting gay or lesbian people. Franklin places at least part of the blame upon a cultural climate that accepts and tolerates harassment of those who are different, particularly homosexuals, and she criticized school curricula that do not present any positive images of homosexuals, thus contributing to the proliferation of negative stereotypes.

THE HIDDEN GAY STUDENTS

Given that so many young gays do not acknowledge their sexual orientation during their junior high or high school years, the high levels of intimidation and harassment reported in these studies may not apply to all gay students. Those gay students who are not at all obvious to their peers and who choose to keep their sexual orientation a secret are much less likely to be the direct targets of taunting and victimization at school. But they will certainly be affected as they observe what happens to their openly or obviously gay peers. On a questionnaire such as the Massachusetts Survey, those students who are aware of or suspect their same-sex attractions but are still secretive about it may not admit to their homosexuality, even though they realize the questionnaire is anonymous. Such students would not show up as gay in the statistics from the survey. However, this does not mean that gay youth who are still in the closet and are not themselves being harassed are unaffected by homophobic taunts and name-calling. It does not take a lot of imagination to suspect that gay youth, even though not personally harassed, will still suffer vicariously as they observe the treatment of students perceived as gay and will feel the same assault to their own identity. And what of the guilt or sense of weakness they may experience when they fail to come to the defense of their secret comrades, when they fail to speak out against antigay slurs and attacks?

INTIMIDATION AND HARASSMENT MAY PROVOKE VIOLENCE IN SCHOOLS

Perhaps it is the case, as is hinted at in the Massachusetts study, that being intimidated on a regular basis in school may provoke aggression and violence on the part of those students who are harassed. Reports in the media during the recent flood of school violence and killings indicated that some of the perpetrators had been taunted about being gay, though no evidence suggests that any of them actually were gay.

Dorothy Espelage and her students at the University of Illinois reported recently (Asiado, Vion, and Espelage,1999) that bullying is rampant in U.S. schools. She suggested that this practice may be a major factor in explaining some of the violence that erupts in schools because of the anger bullying creates in its victims. Her study showed that 81 percent of the students in her study admitted to having bullied classmates during the previous month. Seventy-five percent of the bullies said they themselves had been harassed. Bullying included ridiculing, threatening to hurt, pushing, shoving, slapping, and kicking. The most frequent targets were those who appeared different in any way.

Harassment and victimization on school campuses of those who are different, whether on the basis of sexual orientation or some other characteristic, is not only a form of violence itself but may also provoke violence as a reaction from those who are its victims. The chronic emotional stress created in any child who is taunted and bullied frequently at school is perhaps underestimated in our concern about school violence, although its effects are certainly not limited to those children who are perceived as gay. Anyone who is an outsider, a "loser," at the bottom of the school social hierarchy, is at risk of being bullied and shamed. For most male students, being effeminate or being labeled as homosexual is the ultimate insult, and may mean being relegated to the very bottom rungs of the social hierarchy. It is little wonder that many of those who can pass as heterosexual will monitor every nuance of their public image in order to keep their orientation a secret. Imagine the vigilance required of a child or adolescent who must always present and image that is inconsistent with who he or she actually is.

Andrew Sullivan, in a 1999 article in the *New York Times Magazine* titled "What's So Bad About Hate," also suggested that those who are the victims of hate may retaliate in violent ways. He gave an example of Dylan Klebold and Eric Harris, the Columbine High School assailants in Colorado who were regularly called "faggots" in the halls and classrooms of their school, and concluded that it should not be surprising that persons subjected to ridicule and harassment will sometimes react violently in return. Sullivan does not excuse the actions of Klebold and Harris, but writes that some hates seem more justified than others. Sullivan suggests that those who have been oppressed, tormented, and shamed may be more justified than those who did the original tormenting.

Male athletes are sometimes among those who are most invested in their masculinity, those among whom the "Boy Code" is most highly enforced (Pollack, 1998). They may also be the bullies and are at least sometimes among those who are most intolerant of boys they think are gay or who are effeminate in any way. The male athletes may have been among those who Klebold and Harris believed were shaming them and toward whom their anger was directed.

In a 1999 article in *Time Magazine*, Nancy Gibbs and Timothy Roche wrote about the fact that many students and faculty at Columbine High School claimed that the school was portrayed too negatively in the media and disagreed with the description of the school as rife with harassment of those who were different. Many of those who were interviewed claimed that there was no unusual harassment and that the accusation of cruelty toward some students was greatly exaggerated. However, one of the athletes, in attempting to stand up for his school, revealed more than perhaps he intended or realized in his statements:

> Columbine is a clean, good place except for those rejects. (Klebold and Harris and their friends) . . . Sure we teased them, but what do you expect with kids who come to school with weird hairdos and horns on their hats. It's not just jocks; the whole school's disgusted with them. They're a bunch of homos, grabbing each other's private parts. If you want to get rid of someone, usually you tease 'em. So the whole school would call them homos, and when they did something sick, we'd tell them, "You're sick and that's wrong." (Gibbs and Roche, p. 183)

Chapter 8

Students Tell Us How Schools Can Help

Many gay and lesbian students report feeling unsafe psychologically, and sometimes even physically, just being themselves in the school setting. These students realize that coming out as gay or even being perceived as gay may lead to harassment from their fellow students. Those students who join school-based gay/straight alliances are more "out" and run the risk of being even more vulnerable to harassment. Despite these risks, an increasing number of gay and lesbian high school students are starting to become active in forming and attending such groups. Again, the claim cannot be made that these students are representative of all gay high school students. In fact, most likely they are not. But they have become a source of information about gay youths that we did not have in the past, when most information about what it was like to be a gay child or adolescent came from accounts of adults remembering what they had experienced during their youth.

ACTIONS SCHOOLS CAN TAKE

In my interviews with participants in gay/straight alliances on school campuses, students were outspoken about what they thought schools should do to create a safer, more comfortable climate for their gay students.

Sex Education

Among the ideas suggested by the students were changes in sex education and health curricula. A number of students thought that safe homosexual sex was just as important to discuss as safe heterosexual sex and that AIDS education without reference to homosexuals was discriminatory. Some thought that AIDS prevention would hardly be complete without reference to homosexuals. Eighteen-year-old Flaka said, "They could teach about sexual orientation in sex education. The only thing I have ever been told in school is that ' . . . occasionally there are homosexuals, I don't know why, but we're not going to talk about it.' "

Gay/Straight Alliances

Many students mentioned gay/straight alliances and clubs on school campuses and how these groups need the support of administration and faculty. Even a few faculty members or staff willing to help students start these groups would provide a supportive and reassuring message to gay students. Among the reasons gay students gave for why schools should encourage these groups is that they help gay students feel they are not alone and they provide a safe place where these students can meet others like themselves and talk about the difficulties they are having in resolving the conflict between who they are and what they are being told they should be.

Sensitivity Training for Teachers, Administrators, and Students

Other students suggested sensitivity training for administrators and teachers to help them understand issues related to sexual orientation and how gay students feel in school settings where they are not accepted.

> Open their eyes by having diversity workshops. Bring it to their attention. Hopefully they will become more tolerant. We want acceptance but we will live with tolerance. Teachers and counselors could put up posters which show support, like a big pink triangle or a pride flag. For gay teachers and administrators to be open about being gay, to be role models. This would give me a sense of pride. "She's a teacher; she's gone to college; she's been through all this." I admire my one teacher who is openly gay. I look up to her.

Some students also spoke of having sensitivity or diversity training for students. Seventeen-year-old H. W., for example, said the following:

There should be tolerance classes but they have to be taught by someone the students respect. A lot of schools need tolerance classes for different groups, racial, ethnic, etc. Through knowledge, intolerance and hatred would dissipate. Discuss the topic of sexual orientation in regular classes. Broaden the curriculum, the African experience, etc. Encourage diversity understanding. Allow people to be who they are. You don't have to agree with them.

Seventeen-year-old Ann agreed with H. W., saying:

Educate the other students by going into classrooms and explaining what it is like to be gay in our society, answer their questions. Help them learn to accept us. I would like for the people in our group to go into the junior highs and talk to the eighth graders just before they are going to go into high school. Tell them what they may face and that we are there as a group to help them.

Stop Harassment of Gay Students

A request for administrators and teachers to put a stop to harassment of gay students was mentioned frequently. Ann suggested schools should ". . . encourage teachers to say something when kids in class harass us or call us names." And Flaka said, "Teachers could individually put a stop to name-calling. Don't allow humiliation." Flaka also suggested having policies that make it unacceptable to discriminate against anybody, whether students, faculty, or staff, because of sexual orientation. Some mentioned that it was easier to get gay clubs started when sexual orientation was already a part of a school district's antidiscrimination policy. Sixteen-year-old Kate gave this advice:

Change the antidiscrimination policy to include sexual orientation. They do nothing about verbal harassment but they have racial rules. Teachers could do something about name calling in the classroom. They don't think it's an issue or that it affects anyone in their classroom. They need to admit that faggot is meant as a put down.

Nineteen-year-old Andy said, "Make teachers more aware that, if gay students are being violated, they should do something. It makes the gay youth feel even more frightened and alone when teachers don't do anything." F. F. thought that the most important thing schools could do was to acknowledge that gay students exist and give them support. He said, "We don't need any special treatment. Just don't condemn us. Don't allow any bashing. Create a safe emotional environment." And Samantha said, "Make it known that it's OK to be gay. They can't make the kids like homosexuals. You'll always have homophobia. But they can educate that we are OK. We're not all perverts. Some gays give us a bad name. Educate about sexual orientation."

Open Discussion About Homosexuality in Classes

Some students, including sixteen-year-old Erica, suggested addressing homosexuality directly in the classroom by introducing basic information about sexual orientation and providing opportunities for the topic to be discussed. Erica said she understood that parents of elementary school students might have trouble with this suggestion. Several students thought that one of the most important things teachers could do would be to inform students about famous gay persons so that gay kids would have someone to look up to. Tiger suggested the following: "I believe that the best way [to help gay students] is to introduce sexual orientation into the history and English courses, great emperors, painters, sculptors. Show students gay people can be great. Like if someone had told me that my favorite composers were gay. I didn't want to be like the gays I knew about." Star suggested that a history of the gay community be taught in classrooms and that teachers help present more positive images of gay people.

Normalize Homosexuality

These young people seem to have figured out what schools need to do. The next step is to persuade the schools to listen to what they have to say. These young students seem to be saying that a primary emphasis for schools should be to normalize homosexuality, to get across the simple idea that being homosexual is not really a big deal, and to say that gay youths don't need to be treated any differently than straight youth. But at the same time schools need to be aware that what is going on now tends to either demonize gay students or pretend that they are not there. Neither of these approaches helps to normalize these people, to make them just another part of the student body, or to keep them safe. The media is making more progress than most schools are. For example, in movies and on TV there are now many more openly gay characters who are not twisted and deviant, but are just typical, everyday people who happen to be homosexual.

A GAY FOOTBALL PLAYER COMES OUT

An inspiring story about a gay high school football player, cocaptain of his team, who came out to his team members, was recently reported in an article by Robert Lipsyte in *The New York Times* (April 30, 2000). Football players are, in high school, usually at the very top of the social hierarchy and for one of them to risk his reputation as an athlete and male icon by coming out as gay is a rare event and will probably have a major impact, at least in this one particular school and community.

The caption under Corey Johnson's picture in the newspaper describes him as defying a high school sports stereotype. In the article, the writer calls Johnson a "liberating symbol" and points out how athletic coaches often use homophobia in the socialization of their athletes. After coming out, Johnson was quoted as follows, "Someday I want to get beyond being that gay football captain, but for now I need to get out there and show these machismo athletes who run high schools that you don't have to do drama or be a drum major to be gay. It could be someone who looks just like them."

Before Corey Johnson decided to come out to his team members at the Masconomet High School in Massachusetts, he agonized about his secret. At some point he told a school guidance counselor and his biology teacher that he was bisexual. Later he told his lacrosse coach that he was gay. He began attending his school's gay/straight alliance group, which was composed almost entirely of straight girls. Then he decided to tell his parents. His mother was fearful that her son would be hurt or that people would be mean to him if anyone found out. Then Johnson, along with the school sponsor of the Gay/Straight Alliance, attended a conference of the Gay, Lesbian and Straight Education Network (GLSEN), a national organization that, among other things, promotes safe schools for gay/lesbian/bisexual students. He attended a sports workshop led by Jeff Perrotti, GLSEN's Northeast coordinator. Perrotti discussed the special entitlement of athletes in school settings, and suggested that all students needed to be treated as well as the athletes are.

At that workshop, Johnson revealed that he was a football captain at his high school and he wanted help in coming out. Perrotti was instrumental in working with the school and the parents in planning a strategy for Johnson to come out to his coach and his teammates. More than a year had gone by since Johnson had spoken to his teachers and guidance counselor when he finally told his coach that he was gay and arranged to have a meeting with his team members to tell them. With the support of his coach, Jim Pugh, and the other two starting linebackers on the team, any resistance from parents, team players, or other students was quickly addressed. Johnson graduated from high school the spring of 2000 and planned to go to San Francisco after graduation and work as an intern in the San Francisco GLSEN office.

What better way to normalize gays in high school than to have a captain of the football team come out as gay? It says that gays are among us, that some are the athletes, some are the honor students, some are the drama and the dance students, some are gender atypical, while some are the epitome of masculinity or femininity. And some are just average, ordinary, everyday kids.

Chapter 9

How Individuals Within the School
System Can Help Gay Students

> I think that teachers and administrators are professionals, obligated to accept everybody and treat everybody with respect. That is part of their job. They don't have to like gays, they just have to accept them for who they are and treat them with the same respect they treat everybody else. (High school teacher)

Gay students do not, of course, always, or even usually, identify themselves. But they will be in every school and in every classroom. They are sometimes the lonely outsiders, they are sometimes the "sissies" or the "tomboys," but they also may be the best athletes, the school leaders, the accomplished scholars. It is not necessary for schools to know who is gay to help these students and it should be kept in mind that those gay students who are at the top of the school social heirarchy may be even less likely to acknowledge their orientation than those who run no risk of losing their social prestige since they already have little or none.

If schools are to help change the lives of both their hidden and their open gay students, individual adults in the school system need to stand up for them in whatever way their position and personal situation permits. An especially powerful way to do this, one only available to those individuals who are gay or lesbian themselves, is for them to come out and openly acknowledge their orientation. Gay and straight students alike then get the message that respected adults are not always heterosexuals, that homosexuals can be teachers, principals, nurses, counselors and that they can lead normal lives. Openly gay adults in the school system also convey to the gay students that there is someone they might be able to approach with their questions or concerns.

I am certainly well aware that deciding to be openly gay or lesbian may be extremely difficult, perhaps impossible, due to particular personal circumstances or particular school settings. When the school's antidiscrimination policies for students and faculty do not include sexual orientation, for example, one's very livelihood may be at risk. There may be negative professional and personal consequences even when such policies do exist. But realization of what such an act may mean for the gay children with whom they come in contact has motivated some individuals in some schools to take risks they had never thought they would, and to thereby become role models for those children.

A TEACHER'S COMING-OUT STORY

Barb Mathers is a lesbian and has been an eighth grade Language Arts teacher in Tucson, Arizona, for ten years. She had never tried to conceal her sexual orientation at school, but she had never openly disclosed it unless she were specifically asked. She was always sensitive to the needs of gay kids. She tried to use "teachable moments" to bring issues of sexual orientation into the classroom and incorporated sexual orientation into the curriculum through assignments and discussions regarding diversity and discrimination. She was very aware of how cruel middle school students sometimes were to one another and she observed how those perceived as gay, particularly the male students, were teased and humiliated on a daily basis—sometimes to the point that they would quit coming to school. Mathers believes this kind of social cruelty is more pervasive and intense in middle schools than it is in high schools when students are a little more mature and perhaps striving less for status.

The plight of gay students and those students perceived to be gay increasingly troubled Mathers, particularly as she saw that other teachers and staff often failed to intervene when antigay remarks were made, even though they didn't allow racial or ethnic epithets. Her impression then and now is that many teachers are uncomfortable with this issue and just try to ignore it. Occasionally, individual students came to Mathers in distress over some humiliation that they had endured at school or because of the dawning realization that they were gay or that other kids were calling them gay. Then one of her young students, a girl, came to her in the depths of a depression.

This student had been engaging in self-mutilating behavior and was suicidal. She told Barb that she was gay and would never amount to anything, that she was afraid she was going to go to hell. Barb spontaneously came out to this young girl and told her that she herself was gay and that being gay didn't make a person worthless. The girl's stunned response made Barb realize how important it was for her to be open. She began to think that she had not done enough for these students who sat quietly in her classroom while inside they were living with anxiety and fear of discovery.

She reached a crucial decision. In an e-mail, which she sent to all the faculty and administrators, she wrote about how difficult it is for young gay and lesbian students to deal with all the stresses of emerging adolescence and, in addition, to have to deal with realizing how different they are from their peers. She wrote of how little support these students were getting, and noted that when slurs went on in the halls and in the classrooms, often nothing was done to stop it. She described how these students were sometimes afraid to come to school, afraid of the homophobic remarks, afraid they would be harassed and embarrassed. She also made it quite clear that she understood at a personal level what these students were going through because she had gone through the same thing when she was in school.

Mathers was prompted to come out at work by the evolution in her own thinking about gay children and their needs, by a growing sense of her responsibility as an adult to be a positive role model for these children, and by the very dramatic experience with one particular student. Also, during this same time period, the Director of Student Services, Dr. Alan Storm, had begun to bring the needs of gay and lesbian students to the attention of the school district through in-service training and staff development programs. This gave Mathers a certain sense of support, as did the fact that the school district antidiscrimination policies specifically included sexual orientation. Mathers has no regrets about her decision and there have been no negative repercussions. She has even received messages of support from other teachers, praising her courage and her willingness to take a controversial stand. She feels that she has touched the lives of many young people through bringing the issues to their attention in her classroom and through being willing to take the risk of coming out herself.

When asked about what advice she would give other gay and lesbian teachers, Mathers spoke of how so many of these teachers struggle with the decision about whether to come out. They want to help the kids in their classrooms, but they worry about hurting their careers and the reactions of parents and the community. Her final remark was "It's tough to come out and be honest, but they would be helping a lot of kids if they would do it."

WHAT ELSE CAN TEACHERS DO?

Ironically, heterosexual staff are sometimes in a better position to help gay students than gay and lesbian staff. A heterosexual adult in the school setting does not have the same risks and has less to lose if he or she begins to openly take steps to create a safer environment for gay students. Among the things that any teacher, whether gay or straight, can do are the following:

Stop Derogatory Remarks and Harassment

Teachers should treat derogatory remarks about sexual orientation just as they would such remarks about race, ethnicity, gender, disability, or religion. Labels such as "faggot," "queer," "fairy," "dyke," and "homo" are often used to demean homosexuals and should not be tolerated even in the context of a joke. Specific suggestions as to how to do this are:

1. In a very straightforward way, tell any student making antigay comments or jokes that such remarks are unacceptable in your classroom and in the school. Remind them of antidiscrimination policies if these exist.
2. If the setting is appropriate, ask the student and/or the class to think about how they feel when they are ridiculed or when they believe their peers do not like or do not accept them. Encourage open discussion about this issue.
3. Simply say, "Name-calling is cruel and it hurts." or "In this classroom disrespect toward anyone is not allowed."
4. Be equally straightforward in confronting antigay comments or jokes by faculty or staff.

5. Be aware of the bullying and harassment that happen on the playground and in the hallways and inform students that such behavior will not be tolerated in the school. Children who are being isolated, teased, or bullied by their peers for whatever reason, need to be identified and given attention and support. Bullies need to be identified and given appropriate guidance and consequences.

Allow the Topic to Be Discussed

Allow homosexuality to be discussed comfortably in the classroom. In fact, antigay remarks can be used as an opportunity for doing so. How can you do this?

1. When the words homosexual, gay, lesbian, "faggot," and so on come up in the classroom, respond with factual information. For example:

- Did you know that a small percentage of people (estimates vary from 2 percent to 10 percent) in every society are homosexual, which just means that they are sexually attracted to and fall in love with persons of the same sex?
- Homosexuals are not perverted or sick. They are like everyone else except in their sexual orientation. They are doctors, lawyers, actors, truck drivers, football players, nurses, teachers, politicians.
- We do not know why certain people are homosexual while others are heterosexual. There are a number of theories, but none seem to fully explain the cause of homosexuality.
- No one should be made fun of or discriminated against because he or she is different from the "norm."
- If someone happens to be homosexual it doesn't mean he or she cannot live a happy, successful life.
- Many famous people who have contributed to society are gay, lesbian, or bisexual.

2. Use specific examples of accomplished gay/lesbian/bisexual writers, actors, athletes, and so on in class discussion, acknowledging their sexual or bisexual orientation (e.g., Billy Jean King, Martina

Navratilova, Walt Whitman, Rock Hudson, Christopher Isherwood, Gertrude Stein, Edward Albee, Tennessee Williams, James Baldwin, Allen Ginsberg, and U. S. Representatives Barney Frank and Jim Kolbe).

Be a Model

Demonstrate to your students that you are accepting of all minorities and that a person's character and behavior are what is important, not religion, not color, not gender, not sexual orientation. You can accomplish this by freely discussing the topic of diversity—how human beings are different in many ways—and emphasizing that we should appreciate and respect these differences. Point out that sexual orientation is just another way that people are different. This difference does not make homosexuals better or worse than anyone else.

Include Lesbian and Gay Issues in Your Curricula

Here are some ways you can do this:

1. Discuss these topics when relevant to the specific course (e.g., when studying civil rights, health, sexuality, literature, history).
2. Assign readings that address gay/lesbian issues or include the topic in the list of suggested topics for student research papers or class presentations.
3. Ask outside speakers to present to your class on this topic.
4. Be aware that recent national surveys (Schemo, 2000) indicate that, not only do parents want schools to provide more explicit sex education for their children, but 76 percent of those surveyed even want sex education courses to cover sexual orientation and homosexuality.

Be Aware of Materials and Resources

1. Acquaint yourself with relevant resources in the community, for example, gay/lesbian-friendly agencies, gay youth support groups, groups such as mental health professional associations who may be willing to provide speakers to your classes, and speakers from Parents, Families, and Friends of Lesbians and Gays (PFLAG).

2. Display relevant news items, brochures from gay-related agencies, and appropriate books in your classroom. A pink triangle decal or a rainbow flag on the classroom door is a message of acceptance.
3. Approach your school librarian to request that there are appropriate gay-related books in the library.
4. Many materials and exercises that teachers can use in their classrooms to inform students and increase their awareness about sexual orientation can be accessed through GLSEN (Gay, Lesbian and Straight Education Network) at <www.glsen.org>.

Be Sensitive to Language

Be aware of and sensitive to how our language assumes that everyone is heterosexual.

1. Refer to parents, not just mother and father. The parents may be a lesbian or gay couple.
2. Use non-gender-specific language (e.g. partner or special friend rather than girlfriend, boyfriend, wife, etc.).

WHAT CAN SCHOOL COUNSELORS AND SCHOOL PSYCHOLOGISTS DO?

Counselors and psychologists working in schools often have backgrounds in child development and understand the social and emotional needs of children and adolescents as well as the psychological effects of harassment and discrimination. They may also have been exposed, perhaps more than many teachers and administrators, to factual information about homosexuality and sexual orientation development. School counselors and psychologists who recognize that there is always a small percentage of students within the school population who will eventually identify as gay, are likely to be especially alert to subtle cues and indicators that will help them recognize children who may be developing in this direction and children who may be perceived as gay.

Counselors and psychologists at the elementary school level can help create a more accepting school environment for all children, including those who are gender atypical and especially vulnerable to teasing and bullying. One way may be to provide materials, consultation, and training about sexual orientation and gender stereotypes to teachers and administrators. Another approach is to assist teachers in developing and implementing a set of well-defined classroom guidelines prohibiting harassment and promoting respect toward all students. Counselors and psychologists at the elementary school level could also become involved in designing programs to educate teachers, administrators, and students about the harmful effects on children of teasing and harassment.

Counselors and school psychologists at the junior high and high school level may be called upon to deal more directly with the issue of sexual orientation. Indeed, almost all adolescents have concerns about sexuality and counselors who work with this age group must have the ability to create an accepting atmosphere in which sexuality, both homosexual and heterosexual, can be discussed with ease. If, as a counselor for young people, you are not comfortable with these issues, your ability to help students of this age group will be limited.

It can be very affirming for the gay student if the counselor or school psychologist displays in his or her office names, phone numbers, brochures, and posters for local gay/lesbian support groups and support groups for parents of lesbians and gays. Displaying gay symbols such as the pink triangle, the rainbow flag, and appropriate books are other ways of acknowledging gay youth and their legitimate concerns. Some students may memorize or write down the phone numbers without ever speaking directly about their sexual orientation.

A specific way of opening up communication may be to make casual remarks showing that you are aware of young people having same-sex attractions and that you are not judgmental. Such comments can be made in the context of exploration of the many issues troublesome to adolescents. For example, to an adolescent who is having difficulty communicating his or her reasons for seeking out counseling, you may casually insert "same-sex feelings" as a possible concern. When you ask the youth about his or her concerns and he or she is not forthcoming, you might say something such as, "Are you having problems getting along with friends, depression, poor grades, family problems, problems with the opposite sex, feelings of attraction toward your own sex?" or "Are you having problems with boyfriends or girlfriends?" Such casual inclusions give the youth permission to discuss homosexual feelings by conveying the message that you accept these feelings as legitimate and are likely to be nonjudgmental. For a gay or lesbian young person to hear this message from a counselor is a validation that he or she may never have received before. You may have an impact on many students in this very small way without ever even knowing it. Even if you strongly believe that the student may be gay or lesbian, do not be surprised if they do not respond to such an opening. Their overt response is not so important as the student's inner realization that you must think it's OK to be homosexual.

If an adolescent does acknowledge same-sex concerns, there are helpful ways to respond. Most important is to recognize that the young person has taken a monumental step in acknowledging these feelings to another human being—you may even be the first. Let the youth know that you appreciate and respect the trust placed in you and let him or her know as directly as possible that you do not share the social prejudices toward homosexuality. When a young person has had the courage to reveal homosexual attractions, any hint that you are shocked or disgusted or that you do not want to discuss the issue can be damaging, while an accepting attitude can help alleviate feelings of guilt and abnormality. If you find that you are unable to be nonjudgmental, help the youth find someone to talk to who is perhaps more knowledgeable or understanding.

A word of caution regarding the assessment of sexual orientation: not all adolescents who have fantasies and thoughts involving same-sex attractions will necessarily have a basic homosexual orientation. You should not prematurely label an adolescent as homosexual and should not encourage premature self-labeling. But if you are nonjudgmental and supportive, you can help the young person to clarify and understand his or her feelings and support healthy development and sexual identity, whatever it may turn out to be in the long run. Reassurance should be given that if, indeed, the youth now or eventually identifies as homosexual he or she can still lead a productive, fulfilling life. The adolescent struggling with same-sex feelings needs information about sexual orientation that helps him or her understand that homosexuality is not an abnormal condition, but a natural variation of sexuality. Counselors do not need to be afraid that talking about homosexuality will lead a young person to become gay.

Assessing for Specific Risks

HIV and STDs

Homosexual and bisexual youth are at greater risk than average of acquiring HIV infection and other sexually transmitted diseases (Coleman and Remafedi, 1989). For boys, of course, this is because in this country HIV was first transmitted through male-to-male sexual contact, and gay males still constitute one of the high-risk groups. However, for both boys and girls, the fatalistic, hopeless perception of life some gay youths have can lead to a greater likelihood of their engaging in high-risk, self-destructive sexual behavior. Thus, it is important for a counselor to specifically ask the young person whether he or she is sexually active and to try to determine whether the individual fully understands how HIV and other diseases are transmitted and how to protect himself or herself. Provide information about the risks involved in teen sexual activity and remind the student that one way to avoid the risks is, of course, to delay sexual involvement. However, it is unrealistic and even irresponsible on a counselor's part to assume that all adolescents will make the decision to delay sexual activity. Counselors should be prepared to help students reduce their risk of exposure to STDs in other ways. For example, a gay boy may need help in obtaining condoms and instruction in their use. The school nurse may be an appropriate resource or possibly the local health department, community AIDS agencies, or prevention programs for both males and females. Students may feel more comfortable dealing with someone outside the school system.

Suicide

Numerous research studies have suggested that sexual minority youth may be at much higher risk for suicide than heterosexual youth—possibly two to three or more times higher (Goodenow and Hack, 1998; Jay and Young, 1979; Remafedi, 1987; Remafedi et al., 1998; Roesler and Deisher, 1972). Similar findings have also been reported in a U.S. Department of Health and Human Resources Task Force report (Gibson, 1989). The counselor working with a gay youth may need to assess whether this particular student is a suicidal risk. Issues to explore include the following:

1. Is there any history of substance abuse?
2. Is there any sleep disturbance?
3. Have there been recent changes in appetite or weight (i.e., loss of appetite, overeating, weight loss or gain)?
4. Is there any evidence of a history of physical, sexual, or emotional abuse?
5. Are there any recent significant losses?
6. Does the youth feel sad or feel that life is not worth living?
7. How does the youth feel about being homosexual or bisexual? Is there internalized homophobia?
8. Has anyone in the family or peer group attempted or committed suicide?
9. Has the youth ever thought about hurting himself or herself or ending his or her life?
10. How recently have there been any suicidal thoughts or thoughts of self-harm?
11. Has the youth ever thought about how he or she would commit suicide?
12. Is there a specific suicide plan?
13. Has there ever been a previous suicide attempt?
14. What kind of support system (e.g., family and peers) does the youth have?

If you think the youth may be actively suicidal, you need to inform the youth that you will have to notify his or her parents. Referral and crisis intervention outside the school setting will be needed for suicidal or seriously depressed adolescents.

Harassment at School

As we have already noted, there is a high likelihood that openly gay students or students perceived to be gay will be harassed and victimized in the school setting. It may be very difficult for these students to admit that this is happening to them because they do not want to call attention to the fact that other students believe they are gay. Through sensitive questioning it may be possible to encourage the student to reveal that he or she is being harassed. If you have already established that you are accepting and nonjudgmental, the youth is much more likely to reveal the problem. When this happens, students should be assured that if they are willing to report the perpetrators you will do your best to see that they are protected and that appropriate steps are taken by the administration to discipline the perpetrators. Unless carefully handled this approach could, of course, make matters worse and lead to more extreme harassment of the youth, so it is important to have some sense of how the school administrators are likely to handle the situation. If the school has antidiscrimination policies that include sexual orientation it will be much easier to take the appropriate steps to protect gay students. If there are no such policies, school psychologists and counselors should to approach their school board with a recommendation that the policies be amended to include sexual orientation. However, no student should be harassed or bullied for any reason. An antidiscrimination policy may be an added weapon, but it should also be possible to deal with these situations without one.

Substance Abuse

Substance abuse can be a problem for many youth, but the additional stress gay youth experience as they try to deal with their sexual orientation can sometimes lead to a higher risk of experimentation with drugs and alcohol. Getting high can be a way of feeling better about themselves, of helping them fit in with their peers, of alleviating loneliness and isolation. When the gay youth has a supportive counselor or family or is in a support group with others, there may be less of a need for such behavior. However, even with such support many youth may continue to abuse drugs or alcohol. There are outpatient programs in most communities for young persons with substance abuse issues and referral to one of these programs may be appropriate. Referral for family counseling may also be helpful, particularly if the youth needs and wants help in coming out to parents.

Family Issues

Gay youths seldom have the same type of family support for their minority status that youth from other minorities do. They may fear to reveal their sexual orientation to their families because of possible negative reactions. Some gay and lesbian people never reveal their sexual orientation to their families, even after reaching adulthood.

Children and adolescents usually know when their families are deeply hostile toward homosexuals because they have heard negative remarks and comments openly expressed in their homes. In other families homosexuality is simply never mentioned, as though it does not exist. Even in families that are tolerant and accepting of homosexuals and even though the children do not believe they run any risk of rejection or ridicule, they may be fearful that their parents would be disappointed to learn they have a gay child. Any of these family situations is likely to discourage gay children from letting their parents know what they are going through.

Here are some specific family issues to discuss with a youth who has told you he or she may be gay.

1. Does the family know of the child's concern about sexual orientation?
2. What does the child believe would be the family's reaction if they were to know?
3. Does the adolescent want to tell the family?
4. Does the adolescent want the counselor's help in telling the family?
5. Are there problems in the family happening now because of the secrecy involved?
6. If the family already knows or suspects, what has been their reaction and how can they be helped to deal with the issue?

Most gay adolescents say that telling their parents they think they are gay is very scary and they are uncertain about the wisdom of doing so. The counselor's role is a balancing act. If the youth is encouraged to tell the family, the family might reject or abandon him or her. Yet continued concealment from the family imposes its own risks, as the youth may withdraw from the family system in order to maintain the secret. As a general guideline the counselor should never inform the family against the adolescent's wishes. The wisest course is to follow the youth's lead and support him or her in whatever decision is made. However, in helping the youth reach a decision, the counselor should help prepare him or her for the many possible reactions and help the youth evaluate the relative risks of coming out to the parents compared to the risks of not coming out. Parents' reactions may range from acceptance and support to outright rejection and in some cases abuse or being told to leave the home.

If the family does discover, whether inadvertently or through being told directly, that their child thinks he or she may be gay, it is very likely to precipitate a crisis in which the counselor may become involved. A family in crisis will usually benefit from professional assistance. The school counselor may feel qualified to provide this or may instead wish to refer to outside professionals. Not all mental health professionals are trained to deal effectively with either a gay youth or his or her family. Those who do not understand the extent to which their own attitudes may have been affected by society's negative views of homosexuality and who do not realize the extent to which they themselves have homophobic attitudes may do more harm than good when they become involved with gay children and their families. Mental health professionals who, at some deep level, believe that homosexuals are deviant or immoral or who believe that homosexuals are inferior in some significant way to heterosexuals, should not work with this population. State psychological, psychiatric, or social work professional associations can usually provide referrals to mental health professionals who have special expertise in working with families of gay children and adolescents.

Can Psychotherapy and Religion Help?

Parents may ask school personnel for referral for individual treatment for their gay child. The counselor or psychologist should attempt to discover whether the parents' motive is to have the child "cured." Grave damage can be and has been done to gay/lesbian persons in treatment with ill-informed or prejudiced mental health professionals who have tried to "cure" them of something that is not an illness.

A number of the major national health and mental health organizations have developed an informational brochure (*Just the Facts About Sexual Orientation and Youth,* 1999) warning educators that "reparative therapy," aimed at curing homosexuality, is based on an unfounded and largely discredited theory that homosexuality is a mental disorder. These national organizations agree that homosexuality is not a mental disorder and thus that there is no need for a cure.

I urge counselors to provide this kind of information to parents who have learned they have a gay child. The parents should also be given information about the organization PFLAG (Parents, Families and Friends of Lesbians and Gays), which provides support groups to help them understand and accept their gay child rather than look for treatment to "cure" him or her. Psychotherapy may be needed to help the child deal with the psychological effects of homophobia or to help the family do so.

Some parents react to learning their child is gay by seeking the help of their church to "save" their child from homosexuality. The national organizations just referred to also point out that the use of religion to eliminate homosexual desires, referred to as "transformational ministry," is not universally supported by people of faith and that many religious congregations are now speaking out in support of gay, lesbian, and bisexual people and urging an end to any form of discrimination against them. Parents seeking help for their gay child through religion should also be provided with this information. Some churches now describe themselves as "welcoming congregations" and are reaching out to gay and lesbian members. Perhaps these churches are also beginning to reach out to gay youth.

Peter J. Gomes, Harvard professor and minister of the Harvard Memorial Church, addressed the issue of homophobia and religion in a talk to students in November, 1991, in which he spoke of how overly-literal interpretations of the Bible are used to condemn homosexuality. Reverend Gomes' remarks were quoted by a writer for *The New Yorker* (Boynton, 1996, p. 64) as follows: "Gay people are victims not of the Bible, not of religion, and not of the church, but of people who use religion as a way to devalue and deform those whom they can neither ignore nor convert."

WHAT CAN SCHOOL ADMINISTRATORS AND SCHOOL BOARDS DO?

Probably the single most important thing that school administrators and school boards can do is to review their antidiscrimination policies for both students and personnel to ensure that the policies are inclusive of sexual orientation. The administrator, whether it be the principal of a school or the superintendent of a school district, is likely to have broad access to the appropriate educational materials about sexual orientation and can facilitate the change process by bringing these materials to the attention of the school board. The brochure *Just the Facts About Sexual Orientation and Youth* (1999), provides very succinct information appropriate for both educators and school boards and is an ideal document to begin this process of education. This brochure will help administrators and school boards deal with community controversies about homosexuality and homosexual students. Another very brief, but informative, pamphlet is *Answers to Your Questions About Sexual Orientation and Homosexuality* (American Psychological Association, 1998).

Other approaches to educating school boards would be to contact professional organizations such as state-level psychological or psychiatric associations. These groups may have committees that deal with gay/lesbian issues or at least will have individuals within the organizations who are knowledgeable and who would be willing to speak to school boards and administrators.

In addition to influencing the school board, administrators also set the overall tone in a school and thus are extremely influential in determining how accepting the school will be toward its gay/lesbian students. If harassment of gays is tolerated or ignored by administrators, this attitude will filter through all levels. If diversity education workshops and programs include no mention of sexual orientation, this conveys a message of denial or disinterest, and by omission condones homophobia. The administrator can do a great deal to promote a philosophy of inclusion merely by asking the right questions or making a few suggestions when in-service training topics are being proposed or when diversity issues are discussed in faculty meetings. The administrator can take the lead in inviting relevant speakers to meet with teachers and counselors during in-service training, parent-teacher meetings, or regular faculty meetings. Of course, support groups for gay students and their straight allies should be encouraged and supported.

School boards and school administrators are responsible for preventing harassment and victimization of all students, but they often are less aware of this particular group of students because so many of them hide their sexual orientation and fail to report harassment. It must always be remembered that this is a population that is largely invisible because of shame and homophobia. Steps taken to send the message that gay students are valuable members of the student body, that they will be protected, and that antigay harassment will not be tolerated will reassure both those who are openly gay and those who have not come out.

As chair of the Gay/Lesbian/Bisexual Issues Committee of the Arizona Psychological Association, I have given presentations about sexual orientation in a number of schools. Some of these presentations have been done in collaboration with PFLAG members and other organizations. Often it is not possible to have school board members attend these kinds of presentations. However, on one occasion, at a presentation at Coronado High School in Phoenix, Arizona, a school board member was present and sent me the following letter:

Dear Dr. Baker, Ms. Harvey, and Ms. Bibbins:

After your presentation at Coronado High School last week, many in the audience commended you and thanked you for coming. To those voices—of staff, of students, and of parents—I add my thanks and appreciation. As was clear, the students are crying out for clear information and open discussion of issues related to homosexuality; your presentation not only gave them new factual information but also allowed us all to better understand the social, emotional growth experiences of homosexual young people and their families in today's world. It was important to include your personal family experiences and important to address the myths about homosexuality which are so prevalent in our society.

These are difficult issues to discuss with people, young or old; you did so with great sensitivity and respect for everyone's individual backgrounds. Too often we shy away from difficult discussion and from controversial topics. I believe that adult refusal to discuss issues which our children know are out there and which they hear about in movies and on TV on a regular basis, only leads students to conclude that adults in schools are out of touch with the world and/or that they don't care what young people think about these issues. When students conclude that about schools, it makes teaching any subject extremely difficult. This was an excellent beginning to a discussion which I hope will continue in our schools.

As our school board considers a new sex education curriculum for the district in coming months, I am at least one board member who will be very interested in how we include discussion of these issues within the framework of this community. Again, thanks for coming.

Sincerely,

Susan Goldsmith

Chapter 10

Gay Youth Support Groups

Many cities now offer support groups for gay, lesbian, bisexual, and transgender youth under the sponsorship of community agencies serving the GLBT community. These groups can be life-saving to young gays and lesbians, especially for those who are fearful of being identified by their fellow high school students and thus reluctant to attend a support group that meets on campus. However, I have found that young people who have participated in community-based gay youth support groups often gain the courage to go back to their schools and become involved in support groups in the school setting. A number of the students in the school-based gay/straight alliances told me that they attended the Youth Support Group at Wingspan, Tucson's Lesbian, Gay, Bisexual, and Transgender Community Center before they got the courage to join a group in the school setting. Some even became leaders in starting gay/straight alliances in their schools.

School-based gay/straight alliances usually require the sponsorship of credentialed staff or faculty. Teachers, librarians, school nurses, counselors, and school psychologists are all potential sponsors. The groups sometimes are initiated by students and sometimes by interested adults. The sponsors may be gay or lesbian, but not necessarily. Sometimes a gay teacher and a straight teacher collaborate to sponsor a group. Although resistance has been encountered in some schools when attempts have been made to start these extracurricular groups, under federal guidelines for public schools accepting federal funds, schools may not refuse to allow this type of club if they allow any other student clubs. A school in Utah went to the extreme of discontinuing all student clubs to avoid permitting gay students to form their own club.

STUDENTS SPEAK ABOUT THE GROUPS

The students attending the school-based groups have been uniform in their enthusiasm about the benefits, although they also acknowledge that many of the gay youth in their schools are afraid to join them. Samantha, a sixteen-year-old, told how the support group helped her to come out to her family and to cope with her feelings of self-blame. She was involved in approaching the school newspaper about including an article about their group. Samantha even suggested that the article present an opposing viewpoint from a student who wrote the group a letter stating that groups for gays should not be allowed in the school because gays would be "hitting on the straights." Samantha thought this letter would show how uninformed that kind of thinking is, and she encouraged the group to include it in the article.

Kate, also sixteen, said that the value of the group to her was that they could all talk about prejudice and be with people like themselves. The group also made her feel good because there was a gay teacher who was one of their sponsors and he was someone they could look up to. Andy, age nineteen, spoke of being with other people who have similar thoughts and feelings and learning that there were others like herself. The group helped her become more comfortable with her orientation. Andy also liked being able to help others in the group. Star was one of the students who helped start the group at his school because he thought that there should be a place where gay kids could go to help them ". . . understand about gayness and to think more positively about being gay." Being in the group helped him to feel accepted and get to know himself better. Another group member had a very supportive family and felt that by the time she started going to the group she had already "gone a little past the need for support." However, she wanted to join so that she could help others.

Tiger had gone to the Wingspan gay youth support group prior to joining the group at his school. He spoke of walking by the door of Wingspan and being afraid to go in. Later, a gay relative took him by the hand and walked him in. Everyone was very supportive and he said he felt warmth from the group. This experience helped him gain the courage to later join the support group at his school, where he learned that other students were having the same problems as himself. He wanted to hear that it is OK to be gay and to tell others that it is OK. Tripp liked the group because it was a safe place to talk about all the things that gay kids are dealing with without having to censor themselves. Anne especially liked the group because it was not only for gays and lesbians but for bisexuals and straights. She said that the straight students who come to the meetings sometimes become advocates.

Maria said that she liked being in a room with people like herself, hearing their stories and relating them to her own experiences. She got advice from caring people who have been in the same boat. She liked "just knowing it's there." H. W. liked the idea of knowing who your friends are and getting advice about which teachers you can go to and who your allies are among the students. Being in the group also helped him build a social network, and it was comforting just knowing the group was there. H. W. also belonged to Wingspan, and liked the fact that some people in that group were a little older and could give advice about things not to do and gay-friendly places to go. He also felt that "getting people's different stories" was important. H. W. described Wingspan as another network and recalled how he too had walked past the door of the Wingspan Center for months before he got the courage to go in.

Judy said the group was important to her "Just to know there are others like myself and to know I can help other people. I like to take younger people under my wing." Ivy spoke of wanting to help others because she had such a difficult time herself when she was starting to come out. She was always telling herself that it was wrong and that God was telling her it was wrong. Now that she is more self-accepting she wants to help others. B. H. goes to the group "just to know that it isn't just me." F. F. felt good knowing there is someplace gay kids can go, that they ". . . don't have to stay in a dark corner."

Though these school-based support groups are obviously very helpful to those students who have the courage to join them, they may be almost as helpful to those students who are so fearful of being identified as gay that they would never consider joining. The mere existence of the groups gives the message to these students that the school cares, that there are others like themselves, and that if they change their minds there is a place where they can get help.

In the course of interviewing these students, I also met with adults who were sponsors of the support groups. They came from a variety of backgrounds: one was a school nurse, two were teachers, and one a librarian.

A SCHOOL NURSE

Tam DeWitt, a school nurse, was the first sponsor of Pink Triangle, a gay/straight student group at one of the Tucson, Arizona high schools. DeWitt became interested in this issue when she heard a panel of gay teens speak at a local church about their troubled experiences in high school. She felt moved by their stories to take some sort of action in her own school. Fortunately, her school already had an antidiscrimination policy that explicitly included sexual orientation. DeWitt stressed how important it is for sexual orientation to be included in these policies. The existence of the policy gave her the legal backing and the rationale to begin organizing support and services to gay and lesbian students.

She started by putting up a poster in her office about the youth support group at Wingspan. The poster said, "What would you do if your best friend said he was gay?" and it gave the Wingspan phone number. DeWitt did not stop here. She went on to put a pink triangle in the window to her office and a rainbow colors poster on the door. The pink triangle and the rainbow are symbols of acceptance and pride readily recognizable now by most gay youth; by displaying these symbols, DeWitt was attempting to convey that her office was a safe place for gay students and that she was a safe person to talk to.

Even before she became more attuned to the needs of gay youth, DeWitt played a role in her school regarding how to deal with homosexuality. This was because at one time the sex education curriculum in her school district had recommended that if the subjects of homosexuality or masturbation should come up in the classroom, the topic should not be discussed and the students who brought up these subjects should be referred to the school nurse. The curriculum is no longer so explicit about referring to the school nurse, however, Arizona has an AIDS education statute that puts the topic of homosexuality outside the parameters of discussion. As a result, education in Arizona classrooms about homosexuality or about AIDS prevention for gay students is severely limited. The school nurse is not so inhibited as the faculty in what he or she can discuss with students and, indeed, when DeWitt goes into classrooms now she discusses homosexuality and AIDS prevention quite openly.

DeWitt's posters and symbols in the nursing office led some students to come out to her, and eventually these students asked if she would help them start a support group. She readily agreed to do so and had already reached the conclusion that since sexual orientation involves both health and mental health issues, school nurses are the obvious choice to be leaders in helping create safer school environments for gay and lesbian youth. However, she went on to say that anyone could take the lead: a counselor, a teacher, a librarian, or an administrator. The important thing is that whoever it is should be comfortable with the topic. It can be helpful, but certainly not essential, for the sponsor to be straight, but even better would be a straight person and a gay person together.

The process of gaining approval from administration was slow, but the students persisted and eventually the group became a recognized club like any other on campus. DeWitt had many ideas for anyone who is interested in starting a gay/straight alliance or support group on his or her campus. She recommends starting with getting support of the administrators and keeping administrators informed all along the way. She even informed the principal when she put up the poster. This way, if any complaints come to the principal he or she will be forewarned and prepared.

Those who take a leadership role in whatever way, whether it is to start a group or just to openly show support for gay youth, need to be prepared for backlash from faculty, staff, and possibly parents. DeWitt suggests making the point that you don't have to approve of homosexuality in order to agree that these students need equal rights and equal protection. DeWitt never had any complaints from parents, but if she did she would have referred the parent to the superintendent of schools. A situation such as this could very well arise, and this is why it is so important to have the antidiscrimination policy be explicit in its protection of gay and bisexual students.

DeWitt spoke of the significance of language and how everyone in the school needs to become more sensitive to the language they use with students so they do not appear to be presuming heterosexuality. For example, she recommends not asking an upset female student if she is having trouble with her boyfriend. Instead, use a neutral term such as partner, relationship and so on. In AIDS-education presentations she does not speak of a sexual partner as male or female, but just "your partner."

In speaking of some of the dynamics in groups, DeWitt explained that in the beginning some of the students wanted to be very militant, to protest, to wear T-shirts and carry placards and signs. She urged them to go slowly, not to give other students a reason to be annoyed with them by being overly militant or flamboyant. She recommended behaving better than everybody else and setting an example. This seemed to work, although as more gay youth come out of the closet and insist on recognition, this approach may change simply because of the greater confidence and activism of the younger generation.

At DeWitt's school the majority of students who attended the Pink Triangle meetings were female—something that was true at the other schools also. Everyone, students and adults, whom I have spoken to at the high schools agrees that it is much more difficult for males to come out in high school than it is for females. Overt prejudice toward gay males appears to be much more intense than prejudice toward lesbians, at least at the high school level.

DeWitt believes that, if the school climate toward gay students is to change, in-service training about sexual orientation is essential for school nurses, faculty, administrators, counselors, and staff. Often there has been absolutely no training or education on the topic. One approach is to contact local PFLAG groups and have their members come into the school to make presentations to faculty and staff. Also, the group members themselves are often willing to participate in panel discussions for faculty, parents, or other students. DeWitt has also persuaded a group of local psychologists, including myself, to present an in-service program on the topic to teachers and administrators.

In recognition of World AIDS Day, DeWitt organized a weeklong display of sections of the AIDS Memorial Quilt along with educational materials, poetry, and essays about AIDS written and prepared by students. In coordination with the display she invited speakers, such as parents of persons who died from AIDS, people living with HIV, and AIDS educators to come and speak to students and faculty. Some of the speakers discussed the issue of antigay prejudice. In addition, during the same week, the drama department and the music department put on a student production dealing with the issues of AIDS and homophobia.

AN ENGLISH TEACHER

Guy Velgos is a high school English teacher in Tucson and one of the sponsors of a gay/straight alliance in his school, now called the Arcus Alliance. Velgos had never given any particular thought to gay students until he read an article about sex education in the Tucson *Weekly*. In a section of the article titled "Homophobic High," gay students described being harassed at school and on the way back and forth to school. This touched a nerve in him and he began to think about what these students might be going through. He remembered how, in his small midwestern hometown, while he was in high school, there had been no recognition that homosexuals even existed. They were the "nebulous They." He thought about what a hostile environment it must have been for gay students at that time. He remembered his liberal parents whom he admired because they had always stood up publicly for their beliefs, and he began to realize that he should do the same. He was unclear about what this might entail, and he had no thought of starting a group. Velgos began by trying to figure out a way to give these kids a message of support. His first step was to approach the Wingspan GLBT Community Center and obtain some of their posters announcing the center's gay youth support group.

Velgos displayed these posters in his classrooms and soon a couple of other teachers asked about them and put up posters in their rooms. Students started asking about the posters and making comments, some of which were hostile. A few students remarked that homosexuality is wrong and asked Velgos how he could do such a thing as display such posters in his classroom. There were comments such as, "God made Adam and Eve, not Adam and Steve." When hostile comments were made, Velgos would let the students know that violence, teasing, and name-calling directed toward any group was unacceptable. He told his students that not liking gays was no justification for harassment.

He also used news items to bring up related topics for discussion such as gays in the military, the Matthew Shepard murder, the Stonewall anniversary, and gay-pride marches. He has found that, although not many students speak up during these discussions, they seem interested and listen carefully to those few who do speak.

Eventually a small group of gay students approached him and the school nurse to ask if they would sponsor a club. The students took the initiative and went through the myriad steps that were required. Though it took a concerted effort to overcome a number of roadblocks (mainly just the slowness and reluctance of the administration), eventually the club was officially approved and granted the same rights as other extracurricular clubs.

Velgos spoke of the attitudes of other teachers and he thinks that many of them are glad that somebody is doing this work even though they would not want anything about the topic mandated to their curricula. Many say they don't have enough time to teach what they already have to teach. However, when someone is willing to volunteer to help these kids, many are pleased. Of course, there are also certain teachers who themselves may make antigay remarks or who laugh at gay jokes. He has not heard these teachers himself, but students have mentioned them to him. He thinks that teachers, even without adding anything to their curricula, could help by allowing gay issues that come up in the news to become topics for discussion in the classroom. This tells students that homosexuals are part of the real world and helps to humanize them.

Velgos would like these clubs to be more wide-ranging and accepting and to place more of an emphasis on making them true gay/straight alliances. He believes that an untapped number of supportive straight students exist and could be reached. He likes the idea of trying to make everybody welcome in order to calm fears of admitting to being gay or being thought to be gay. He suggests keeping meetings informal and trying to keep the atmosphere friendly. Having food really helps. Heavy issues do not have to be discussed. The important thing is to reduce tension and help students feel comfortable.

The school in which he teaches may be somewhat of an exception in its acceptance of diversity and its rather gay-friendly atmosphere. It has an ethnically and socioeconomically diverse population, which may help in promoting an especially tolerant atmosphere for sexual minorities as well as other minority groups.

Velgos admires these gay students who are now willing to come out in high school. He calls them amazing and wonderful.

A CHEMISTRY TEACHER

Gayle Brickert-Albrecht, a high school chemistry teacher in Tucson, is one of the sponsors of a school-based gay/straight alliance. She is openly lesbian and cosponsors the group with a straight teacher. Although she had never concealed her orientation at school, neither had she been outspoken about it. When it came to her attention that there were some gay-identified students on campus who wanted to have a group, she decided that this was her opportunity to step out and be supportive in a more personal way, to be somebody who was both out and very open about it. She felt that somebody needed to take on the cause of these students, to be supportive, and help provide them a safe haven. Any group of students, not just gays, who are out of the mainstream and are being rejected or mistreated in some way deserves the same sort of attention and protection. However, gays in particular are especially likely to be harassed because of the homophobic atmosphere in most schools.

This teacher understands why so many gay and lesbian teachers and administrators do not come out in the school setting. Though there have been some negative repercussions, she herself has experienced personal growth as a result of coming out. She also believes that she is a better person as a result of her involvement with her gay and lesbian students. She was not fearful that she would lose her job because she has an excellent record in the school district and has earned many accolades. If there had been an attempt to fire her she thinks it would have been unsuccessful because it would be blatant discrimination. She wishes that more teachers and administrators were able to come out and be models for the gay students, but even when there are teachers in a school whom everybody knows to be gay, there seems to be a tacit understanding that it is supposed to be kept a secret. When these teachers aquiesce to such unspoken rules, it is damaging and disheartening to the gay students. The message conveyed is that known homosexuals are not acceptable as teachers or administrators. As it is in the military, so it is in the schools: "don't ask, don't tell."

When someone in the school does take a stand and openly advocates for gay kids there are many different reactions on the part of other teachers. The most positive group seems to be the English teachers, perhaps because their subject entails the study of humainty in all its myriad forms. Some teachers are positive and supportive, but remain rather secretive about it. There are certain teachers, even some who are gay, who are embarrassed and disapproving. Students may also make negative remarks about a teacher who is out.

This teacher believes that there are many seemingly small but critical ways in which teachers can support gay students. They can model tolerance toward all kinds of diversity, not just sexual diversity. They can refuse to accept homophobic remarks or attitudes in the classroom. Teachers can also advocate to administration for in-service training on diversity. Such training should include how to respond to discrimination and intolerance in the classroom. Teachers are often afraid they will be labeled gay if they intervene when homophobic remarks are made. Teachers also ignore such remarks because they are uncomfortable with their own sexuality, they don't know what to say, or even because they just don't like conflict or confrontation. Teachers who wish to become more involved in helping gay youth may do something as simple as displaying relevant posters and brochures. Putting this material on display and making it openly available in the classroom means that students do not have to ask and conveys a message that the teacher is supportive.

Many administrators and teachers are reluctant to address the issue of gay students. They feel uncomfortable, they foresee parental backlash and religious and political ramifications. Leaving the issue alone and letting the kids deal with it after they leave high school is an approach favored by many. However, Brickert-Albrecht worries about how little recognition there is of how difficult it is developmentally for these gay adolescents, who struggle every day to try to understand themselves and figure out how they are going to fit into a world that seems made only for heterosexuals. She thinks that administrators and faculty need a Homophobia 101 course emphasizing how homophobia affects gay youths and straight youths. Even teachers and administrators who are more accepting of homosexuality often do not feel comfortable dealing with the issue in the school setting. They are still professionally obligated, however, to treat everybody with respect. That is part of their job. They do not even have to like gays, they just have to treat them with the same respect they treat everybody else.

In Brickert-Albrecht's experience, the general climate for gay students is better at her school than it is in most other high schools in the community. This is likely because of the diversity of the student body—ethnically, racially, and socioeconomically—and the diversity of the faculty. Also, this high school is known for its Performing Arts Department, which tends to attract a more sophisticated, diverse group of students. The kids who are most visibly gay are the ones who get the verbal harassment, but there is seldom, if ever, any physical harassment. The word faggot is pervasive, however. Boys who are flamboyantly effeminate are the most frequent targets of harassment.

The major purpose of a support group for these students is to counteract the atmosphere that is sometimes present in the halls and on the athletic field. Even gay kids who do not attend the group still know there is a place for them if they want it, and that there is a group of students who are self-confident and out. When she was asked about the students who are the stars (i.e., the football captains, the cheerleaders, the valedictorians, the class presidents, and so forth who might also be gay and who are sometimes less likely to come out in high school), Brickert-Albrecht said that student leaders who are gay may be the ones most at risk. Their identity is their public persona and they are afraid to lose that identity. Many of them are caught up in being successful and being admired. She thinks they may be the ones at most at risk for suicide.

Then there are the students who do not come out as gay but who seem to be having identity issues. Her experience has been that some of the students who dressed all in black, adopted the "Goth" style, and were somewhat introverted, after high school have turned out to be gay. Perhaps someone in the school might have been alert to what these students were communicating by adopting an identity that was so different from most of their peers. She is not suggesting that such students are always gay, but they may be asking for some sort of attention or support and a teacher might take this cue to make a special effort to reach out to them.

Brickert-Albrecht believes that having a straight sponsor along with a gay or lesbian sponsor may help alleviate the fears of administration and also sets the tone for a more broadly encompassing group. She acknowledges that it is difficult to get the straight kids to come to the group. Usually they only come to accompany a gay friend. So far nobody who is not already a friend of a gay person has attended the group.

A LIBRARIAN

Sally Hansen is a librarian in another Tucson school. She was one of two sponsors who helped students start the first gay/straight alliance at her school. Hansen has always been supportive of diversity and equal rights and has always thought that one human being has as much to contribute to society as any other human being; but she never thought, as a public school educator, that she would become a sponsor of a gay group. The interest and the motivation came from the students themselves and evolved over time.

Hansen had always made the library a welcoming place for gay students by having appropriate books available and on display, and she was open to engaging in conversations with kids who seemed lonely for whatever reason. Soon three or four gay students were hanging out in the library a lot because they felt it was a safe and comfortable place. These students approached her about starting a club. She agreed, along with one of the teachers, to be their sponsor and helped them work through the process of gaining official standing for the club. They called it the Spectrum Alliance. Around the same time, a counselor had started a counseling group for gay students and eventually these students got in touch with the library group and the Spectrum Alliance grew. Hansen feels that it was the friendly atmosphere established in the library and by the counselor that helped the group evolve as it did. Currently usually ten to twelve students attend the meetings, and some are straight friends who are there to be supportive.

Hansen pointed out that these kinds of groups cannot really get started unless some gay kids in the school are already out and self-identified. Students who do not want to be out at school would find it much too risky to attend a group like this. She suggests that students who are afraid to be identified at school can attend support groups in the community, which are often found at gay/lesbian community centers. However, for those closeted gay students who do not join either a school-based group or a community-based group, Hansen believes that the presence of these groups on school campuses is reassuring and comforting to them. Several of these students have told Hansen that the group is helpful to them in that it identifies teachers and counselors who are supportive and it contributes to a more open, accepting atmosphere in the school. The presence of the group tells the closeted students that they are not totally alone.

School librarians can play a significant role in the lives of gay students, whether or not they have anything to do with helping to start clubs or support groups. In her experience, Hansen has found that many librarians tend to be liberal, anticensorship, and are especially likely to be supportive of all minorities. Because of these qualities, librarians can make their libraries safe havens for any students who are not in the mainstream and who fear being harassed in the bathrooms, in the cafeteria, or in the halls. Displaying symbols such as the pink triangle and the rainbow flag help create this atmosphere, as does having brochures and notices about gay support groups in the community, PFLAG (Parents, Families and Friends of Lesbians and Gays) meetings, phone numbers of crisis groups, Al-Anon meetings, and so forth. It is in the library that students can surreptitiously pick up these materials. Even in the school counselor's office, they have to enter the office in order to obtain information, but in the library they do not have to reveal anything about themselves.

Hansen stresses that librarians who wish to connect with gay students should strive to develop a good collection of literature that is friendly to gay kids—both fiction and nonfiction. Librarians wishing to start or expand their collections may refer to the Gay Lesbian Straight Education Network (GLSEN) at <http://www.glsen.org> for a bibliography of gay fiction and nonfiction appropriate for youth. Beyond just having the collection available, special displays of appropriate books at particular times of the year, for example, during Gay Pride Month (October), are recommended, as well as having displays of relevant new books from time to time. All of these approaches help to create an atmosphere that encourages gay students to talk openly. Once that happens, the librarian can offer to help the student find literature that is of particular interest to him or her and even obtain books that the youth may have heard of but are not presently a part of the collection.

Hansen feels that in her school, probably at least half of the teachers and administrators are quite positive about trying to help gay students. Now at least eight or ten teachers have put pink triangles on their doors. Three out of the five counselors have pink triangles in their offices. Some teachers, even though they might really believe that these kids should have equal protection, would rather not have the hassle of dealing with the issue. Probably some techers are homophobic and/or antigay, but overtly displaying such attitudes is not acceptable in the school.

The director of student services at Hansen's school, Dr. Alan Storm, has played an extremely important role in creating this atmosphere by constantly reminding teachers and administrators of their responsibilities in regard to gay students. He reminds them that allowing students to use terms such as "faggot" can get a teacher into legal difficulty, and failing to protect students from harassment can lead to lawsuits against schools and administrators. He informs them of the Nabozny case, in which a gay student in Wisconsin who was constantly harassed sued the school district and the individual administrators for failing to protect him from verbal and physical harassment. Since the Wisconsin school district did have in place an antidiscrimination policy that included sexual orientation, the district itself was not held liable, but the three individual administrators were court ordered to make financial restitution of $900,000 to the student.

No particular difficulty occurred in getting Spectrum Alliance started at Hansen's school, but there was little positive support for it either. However, as a result of school policy, the in-service training that has been done, and the presence of the gay/straight alliance, most teachers are now quite careful not to allow harassment in the classroom, and no physical altercations involving gay students have occurred during the 1999-2000 school year. The student body is fairly tolerant but not entirely. There still are homophobic students, and the possibility always exists that openly gay students, especially the males, will be harassed verbally or physically. There are some very proactive teachers, however. One teacher who was having trouble with a couple of very homophobic boys in her classroom asked Hansen to come in and talk to the class about sexual orientation.

Despite the progress that has been made, Hansen feels that when gay kids at this school complain about minor incidents, often nothing is done, even though more serious harassment will get handled. There certainly is room for improvement. For example, if the word "faggot" is used in the classroom and the teacher does nothing, the administrators could be more proactive—talking to the particular teacher on a one-to-one basis rather than just ignoring the complaint. Hansen believes that, at her particular school, there has already been fairly intensive in-service training of teachers regarding sexual orientation issues and that what is needed now is a more proactive administration. She does think that training of teachers and students should continue through such mechanisms as diversity workshops, which include sexual orientation as well as the usual racial and ethnic issues.

Hansen commented further on the particular difficulties encountered by openly gay male students as compared to the females. Incidents of physical harassment, i.e. pushing and shoving, have involved only boys. Girls showing affection or being openly out as lesbians are much more acceptable than gay boys, both to male and to female students. She attributes this to the fact that we raise girls to be affectionate with each other and so it is not a shock to see hand holding or hugging between girls as it is between boys. Girls can be physically affectionate in public without criticism and it is not even presumed that they are gay. The greater physical aggressiveness of males toward one another may be another factor. Ms. Hansen is involved in the school athletic programs as a tennis coach and she pointed out that the coaches of boys' teams tell her that, on out of town overnight team trips, boys in the same rooms will never sleep in the same bed with another boy whereas the girls do not hesitate to do so.

Comments

Sally Hansen, Guy Velgos, Tam DeWitt, and Gayle Brickert-Albrecht are to be commended for their work in the schools to help support gay students. Their willingness to stand up for these boys and girls has probably changed the lives of more students than they are even aware of, students who participated in their groups of course, but also those who quietly observed their existence.

Chapter 11

A School Climate Survey

BACKGROUND

The Gay Lesbian Straight Education Network (GLSEN) is a national organization of educators and their supporters working to end antigay prejudice in America's schools. GLSEN has developed a questionnaire called the School Climate Survey which has been used to measure various aspects of the social climate for gay/lesbian/bisexual/transgendered students (GLBT) in school settings. The Tucson, Arizona chapter of GLSEN cooperated with a local gay youth support group and its sponsors to administer this survey to 496 students in a local high school. The survey asked students to report how frequently they heard words such as "faggot," "dyke," "queer" and so forth used in their school. The results indicated that such remarks were extremely common and seldom did anyone, students or faculty, take action to intervene or put a stop to the remarks.

In responding to this survey, 88.5 percent of the students reported that they frequently or sometimes heard these words used in their school. And 82.5 percent reported that rarely or never did they observe anyone taking action to intervene when these words were used. Students reported hearing the words in classrooms, on the athletic field, in the hallways, in the cafeteria and in the bathroom or locker room. The students were also asked whether they thought that gay, lesbian, bisexual, or transgendered students would feel safe at their school. Of the total number of students completing the survey, 65 percent said "Yes" and 35 percent said "No."

WHY STUDENTS DID OR DID NOT INTERVENE

In addition to those questions that could be summarized numerically, the students were also asked several open-ended questions.

Among these questions were the following: "If you were the one who intervened (when you heard the words "faggot," "dyke," etc.), why did you do so?" and "If you chose not to intervene, why didn't you?"

Students Who Intervened

Not everyone responded to these open-ended questions, but of those who did and who chose to intervene, there were several categories of responses. I will include representative answers from each of the categories.

Category 1: A General Principle, or the Right Thing to Do

- "Because people need to respect other people."
- "Because they are discriminative [sic] words that hurt people's feelings. I would do the same thing if I heard derogatory racist comments."
- "Because I thought that it was wrong to let someone say those things and just sit there while everyone laughed."
- "Because who are we to judge one another?"
- "Because I do not feel it is right to put anyone down because they are different. Everyone is equal and should be treated that way."
- "It is just not right to degrade a person (especially like that)."

Category 2: To Show Support for Friends or Family

These responses were primarily to show support for a friend or fellow student or because the student has a family member who is gay.

- "I did it because it was one of my friends so I did something about it."
- "Because my brother is gay."
- "The reason I intervened is because I have many friends that are gay and I try to stand up for them."
- "Because they were talking about some person that was a friend of mine."
- "To help a friend."
- "Because some of my friends are lesbians."
- "I intervened because I have friends and relatives who are gay."

Category 3: To Keep the Situation from Escalating

- "Because it was going to cause a fight/rumble for no good reason."
- "The situation was getting too hectic."
- "If there's a problem, it's best to solve it right away instead of waiting until it is uncontrollable."

Category 4: Sympathy for Hurt Feelings

- "It isn't nice to call people names like that, it hurts the self-esteem of that person."
- "Because I feel sorry for the person that was being made fun of."
- "It is wrong. Everyone is human and has feelings. No matter if they're gay, bisexual, etc."
- "Because I don't think it's fair to someone to be saying things like that to people who are gay. It's the same as calling someone a racial name and hurts just as much."
- "Just because someone's different it doesn't mean that they don't have feelings and it doesn't mean they're not a good person."

Category 5: Self-Defense

- "I intervened to defend myself."
- "Because sometimes they say things about me."
- "Because it was about me."
- "Someone called me a "dyke" and I stood up for myself and I stood up for my friends."

Students Who Did Not Intervene

Among those who did not intervene when they heard the negative words, most responses fit fairly well into the following categories:

Category 1: It's None of My Business or I Don't Care

- "They do not concern me."
- "Because I don't care if these words are used."
- "Because I don't really care what they say about those people. It's not my business."

- "Because I don't care."
- "Because it's none of my business and disgusting."
- "It's not really important to me."
- "Don't give a shit."

Category 2: The Words Aren't Meant to Offend

- "Because we use these words just for playing around."
- "Because usually the words are used jokingly and not meant to hurt others."
- "Although they're degrading words, we were using them jokingly, not to offend."
- "These words are not hate-filled or meant to hurt, they are used in the context of joking among friends. They are insensitive, not cruel."
- "I choose not to intervene when it is meant as a casual insult between friends. Also some people are proud to wear those names."

Category 3: Afraid of Getting Hurt

- "Because if I did I would get beat up."
- "I feel really shy or stupid because most of them are all bigger than me. I just try to stay away and not pay attention to what they're saying. Sometimes it's just a joke."
- "Because I'm scared."
- "I do not want to be made fun of."

Category 4: Fear of Being Thought Gay

- "Because they will think I'm gay."
- "Because it will make me look like a fruit if I intervene."
- "Afraid people will think I'm like that."
- "I didn't intervene because I was afraid my friends would associate me with those words thereafter."

Category 5: Overt Dislike of Gays

- "Because faggots are a disgrace."
- "Because I hate fags. I'm homophobic."
- "I don't give a fuck, let them all die, faggots."

WHY GAY STUDENTS WOULD OR WOULD NOT FEEL SAFE IN SCHOOL

Why Gay Students Would Feel Safe

Among the 65 percent who answered that they thought gay, lesbian, bisexual and transgendered students would feel safe at their school, some wrote in why they thought that way. Their answers fell into several main categories. Here are a few examples from their answers.

Category 1: An Overall School Climate of Tolerance
and Acceptance

- "Yes, the majority of the students respect differences, and there is always teachers around if you're in need of help."
- "Yes, because this school is very diverse and I don't see any reason not to feel safe."
- "Yes, because people respect them."
- "Yes, this is a unique school because of all the differences we have, including the many gay, lesbian, bisexual, and transgenders we have."

Category 2: The Presence of a Support Group or Club
on Campus

- "Yes, because they have the club here so that's saying anyone is welcome no matter what sex you are or want to be."
- "Yes, because there are a ton of liberal people at this school, some of which have started the club."
- "Yes, there are support groups and everyone is pretty much open-minded and if they aren't then they keep their mouth shut."

Category 3: Because There Is Not Likely to Be
Any Physical Harassment of Gays

- "Yes, because no one will hurt them, maybe but rarely."
- "Yes, nobody does anything physically, just verbally."
- "Yes, they might get teased but probably not get beat up."
- "Yes, [they would be safe] but not comfortable."

- "Yes, they would not be beaten up just resented a little."
- "Yes, there is no reason to be afraid. Everyone leaves these creatures alone."
- "Yes, it's an OK environment. I suppose you get the same treatment just about anywhere. There isn't violence toward gays or real gay bashing. Strictly joking most of the time."

Why Gay Students Would Not Feel Safe

Among the 35 percent who answered No, that gay students would not feel safe at school, the answers fell into the following categories:

Category 1: They May Be Physically Harmed

- "No, too many people will beat them."
- "No, I have seen many narrow-minded students discuss with each other about how they hate gays and lesbians. And they would beat them up if they see one."
- "No, people would probably kill them."
- "No, because people like me will kick their ass."
- "No, because they might get hurt or killed."

Category 2: They Will Be Shamed, Humiliated, Rejected, or Teased

- "No, because all the school will look at them a lot and talk about them too."
- "No, because they are always ridiculed and offended."
- "No, because being called names is common."
- "No, because so many kids say things like dyke, fag, or queer that homosexual kids would feel ashamed."
- "No, because they'll make fun of you just because you even resemble gay."
- "No, because people would make fun of them. Not only the students but the monitors and staff. They would talk about them behind their back."

Category 3: Hostile Feelings Toward Homosexuals

- "No, lots of students just don't care and hate GLBT."
- "No, because there better not be a faggot at our school."

- "No, because there are so many people that hate them."
- "No, because a lot of people think that it is disgusting to like someone of your own sex. If they knew of a guy that was gay they would not want to be around him because they would not want him to hit on them."

SUMMARY

The social climate for GLBT students on this one particular campus, based on the responses of nearly 500 students, suggests that the majority of the students (65 percent) thought that the gay students were safe in a physical sense. However, another percentage (35 percent) thought that they were not and that they might be exposed to verbal taunts, social disapproval, and even physical danger. The pejorative words "faggot," "dyke," and "queer" were pervasive on this campus, although some students thought that the words were being used only in a joking or playful manner and were not meant to be hurtful. It was rare that anyone intervened when the derogatory words were overheard, with the vast majority of the students responding that either "Never" or "Rarely" had they observed anyone do so.

This survey was not worded in a way that allowed a quantitative assessment of student attitudes toward homosexuals, as it primarily looked at the frequency with which negatively toned words referring to homosexuals were used, whether anyone intervened when the words were used, and whether gay students would feel safe in the school setting. However, many students did reveal something about their attitudes in their responses to the open-ended questions. There appeared to be a small element in the student body that truly harbored extremely hostile attitudes toward gays and would prefer not to have to be exposed to them. However, a larger number of students expressed positive attitudes toward homosexuals and believed they should be treated with the same respect as all other students. Other students appeared to be indifferent.

We can only speculate as to the factors that might differentiate the tolerant students from the intolerant, the homophobic from the accepting. Although the data here do not provide evidence for any particular explanation, certain theories are intriguing. For example, it was interesting to note that a number of students who intervened when they overheard demeaning remarks being made to or about gays had gay friends or gay family members. In other words, having a personal relationship with someone who is openly gay may lead to more positive attitudes toward gays in general. There is considerable evidence to support this hypothesis (D'Augelli and Rose, 1990; Herek, 1988, 1994).

Maturity and thoughtfulness were evident in the answers of some of the students who intervened to stop antigay remarks because of their ethical or moral principles or empathy for the individual being harassed. Students like these, with some guidance and support from administrators and faculty, have the potential to be role models and leaders who could influence other students toward greater acceptance of and kindness toward those kids who do not "fit." This is a group that is perhaps already influential in helping to prevent violence in their schools.

Another point that emerged from this study has to do with the particular school where the survey was conducted. A number of students mentioned that this particular school was especially tolerant and supportive of ethnic, racial, and sexual diversity. If that is so, then there may certainly be other schools where the climate might be much more threatening for gay youth. The presence in the school of a gay/straight alliance or support group might be one factor in helping to explain the tolerant atmosphere, but perhaps there had to have been more tolerance already for the students to feel safe enough to form such a group. At any rate, the presence of the group was mentioned by a number of the students as being the reason GLBT students might feel safe at this school.

Another interesting finding indicated that students sensed that negative remarks about a given group, in this case, homosexuals, could possibly escalate into violence, and this was the basis of their decision to intervene. Again, this is a group of students who already may be playing a protective role when antigay tensions and resentments arise between students.

The positive attitudes of many of the students toward GLBT persons was reassuring, as was the recognition of how hurtful it must be for those gay students who are taunted and the willingness of some to actually intervene and stand up for the person being victimized. The insights of a few students who appeared to realize that intervening in these situations could de-escalate tension and potential violence is particularly encouraging. We cannot be completely reassured, however, when 35 percent of the students believed that GLBT students did not feel safe on this campus and a number of individuals openly expressed their disgust toward and hatred of homosexuals.

Work remains to be done, and from this survey it appears that a specific group of students might have the potential to become leaders in helping to reduce prejudice toward gay students and any others who are being harassed. For example, if that subset of the student population who emphasized equal rights for all students in their answers and who had the courage to stand up for those in need of protection could be identified, a program for training and mentoring such students might possibly be developed in the school setting.

Such a program could help these special students to build upon the empathic and leadership skills they already appear to possess to help make their school climates safer for all students, gay or nongay, who may be targets of discrimination.

Chapter 12

Transcending the Stigma

ARE GAYS AND LESBIANS EXCEPTIONAL?

Anthony D'Augelli (1998b) and Rich Savin-Willaims (1998), in an American Psychological Association symposium, both argued that the direction of research involving GLB youth needs to change. In Savin-Williams' view, previous research has been overly problem-focused and may have resulted in repathologizing these youth. He questioned why we aren't attending to the normal GLB youths and studying the factors that contribute to their resiliency. He suggested that perhaps even the majority of GLB youth may not have the high-risk pattern which is: Being early identifiers, being gender atypical, coming from dysfunctional family backgrounds, and perhaps most important of all, having suffered school harassment. When none of these factors is present, perhaps the negative impact of stigma and discrimination can be overcome and may even serve as an impetus to outstanding achievement and life satisfaction.

Savin-Williams argued further that we need to recognize the diversity of the gay population and the uniqueness of individual gays and lesbians to begin to understand why so many gays grow up to live happy and productive lives in spite of living as members of a stigmatized minority. To better understand why this is so, we need to know more about the precise factors that make significant differences in the lives of gay children as they grow up, the factors that will determine whether the stigma of homosexuality will affect them adversely or whether it may, on the contrary, have positive effects.

D'Augelli (1998b) further argued that the way social problems are perceived and framed may tend to prevent rather than provide solutions. In regard to the problem of gay youth, he recommended more contextual analyses, and framing the problem as residing not in the youth but, instead, in the community, the family, and the school. For example, he sees moving gay youth to separate schools as a less desirable approach than making institutional changes in the schools they attend and intervening at the system level. He believes that preventing youth from being attacked is a first essential step and that we must more clearly identify and combat the social and community barriers to healthy development for gay youth. He stresses the importance of modifying social attitudes through such mechanisms as PFLAG and Gay/Straight Alliances.

D'Augelli (1994) has written elsewhere and most convincingly about the many gays who grow up to lead rich and fulfilling lives, despite prejudice and barriers. He writes of gay and lesbian development as an example of an exceptional process. Elaborating on this theme, D'Augelli argues that those lesbians and gays who have been able to achieve personal fulfillment in their lives have often developed special competencies and strengths. He believes that perhaps gays develop these distinctive coping skills and personal strengths as a direct result of having had to deal with the stresses of living their lives against the norm, and of having to question their worth and their normality at every step in their development. Somehow, the majority of them devise effective strategies to survive and often excel against difficult odds. Being gay, for some, might be experienced as a kind of gift.

D'Augelli suggests that looking at lesbian and gay development as exceptional may prove to be a useful perspective in examining how some individuals find creative and successful solutions to the predicament of living as homosexuals in a heterosexual world. In D'Augelli's view, the successes that gays achieve in their lives are examples of the human ability to create an identity under circumstances that are unusually demanding. The insights gleaned from such an approach might even offer a better understanding of the ways many children, not just gay children, learn coping skills. Examining homosexual development from this perspective might provide an avenue for helping to identify the significant variables that enable some children to overcome major obstacles in their lives while others, even some growing up in the best of environments, are unable to cope with minor difficulties.

Although D'Augelli writes about the exceptional and fulfilling lives of gays, he makes it clear that he does not wish to minimize the victimization that many of them experience, cultural and institutional victimization as noted earlier, as well as direct verbal and physical attacks. He refers especially to how these practices affect gay youth and how victimization may interfere with emotional and social development. He notes that as young gays and lesbians are coming out at earlier ages they are becoming more vulnerable to being victimized. One of the costs of earlier coming out by this generation of gay people, some of whom are highly visible and outspoken, is this greater likelihood that they will be harassed by their peers and even by their parents.

Until recently, few adolescents chose to come out as gay while they were still in high school and so we knew less about how harassment affected them during this period of development. But recent studies are beginning to help us learn more about the effects on youth of harassment due to sexual orientation. Some of these studies have already been mentioned. One of the studies (D'Augelli, 1999) pointed out that those students who were frequently victimized and harassed by their fellow students had a higher rate of mental health symptoms than those who were infrequently or never harassed. Similar findings were noted in the other studies. Being victimized and harassed by peers is probably one of the biggest risk factors faced by gay youth and is likely related to the higher suicide rate of these youth compared to nongay youth.

To become one of D'Augelli's exceptional gay adults with unusual strengths and competencies may be much more difficult for those children and adolescents who have been the frequent victims of gay harassment or gay bashing. We do know that gender atypical males, especially the extremely effeminate males, are especially at risk of victimization and the earlier they are identified, either through their being outed by others or by coming out voluntarily, the higher the level and the greater the frequency of harassment.

D'Augelli (1998a) reminds us that we must not forget that lesbian, gay, and bisexual youth are almost always the potential targets of victimization and that we should move forward in our attempts to try to prevent the damage that harsh treatment and prejudice can inflict. He presses for further research to study in more depth the effects of victimization on individual development, the factors that increase its negative effects, and the factors that are protective. He stresses that we need to identify the variables that will tell us why some gay, lesbian, and bisexual youth are able to overcome stigma and discrimination and grow up to become well-adjusted, even exceptional, adults. No doubt, as has been stressed throughout this book, the social environment is critical—the family, neighborhood, schools, churches, media, and the legal system. But we need to identify more precisely the specific ways in which these environments, which are so often homophobic and heterosexist, affect gay and lesbian children and adolescents.

However, though we may lack detailed knowledge about the specific factors that lead some gay youths to despair and suicide and others to successful, productive lives, we do know enough about human development to know that all children and adolescents need safe and supportive family, school, and neighborhood environments. Gay children need environments in which they are not shamed or humiliated and in which they are not treated as outcasts, or expected to remain quiet about who they are. In a conference symposium on the topic of building resiliency in lesbian, gay, and bisexual youth, the discussants (Wilcox and Tharinger, 1996) described some of the factors they believe are likely to contribute to the positive development of gay youth. These factors included a significant attachment with at least one adult, availability of appropriate challenges, access to knowledge about sexual orientation, peers and parents who are affirming and supportive, coping skills, and supportive early childhood experiences.

D'Augelli (1994) believes that research on lesbian and gay male development and the factors that inhibit or enhance it should ideally be longitudinal. Longitudinal studies could follow families over time, from the conception of a child through early childhood and into adulthood and could assess at certain developmental points the kind and degree of affectional and sexual interests as they change over time. D'Augelli recognizes the extraordinary difficulties and expense involved in this type of research and suggests another approach that would be easier and less costly, to include an assessment of sexual orientation or affectional status in all developmental research.

WHAT'S GOOD ABOUT BEING GAY?

Just as D'Augelli and Savin-Williams argue, some youth say that being gay is not just a series of humiliations and disappointments. Though they have all had many of these kinds of experiences, their sexual orientation has also helped them gain perspectives and self-understanding that they might otherwise not have achieved. Among the people I interviewed, though they freely discussed the difficulties and sometimes the trauma of growing up gay, many still had positive things to say about being homosexual. Again, I caution that these individuals may be unlike the average gay youth in at least some ways. As participants in gay/straight alliances at school and in community support groups, they are a self-selected group and we do not know how they may differ from youth who might be too ashamed or too fearful to join a group either on or off the school campus. Also, the experience of having participated in a support group would likely help them view the gay experience more positively than young gays and lesbians who are still secretive.

Here are some of their responses to the question, "What are the positive things about being gay or lesbian?"

Carrie thinks that being gay can strengthen your spirit if you've accepted yourself. She thinks it has made her more self-accepting and more compassionate. Carrie writes poetry and thinks that the gay perspective helps her writing.

For Erica, being gay helps her feel more independent because she says she is not like those girls who need to constantly be with a guy to build their self-esteem. She said, "some girls sleep with guys just to feel good about themselves. I came to the realization I don't have to have a boyfriend. I don't have to change." Erica thinks she is maternal and would really like to have children sometime, perhaps in ten or twenty years.

Judy spoke of how easy it is to look just at the negatives of being lesbian, rather than at the positives. She feels that people are antigay because they just do not understand how you can love someone of the same gender. She thinks she can be a role model, an influence on others, by giving a positive impression of gays to straight people.

Ivy has learned that all people deserve to be treated equally, and that what is wrong in this society is nonacceptance.

B. H. says that because he is gay he has learned he can live his life in a way that he can control and that he would not choose to be straight even if he could.

Mary feels she has a better understanding of minorities and all people who have been oppressed—the struggles they must experience. She thinks that being gay can make you more accepting of everybody in general and can help you to be more open-minded.

F. F. thinks that when you grow up as a gay person you're more likely to be open-minded and less judgmental, more accepting of other people. F. F. acknowledged that he likes the idea of being different; he doesn't want to be "Joe Average." He likes to be noticed for his differentness and thinks the most important thing in life is for people to love you.

Maria said she wouldn't have to worry about pregnancy. She spoke also of being a voice for a minority by being lesbian and out. Maria feels that she is helping others. She said that at school people who were gay and afraid to come out sometimes came up and thanked her for her being out and for getting the gay group started. She spoke of the gay culture as being "another culture I have added to my life." She talked of gays being the most hated group and yet having all of these positive accomplishments.

Here are some additional thoughts about the positives of being gay from adults.

> One of the by-products of ostacization is that as an outcast, you don't fit, you have to figure out an identity and your self-esteem is not as dependent on other people. Your self-worth has to be generated by yourself. You learn to examine yourself and everything else more carefully. You become sensitive to other outsiders. I feel I have become a more fully developed man. (Jason)

> Since you don't fit in completely you are likely to be more observant of other people and more sensitive. You are trying to figure out a way to fit in so you watch more closely. You can't move uncensored through the world. It can be character building. Once you have gotten through the difficulties you can be stronger, more sensitive to other people. (Maury)

> Growing up with a sense of otherness taught me to be a critic of the culture, to step outside and see from a different perspective. It allowed me to give up other notions of what is acceptable and taught me a tremendous appreciation of cultural variance. There is also in homosexuals a cool way of blending the masculine and feminine aspects of one's self. We are bridges between the sexes. I can see things from both the masculine and feminine perspectives. Incorporating the feminine aspects in my personality makes me a more gentle, nurturant, and compassionate person, the androgynous blending. Actually, every person has

this potential. Also, I've discovered a very firm and strong sense of myself, who I am and what I stand for. When you have to question yourself every day of your life—those questions "Do I deserve to live?" "Am I really a pervert?" "Will I go to hell?" "Will I be locked up?" "Should I be beaten up?" These existential questions, when you come out of it you are so much stronger, not just about your sexuality but about other aspects. After that you are inner granite. (Rich)

These thoughts about character being built through the confronting of adversity and the overcoming of it, as well as D'Augelli's comments about the strength which many gays seem to develop through coping with homophobia, makes one wonder if gays were to become totally accepted in our society and had no special barriers to overcome, would something positive be lost? Rich's response to this question was that perhaps something would be lost, but he believes more would be gained. He believes that the elimination of gender stereotypes, which contribute so powerfully to the widespread prejudice toward homosexuals, would encourage us all to more freely embrace all aspects of ourselves, the feminine and the masculine, without fear of being labeled abnormal.

Gay children can grow up to be well-adjusted, responsible, even outstanding individuals; they can grow up filled with shame and despair; or they can grow up to be something in between. The consequences of growing up gay will depend on a complex mixture of factors, many of which I have tried to examine in this book. Those who have understanding parents, a strong support system, have not been victimized too severely, and who have coping skills and inborn strengths are less likely to be vulnerable to the prejudice they still face in society. Unfortunately, many young gays and lesbians, because these protective factors are missing from their lives, are highly vulnerable to the daily humiliations and hostility they endure.

Chapter 13

Enlightened Mayor Seeks Acceptance
for Gay Youths

Sometimes just one person in a leadership role, a person who has some imagination and is willing to take a few risks, can initiate an avalanche of change in a community. As an example, a courageous and visionary mayor in Tucson, Arizona, horrified by the murder of Matthew Shepard, the twenty-one-year-old college student killed in Laramie, Wyoming, in October, 1998 because he was gay, decided to alert his community to the dangers faced by sexual minorities when the psychological climate foments hatred toward them. Mayor George Miller, through his subsequent actions, may have pushed public opinion about homosexuality to a "tipping point" (see Gladwell's concept in Chapter 18), in at least one Arizona community.

On the night of October 27, 1998, Mayor Miller attended a vigil for Matthew Shepard held on the University of Arizona campus, where he spoke movingly to an assembled crowd of mourners, condemning prejudice toward sexual minorities and declaring his personal commitment to making Tucson a safer place for them. That night the mayor spoke fervently to members of the gay community, urging them to contact his office the next day to help him decide what this city needed to do to protect its gay citizens and prevent such occurrences as the one in Wyoming. This was not the usual public posturing of a politician, but a dramatic and sincere outreach to the gay community, as evidenced by Mayor Miller's behavior in the weeks and months following that evening.

Within days the mayor had organized a meeting in his office, gathering together approximately forty leaders from the gay/lesbian community and gay-related agencies. The mayor asked the group for specific recommendations that would help him to create a safer community for Tucson's gay, lesbian, bisexual, and transgendered people, particularly its youth. He called the group the Mayor's GLBT Task Force and offered the power of his office to help stop discrimination and harassment of gay people and to counteract the homophobia still evident in Tucson. Mayor Miller became an icon of political advocacy for the gay community because of his immediate and compassionate response to the Matthew Shepard murder.

Out of that initial meeting in the mayor's office emerged a plan to form three subcommittees of the task force (i.e., Legal, Social Services, and Education) recommending that these committees serve as advisory/action groups to the mayor. Mayor Miller requested that each of the committees develop immediate and long-range goals aimed at reducing antigay discrimination and helping the Tucson community become a safer place for sexual minorities. Generous assistance was provided to the three subcommittees from the mayor's office.

Through the efforts of the legal subcommittee, a city ordinance prohibiting discrimination based on a number of categories, including sexual preference, was revised, swapping the word preference for orientation and also, most importantly, extending protection against discrimination based on gender identity. In other words, transgendered people were also to be included as a protected class in the city ordinance. Some believe this is the first antidiscrimination ordinance or law in the country to include transgender as a category of nondiscrimination. In addition, the revised ordinance added a requirement that businesses and housing providers within the city post the ordinance on their bulletin boards alerting employees, customers, and tenants of its requirements. Further, the ordinance now calls for significant monetary penalties for any level of discrimination. The committee also worked on a repeal of Arizona's archaic sex laws (an effort that was helpful in ending these laws), lobbied for equal protection for same-sex victims of domestic violence and against various other antihomosexual bills that have come up from time to time in the Arizona legislature. The domestic violence law in fact has, as a result of these efforts, been revised in a way that now gives some legal protections to same-sex victims.

The social services subcommittee has conducted a survey of social service, mental health, and health-related community agencies to determine the level of awareness regarding sensitivity to the needs of lesbian, gay, bisexual, and transgendered persons and the availability of services for this population. Based on the results of this survey the committee developed guidelines outlining appropriate agency practices and policies for serving sexual minority populations and is distributing these guidelines in the community. This committee is also interested in trying to develop a specialized clinic for gay, lesbian, bisexual, and transgendered persons and identifying those health providers who are willing to volunteer their services to the clinic.

The education subcommittee has focused a great deal of its attention on local public school districts in an effort to increase their awareness of the presence and needs of their sexual minority students. Change in the schools was a particular interest of Mayor Miller's, and led to his invitation to the superintendents and the school boards of the four major school districts within the Tucson community to attend an open meeting with him and the education subcommittee, a meeting that presented information about the needs of gay youth and how the schools could help make their campuses more tolerable for these students. In his letter inviting the schools to the meeting, Mayor Miller described the creation of the committee and noted that slurs and epithets that attack young people for their color, race, ethnicity, religion, socioeconomic status, gender, or sexual orientation should not be tolerated. He asked the schools for their assistance in improving the climate for sexual minorities in school settings.

In that meeting general information about sexual orientation was presented, as well as information about the prevalence of antigay harassment on school campuses and about concrete steps that schools could take to make their campuses safe for their gay, lesbian, bisexual, and transgender students. Those present were asked to schedule a time on the agenda of their school board meetings so that the entire membership of the boards could be informed by the committee about the purposes of the mayor's task force and hear suggestions about how to reduce intolerance in the school setting and make their campuses safer for gay students. At these subsequent presentations to school governing boards in the Tucson community the committee recommended four simple steps that schools could take:

1. Include sexual orientation in school district antidiscrimination policies.

2. Provide diversity training (including sexual orientation) to students and faculty.
3. Designate a liaison at each high school in each school district to be available to GLBT students and to the committee.
4. Designate a "safe zone" for GLBT students at each high school.

The committee developed a set of recommended guidelines to be followed in homophobia awareness training.

The most important accomplishment of this entire process has been the transformation of the Mayor's GLBT Task Force into a permanent City of Tucson GLBT Commission. This required sustained work on the part of the mayor and all three subcommittees, whose members met with Tucson City Council members to gain their support for establishing a permanent commission dedicated to the protection of the civil rights of GLBT individuals. The Council did, indeed, approve the establishment of the Commission approximately one year following the mayor's amazing announcement at the Matthew Shepard vigil.

Mayor George Miller, now retired from office, will long be remembered by the GLBT community in Tucson, Arizona, and the actions of this one man will benefit current and future generations of gay youths as well as GLBT adults. A determined man with a vision moved a community to a level of awareness that might have taken many more years to reach without the example of his spontaneous and compassionate response to the brutal murder of one gay man.

Chapter 14

For Mental Health Professionals

Just as one political leader stood up for gay rights and made a difference, so too, can individual mental health professionals. This is a group that knows more than most about the psychological damage that can result from discrimination and prejudice and it is a group that is also in a position to make changes in their professions and in their communities. Sometimes, though, psychologists, social workers, psychiatrists, and counselors have had only limited training in issues related to sexual orientation. This may be particularly true for those who received their training when homosexuality was viewed as a mental illness or those who have received their training in contemporary programs that ignore sexual orientation as an issue.

Clinical training during the era prior to the 1970s was incompatible with current scientific findings about homosexuality, since it was based on the theory that homosexuality was a mental disorder. Psychologists and other therapists in training learned about therapeutic approaches to help homosexual patients change their sexual orientation rather than learning about how to help these patients overcome the effects of stigma and shame. Unfortunately, there are still mental health professionals who have not been trained appropriately and who do not have a clear understanding of how homophobia and anti-gay harassment can affect gay and lesbian persons.

Attempts to address deficiencies in professional training have been initiated by most national mental health organizations, for example, the American Psychological Association, the American Psychiatric Association, the National Association of School Psychologists, and the National Association of Social Workers. These organizations, among others, have taken major steps to correct common misconceptions about homosexuality and to educate their members about sexual orientation issues. All of these associations have adopted policy statements or resolutions that warn of the potential dangers of "reparative" therapies, which attempt to cure homosexuals, and all have taken a strong stance against any depiction of homosexuality as a mental disorder. The American Psychological Association and the National Association of School Psychologists have adopted policies specifically regarding the needs of gay youth in the schools. Some state professional organizations, including the Arizona Psychological Association, the Georgia Psychological Association, and the Pennsylvania Psychological Association, have adopted policy statements about the needs of gay youth in the schools similar to the policy adopted by the American Psychological Association.

The official policies of these national and state mental health organizations have the potential to shape public opinion and influence the practices of mental health professionals. A broader dissemination of the policies would help to reduce homophobia and improve the skills of clinical practitioners who are working with gay youth and gay adults. All mental health professionals need to become familiar with the relevant policies of their national organizations and help disseminate them. Mental health professionals also need to further educate themselves about sexual orientation through continuing education programs and conferences, through reading and study of current research, and through becoming familiar with GLBT resources in their local communities (for example, Parents, Families, and Friends of Lesbians and Gays (PFLAG); the Gay, Lesbian, and Straight Education Network (GLSEN); and any GLBT community centers).

A number of state psychological associations now have gay/lesbian/bisexual issues committees and the Maryland Psychological Association has recently expanded the role of its Committee on Gay/Lesbian Concerns by changing the name of the committee to the Committee on Sexual Orientation and Gender Diversity Issues. This may be the only state psychological association that has acknowledged a need to attend to transgender issues. The American Psychological Association has Division 44—Society for the Psychological Study of Lesbian, Gay, and Bisexual Issues. Most other professional organizations also have relevant divisions or committees. Those who are particularly interested in sexual orientation issues are encouraged to affiliate with these groups.

The American Psychological Association has recently published a document titled *Guidelines for Psychotherapy with Lesbian, Gay and*

Bisexual Clients. These comprehensive guidelines were developed by the APA Division 44 Committee on Lesbian, Gay, and Bisexual Concerns Joint Task Force (2000) and approved by the APA Council of Representatives. Major aims of the document are to educate psychologists about the appropriate treatment of lesbian, gay, and bisexual clients and to familiarize them with the relevant scientific literature in order to ensure high-quality professional practice. The document emphasizes the need for psychologists to help their gay clients overcome the effects of social stigmatization. A specific section in the document addresses lesbian, gay, and bisexual youth and calls attention to their difficulties in moving through the developmental tasks of adolescence. References are given in the document for appropriate therapeutic strategies for working with this population (Browning, 1987; Coleman and Remafedi, 1989; Gonsiorek, 1988; Ryan and Futterman, 1998). Any mental health professional who treats gay people needs to become familiar with this document, as do those who work with families who have gay members.

Another valuable document, already referred to in earlier chapters, is *Just the Facts About Sexual Orientation and Youth: A Primer for Principals, Educators and School Personnel* (1999). This document was endorsed by the major health and mental health professional organizations in the country as well as by several educational and religious organizations. It was distributed to school superintendents in every school district in the United States for the purpose of informing them of basic facts about sexual orientation development and the need to provide gay youth with safe and supportive school environments. The document includes a brief explanation of current theories about homosexual development and urges schools to provide a safe and supportive environment for these students. Becoming familiar with this document and helping to bring it to the attention of educators is another way mental health professionals can play a role in helping those children who are gay, lesbian, or bisexual.

Mental health professionals who are gay themselves or who have family members who are gay may wish to become even more closely involved in helping gay children and adolescents. Throughout this book I have written of the significant impact that schools can have and of the need for schools to become more sensitive to the needs of gay students. Mental health professionals with a special interest in sexual orientation issues could help gay children navigate the school setting through becoming involved in in-service training for teachers and administrators or making educational presentations to parent groups and school governing boards. Those who are in clinical practice can help to make other mental health professionals aware of the APA *Guidelines for Psychotherapy with Lesbian, Gay, and Bisexual Clients,* and of the positions that most mental health professional organizations have taken against "reparative" therapies.

Chapter 15

Legal and Social Policy Barriers and How They Affect Gay Children

THE RIGHT TO MARRY

Laws and public policies that discriminate against gays and lesbians or that fail to protect them are among the powerful negative messages we send to children who are growing up gay. When the laws that govern our country reinforce the notion that homosexuals are inferior to heterosexuals, how can a gay child or adolescent grow up with the hope that he or she can live a normal life? Among the laws discriminating against homosexuals, perhaps one of the most significant and most injurious in its implications is the denial of the right to marry one's beloved of the same sex. Some in the gay civil rights movement do not desire to push this particular legal agenda, saying that the model of heterosexual marriage is not so desirable nor something they wish to emulate in their own relationships. Some also believe that other, perhaps more important, causes will be neglected if resources are directed toward this one.

However, denying same-sex couples the right to marry deprives them of one of the very basic human rights, and in so doing tells gay people that their relationships have no civil or social status. There are consistent findings (Diener et al., 1999) that happiness and feelings of well-being are closely linked to being married and that married women and men are significantly happier than singles. Should we deny gays and lesbians a major source of life's happiness simply because they fall in love with someone of the same gender?

Andrew Sullivan, in his book *Love Undetectable* (1998), has written compellingly on this topic, saying that the denial of the right of gays to marry whom they love implies that ". . . at the deepest emotional level, homosexual persons are simply lesser than heterosexual persons and that, at a political level, homosexual citizens are simply lesser than heterosexual citizens" (p. 77). Sullivan refers in his book to the ruling by former Chief Justice Warren of the U.S. Supreme Court in the case of *Loving v. Virginia*. In this case, which overturned the ban on interracial marriage, Chief Justice Warren, in the majority opinion, wrote the following, "The right to marry or not marry resides with the individual and cannot be infringed by the State." Sullivan concluded that just as the legal ban on interracial marriage was a statement about the perceived inferiority of blacks to whites, so is the ban on gay marriage a statement about the perceived inferiority of homosexuals to heterosexuals. The *Loving v. Virginia* U.S. Supreme Court ruling, by the words used in the majority opinion, would certainly seem to apply as well to gays, but the current court, were this issue to come before it, might not agree.

To a child growing up gay, lesbian, or bisexual, the stark statement of the law that he or she will never be able to marry who he or she loves, reveals a cruel message. It tells these youth that they can never have a fully meaningful relationship that is sanctioned by our laws and by our society. It tells these youths that they are somehow so different from "normal" people that the right to marry, to which everyone else is entitled, is one that will forever be denied to them.

Marriage is a symbol, one conveying a significant social meaning. Symbols reinforce and guide public acts and are instruments of teaching. They send a signal of what our public values are. Marriage is a symbol so powerful that, if you examined its ramifications carefully, you would be forced to at least consider that even if every other legal privilege and right were eventually extended to sexual minorities, leaving out the right to marry would forever condemn gay people to second-class citizenship and would remind gay children of what society thinks of them.

Denying gays the right to marry also affects the children of gay couples, as Michael Wald, a professor at Stanford University Law School, stated in an Associated Press Wire Service interview on December 16, 1999. Professor Wald, who specializes in the effects of public policies on children, pointed out that these children could feel ostracized by society when their parents' unions are considered invalid.

A dramatic movement toward recognizing the need to legally validate homosexual relationships has recently taken place in the state of Vermont. The Vermont Supreme Court inflamed the debate about gay marriages in its unexpected decision on December 20, 1999, that gay couples in Vermont were being unconstitutionally denied the benefits of marriage. The court left it up to the legislature to remedy this. Subsequent public hearings and demonstrations on both sides left state legislators, many of whom were opposed to the concept of gay marriage, in disarray. The solution, after much agonizing and soul searching by the legislators, was the passage of a bill by both houses of the legislature that was signed into law by the governor in April of 2000. This law now permits gay couples to enter into civil unions, a status that is supposedly separate but equal to marriage. These unions, like civil marriage, make gay couples who have entered into them eligible for all state benefits accruing to married couples; require a license; and require being certified by a justice of the peace, a judge, or a clergyperson. Certain federal rights may still, however, be beyond the purview of this new statute, for example, Social Security benefits and federal tax advantages.

Though this new state law is a major step toward recognizing the validity of committed gay relationships, marriage itself still remains beyond the grasp of gay couples in our country. In fact, the U.S. Congress had already passed the so-called Defense of Marriage Act prior to the Vermont decision. This act purports to deny federal recognition of same-sex marriages. As of November 1999, thirty states had adopted some form of antigay marriage law, and similar measures were being introduced in a number of other states (Lambda Legal Defense and Education Fund, 1999). Whether these antimarriage recognition laws apply to civil unions or are constitutionally enforceable remains to be seen.

The closest that any state has come to granting legal sanction to gay marriages was in Hawaii in December 1996, when a Hawaii court ruled that lesbian and gay couples should be allowed to marry. This ruling was appealed, however, and in the meantime an amendment to the state constitution was passed banning same-sex marriages. When the case was heard in December 1999 by the Hawaii Supreme Court, the state constitutional amendment was used to justify that court's decision to turn down the appeal, thus closing the door in that state to same-sex marriages, at least for now.

ANTIDISCRIMINATION LEGISLATION

Denying same-sex couples the legal right to marry is only one of the many ways in which gay people are reminded that they do not have the same status in society as heterosexuals. Federal law and most state laws still do not include sexual orientation as one of the classes of persons entitled to protection from discrimination in the areas of employment, housing, and public accommodations. The majority of states do not have laws protecting the rights of homosexuals in regard to family issues such as adoption, custody, guardianship, and so forth. However, a dozen states and many local communities have passed laws and ordinances that directly or indirectly protect against sexual orientation discrimination.

Now this issue may seem of only remote interest to children. Nevertheless, as they mature into adolescence and a greater awareness of their own sexual orientation, they may begin to realize that there are laws that specifically discriminate against those like themselves and once again be reminded that others perceive that something is wrong with them.

Though ordinances and statutes actively prohibiting legal protections based on sexual orientation are still on the books in a number of states and communities, a 1996 U.S. Supreme Court decision, *Romer v. Evans,* ruled that such laws are unconstitutional. In this decision the Court struck down a Colorado constitutional amendment that would have repealed any legal protection for homosexuals and prevented passage of any such laws in the future. The amendment was struck down because the Court deemed that it denied constitutional protection to a particular group of people. Justice Anthony Kennedy wrote the majority opinion and said that no state ". . . can deem a class of persons a stranger to its laws."

This decision will certainly be used to challenge such statues and ordinances in other states and communities. For example, three states, Florida, Utah, and Mississippi, have passed bills specifically banning gay couples from adopting children, and many other states achieve the same goal by banning any unmarried couples from adopting, thereby ipso facto excluding gay couples. It will be surprising if such statutes are not challenged sometime in the future as being unconstitutional.

The *Romer v. Evans* decision, though far-reaching in protecting gay rights, applies only to laws that overtly deny gays certain rights. The decision leaves open the question of whether homosexuals must be specifically included as a protected class in regard to laws and public policies. Many states, even those with strong laws against discrimination in employment, housing, and public accommodations, do not include sexual orientation as a protected class. At the time of this writing, only eleven states, along with the District of Columbia, actually include sexual orientation in their prohibitions against employment and housing discrimination. These states are California, Connecticut, Hawaii, Massachusetts, Minnesota, Nevada, New Hampshire, New Jersey, Rhode Island, Vermont, Wisconsin, and Maryland. Even federal nondiscrimination laws do not mention sexual orientation, although attempts have been made for many years by certain congressmen and senators, primarily Democrats, to try to pass an Employment Non-Discrimination Act, which includes sexual orientation. However, even though this act has failed to get through Congress, President Clinton, in 1998, issued an executive order to prohibit discrimination in the federal civilian workforce based on sexual orientation. Indeed, President Clinton was the first U.S. president to speak out publicly on gay and lesbian issues.

ANTIDISCRIMINATION POLICIES IN THE SCHOOLS

For children and adolescents it is the educational policies regarding gay, lesbian, and bisexual students and teachers that have the most immediate impact upon their lives. Though a number of local school districts have added sexual orientation to their nondiscrimination policies and procedures, these are still in the minority. And only four states specifically prohibit harassment and discrimination of students and teachers based on sexual orientation. California is the most recent (October, 1999) to join Wisconsin, Massachusetts, and Connecticut in enacting such legislation.

There is some protection, however, for gay students, even in schools in the states where sexual orientation is not included in their nondiscrimination policies. In 1998, in Fayetteville, Arkansas, a seventeen-year-old student and his parents filed a sex discrimination complaint to the Office of Civil Rights (OCR) of the U. S. Department of Education. The OCR monitors compliance in schools with Title IX, a federal statute that prohibits sex discrimination, including sexual harassment, in schools receiving federal funds. This young student, William Wagner, had been harassed at school over a period of several years—harassment which resulted in physical injuries, not to mention psychological injuries. The school's failure to protect their son led William's parents to withdraw him from school and file a complaint with the legal assistance of Lambda Legal Defense and Education Fund, a legal group that works specifically on issues of civil rights for gays and lesbians.

Shortly after the Wagners' complaint, the OCR revised the Title IX guidelines to add explicit reference to "gay or lesbian students" as also being covered by federal prohibitions against sexual harassment. The OCR proceeded to reach an agreement with the Fayetteville Public Schools that required the school district to overhaul its policies and procedures and to train faculty, staff, and students in regard to the issues of harassment directed at gay or lesbian students. Thus, the Title IX federal statute can be used to require public schools receiving federal funding to protect their gay students from harassment.

Gay students are also protected by the Fourteenth Amendment, which requires equal treatment under the law. The *Romer vs. Evans* Supreme Court decision referred to earlier would clearly apply to gay students despite the fact that many in our country have negative opinions about homosexuals.

In the document, *Just the Facts About Sexual Orientation and Youth* (1999), these protections for gay students have been pointed out through the following statements:

> The legal mandate of equality for gay and non-gay students alike is not limited to circumstances of harassment; it applies to all decisions a public school official might make that would treat lesbian, gay, and bisexual students differently. School officials should follow the law by ensuring that the factor of real or perceived sexual orientation does not result in a decision that treats these students as less than equal to other students on the basis of sexual orientation. (p. 9)

The document goes on to note that there are increasing numbers of gay/straight alliances in schools and that from a legal standpoint these groups need to be treated in the same manner as any other student groups.

Another remedy for gay students who have been discriminated against or harassed in the school setting now lies in the civil courts. I have already referred, for example, to a 1996 civil suit brought before the federal Seventh Circuit Court of Appeals in Wisconsin (Logue and Buckel, 1996). In this suit a young man, Jamie Nabozny, sued his former school district and the administrators of the middle school and high school he had attended. Jamie claimed that the schools did not protect him from repeated harassment and assault by other students because he was gay. The case had previously been dismissed without a hearing by the federal district court in Madison, Wisconsin, and the Lambda Legal Defense and Education Fund took the case on appeal. The Seventh Circuit Court agreed to hear the case, noting in its unanimous decision the fact that Jamie had valid equal protection claims based on sexual orientation and gender discrimination. The Circuit Court used the previous Supreme Court *Romer v. Evans* decision to support its equal protection ruling in this case.

Jamie testified during the trial that he had been shoved, spit upon, beaten, and urinated upon by other students over a period of several years in both middle school and high school. The schools failed to put a stop to the abuse, finally causing Jamie to drop out of school and pursue a GED. The jury found that the school district itself was not liable because it had a policy in place prohibiting discrimination based on sexual orientation. However, the three administrators were found liable by the jury for their failure to protect the student. In a settlement before the jury had the chance to determine damages, an agreement was reached, awarding $900,000 to Jamie. The results of this case send a clear message about antigay violence in the schools and the responsibility of school administrators to prevent abuse and harassment of all their students.

Bringing civil suits against school administrators, forcing them to provide protection to gay students should certainly not be necessary, but when leadership from individual school districts and school administrators is lacking, the leadership may have to come from higher levels. State political leaders, such as governors and superintendents of public instruction, have the power, if they choose to exercise it, to recommend policies of various kinds for all public schools. An example of this kind of leadership has been referred to in an earlier chapter

describing the Governor's Commission on Gay and Lesbian Youth in
Massachusetts. Governor William Weld, concerned over statistics on
the prevalence of gay youth suicide, took active steps to identify the
dangers facing gay and lesbian students in the public schools and to
make recommendations and provide funding for implementing policies to protect these students. Massachusetts is now probably the safest state in the country for gay students.

DON'T ASK, DON'T TELL: GAYS IN THE MILITARY

In 1999, the violent murder of a gay soldier by another soldier on
an Army base brought to public attention once again another policy
that has reminded gays of how they are perceived by the broader society and tells gay youth wondering about a career that the armed services may not be an affirming or even a safe place for them. In the early
1990s, conflict over gays in the military was frequently in the public
eye and General Colin Powell, who was then chairman of the U.S.
Joint Chiefs of Staff, proclaimed quite publicly that allowing openly
gay individuals to serve in the armed forces would destroy morale
and jeopardize the effectiveness of the military.

Bill Clinton, openly courting the gay vote in his presidential cam-
paign, made commitments to lift the ban on gays in the military, and
he attempted to follow through on this promise after his election.
However, he was subjected to extreme pressure from Congress and
from the generals, leading him to back off. Instead the infamous, hypocritical policy known as "Don't ask, don't tell, don't pursue" was
adopted in all branches of the armed services. This policy merely
stated that if you don't say that you are gay and you stay in the closet,
you should not be asked about your sexual orientation and you can
continue to serve. The policy is one of blatant prejudice and it has
been quite successful in one sense, which may have been what its cre-
ators wanted. It has led to more discharges on the basis of sexual orientation than had occurred prior to the policy's adoption, when just
the discovery that a member of the armed services was gay was
enough to get him or her discharged.

A recent survey of more than 71,000 officers and enlisted personnel by the Pentagon's inspector general revealed that 37 percent of
those responding reported having witnessed or experienced harassment based on sexual orientation in the past year. A legal aid group,

the Servicemembers Legal Defense Network, has reported that incidents of verbal abuse and physical assaults against gay and lesbian service members more than doubled from 1998 to 1999 and discharges were 13 percent higher in 1999 than in 1993 (Vistica, 2000).

ARCHAIC SEX LAWS

There are still a number of states with laws on the books outlawing sodomy, oral sex, and various other forms of adult consensual sex. Such laws sometimes, for example in Arizona, use terms such as "Crime Against Nature" or "Lewd and Lascivious Acts" (Arizona's law has recently been repealed). Despite the fact that these laws typically apply equally to heterosexual activity, they have been mischaracterized and employed in various ways to penalize homosexuals. The implication is that any homosexual must by his or her very nature be breaking these laws. The issue has been brought up in child custody cases, for example, to argue that a homosexual parent should not have custody of a child because the parent is obviously breaking the law just by being homosexual. Of course, not mentioned in such cases is that many heterosexuals engage in the banned sexual acts and the same argument is not used against them. In fact, in some states the laws apply only to homosexuals.

Not all homosexuals engage in anal or oral sex and one's sexual orientation does not define one's actual sexual practices. However, the objection to these laws is that they are applied prejudicially against homosexuals and are meant to do so. These laws again send a message to gay youth, when they reach the age where they become aware of them and understand their intent, telling them that their sexual behavior may be a criminal offense.

Court challenges against these so-called "sodomy" laws are among the current goals of the Lambda Legal Defense and Education Fund. It is in the states where the laws apply only to homosexuals where Lambda hopes to first challenge the laws on the basis of constitutional equal-protection rights. Although privacy rights are also violated by these laws, they are likely to be easier to challenge on the basis of equal-protection rights. Arizona recently repealed its sodomy law.

BOY SCOUT POLICIES

The Boy Scouts of America have long held to a tradition of excluding known homosexuals from the right to be in their organization, whether as leaders or as members, though this policy has never been specifically delineated in the organization's official manuals. Linda Greenhouse, writing in *The New York Times* (April 16, 2000 and April 27, 2000) about a case which recently came before the U.S. Supreme Court, reports that approximately ten years ago, James Dale, an Eagle Scout assistant scoutmaster, was expelled by the Boy Scouts after the organization discovered he was gay from a newspaper article about a gay students' group he was involved in at Rutgers University.

Dale filed a suit against the Boy Scouts, using as a basis New Jersey's antidiscrimination laws. New Jersey is one of the few states whose laws forbid discrimination in organizations of public accommodation based on sexual orientation. In 1999, the New Jersey Supreme Court denied the Boy Scouts' claim that the First Amendment freedom of association clause allowed them to exclude homosexuals and ruled in Dale's favor. The New Jersey court's argument was that the Boy Scouts is a "public accommodation" covered by the state antidiscrimination laws, and so could not discriminate on the basis of Dale's sexual orientation.

The Boy Scouts appealed and the case came before the U.S. Supreme Court. Greenhouse, in *The New York Times* article, pointed out that the case galvanized the religious right on the Boy Scouts' side and various other civil rights and professional organizations—including the American Psychological Association, which filed an amicus brief—on Dale's side. She quoted Dale as saying that ". . . learning someone is gay tells you nothing about his or her political party, religious beliefs, lifestyle, or moral code. . ." while the Scouts argued that Dale's sexual orientation represented a repudiation of the "scouting values" that he is obligated to exemplify.

In June 2000, the Supreme Court reached a five-to-four decision in the case, giving the Scouts the right to ban Dale and any other open homosexual from leadership positions. The decision stated that the Boy Scouts' rights of free expression and free association would be violated if they were forced to accept gay Scout leaders. The Scouts' discriminatory policy is now protected by the courts. The court decision, although it does not refer specifically to whether the Scouts can exclude gay boys from membership, certainly implies that and tells gay boys that they can never aspire to leadership in the organization.

The Boy Scouts, long touted as an organization open to all boys who want to join, has now been challenged and is being forced to admit that "all boys" does not include homosexual boys. What about a boy who may join the Scouts at an early age and during adolescence realizes that he is gay? Is he supposed to go to his Scout leader and confess, or is he supposed to pretend to be heterosexual and give up any ideas he might have of being a Scout leader in the future, or is he supposed to just quietly keep his secret and feel guilty for not meeting the "moral" code of the Scouts?

POLICIES ABOUT AIDS

In 1991, the National Commission on Acquired Immune Deficiency Syndrome issued a report, *America Living with AIDS,* calling attention to the failure of the nation, including political leaders and medical leaders, to help prevent the spread of AIDS. The report pointed out how prejudice toward homosexuality was a major factor in the failure to address the AIDS crisis early on. The Commission also warned of the dangers of restricting open discussion of AIDS issues:

> Yet AIDS education and prevention efforts continue to be stymied by an unwillingness to talk frankly about sexual and drug use behaviors that risk the spread of HIV. . . . Reticence about discussing sex has become an obstacle to the implementation of lifesaving prevention programs. This withholding of potentially lifesaving information raises serious ethical problems. (p. 21)

Despite this warning, and many years later, this same reluctance to provide accurate information in clear and simple language about HIV/AIDS, especially to youth and even more especially to gay youth, continues. For example, in Arizona, an AIDS education statute makes AIDS education voluntary. Schools may choose not to provide AIDS education at all. Given the lethality of this disease and its epidemic proportions it seems unethical, at the very least, to make AIDS education merely a choice that schools may or may not make. It is simply tragic for us to fail to give our youth the information that may save their lives because we are squeamish about discussing sex—particularly gay sex. In addition, the statute goes on to say that when schools do choose to offer AIDS education, certain restrictions apply. Three statements in the statute are clearly meant to specifically restrict the information regarding AIDS prevention for gay youth, a particularly troublesome fact given that gay males are still the highest-risk population for HIV infection in this country. The three statements in the Arizona Revised Statutes are:

No district shall include in its course of study instruction which:

1. Promotes a homosexual lifestyle.
2. Portrays homosexuality as a positive alternative lifestyle.
3. Suggests that some methods of sex are safe methods of homosexual sex.

Most teachers reading these restrictions and trying to figure out how to educate gay youth about sexuality and about HIV/AIDS prevention will be hesitant to even mention the word "homosexual." The negativity toward homosexuals in the statute is blatant and is just one more message to our gay youth that we do not want to talk about who they really are and that the schools and the state want them to remain invisible and silent. The fact that their homosexual orientation is so closely tied in the public eye to a stigmatized disease is just one more blow to their self-image and one more added stress in their lives.

ANTIGAY HATE CRIMES

One of the better-known researchers in the area of antigay hate crimes is Gregory M. Herek. For a seminal article in *American Psychologist* (1989), Herek collected statistics from numerous sources, including his own research, and pointed out the pervasiveness of the problem, the serious psychological as well as physical harm resulting from antigay crimes, and how such crimes foster a climate of fear among gays and lesbians. Over the years various national and state legislative bodies have enacted hate crimes legislation that specifically permits more severe criminal penalties when the crime is one of bias against a certain identifiable group of people. But the legislation often does not include sexual orientation of the victim as a basis for identifying the crime as a hate crime.

President Clinton was a strong supporter of national hate crime legislation that would include those crimes committed due to the victim's sexual orientation, and he called upon Congress at numerous times to pass such legislation. So far this has not happened, although the U.S. Senate recently passed an unrelated bill including a hate crimes legislation amendment, one which added sexual orientation and disability to the groups being protected. By September 2000, this bill had come to a nonbinding vote in the House of Representatives, where it passed 232 for and 192 against. The legislation has still not passed.

We must certainly consider that gay youth are likely to be affected by antigay hate crimes, both when they are victims themselves, and when they come to realize that people are beaten up or even killed just because they are gay. When gay youth are themselves actual victims of hate crimes, including those attacks in the school setting, they are less likely than other youth to report such crimes. Failing to include sexual orientation in hate crime legislation suggests that homosexuals constitute a group that does not deserve the same protection as other minorities and sends a powerful message to gay youth as well as gay adults.

CHANGING LAWS AND POLICIES CAN HELP OUR GAY CHILDREN

Thus we see that the larger society, in the forms of its laws, its policies, and its practices, continues in many instances, and despite certain constitutional protections to the contrary, to tell its gay members that they are of less worth than their heterosexual friends, neighbors, and families. We see why the gay civil rights movement is so important for gay children and adolescents. Gay activists, in their demands that we change those laws and public policies that discriminate against sexual minorities and in ensuring that protective laws and policies are enforced, tell gay youths that they have supporters and tell them that they are not morally inferior, that nothing is wrong with them, and that they will be able to fulfill their dreams.

Chapter 16

Transgender Identity

Transgender is a term that refers to a range of gender-atypical sexual identities. The term describes a group of individuals who do not exactly fit into the stereotypes of what it means to be male or female in a given society. This group is rather poorly understood and has probably experienced even more stigma than have gays and lesbians. Such individuals are relatively rare compared to the estimates of the incidence of homosexuality in the population. However, exact data are difficult to obtain and the incidence can only be guessed at.

Some in the gay community are reluctant to include transgendered persons in their political or social movements for fear that the public is only beginning to be more tolerant of homosexuality and that to include this "exotic" group may alienate some of those in the heterosexual community who support gay rights and gay equality. Some in the transgender community do not necessarily want to be brought into the gay community for various reasons, including the fact that many of these individuals do not consider themselves homosexual.

We know so little about transgendered persons and the range of experiences and identities that they exemplify, but the little we do know suggests that as children they may be more conflicted and confused than are children who will grow up to be gay or lesbian. The discrimination in society toward children who do not behave or look the way we expect them to look and behave according to their gender can be even more extreme than antigay discrimination.

I include this chapter on transgender identity because the effects of the prejudice and the basis of the prejudice toward transgendered persons is similar to that which gays experience. Children who are struggling with their gender identity are also children who may need the kind of help we are discussing in this book. To give a few definitions to begin this topic, I will refer to the work of Caitlin Ryan and Donna

Futterman (1998). These authors suggest the following classification for transgendered persons.

GENDER BENDERS

Gender benders may behave or dress in a gender-atypical way in order to make a political statement or to express their difference from conventional society. Some others are referred to as cross-dressers and their motivation is not dissatisfaction with being male or female, but instead is often to entertain others, for example, as "drag queens" or just for fun at parties and so forth. These particular cross-dressers are usually homosexual but are not necessarily so.

TRANSVESTITES

The term transvestite is primarily used for individuals who cross-dress only for purposes of sexual gratification. Although a distinction has not always been made between those individuals who cross-dress (i.e., generally males who dress as females for sexual arousal, and those who cross-dress for entertainment, as in "drag" shows or just for fun), this distinction is now being made by most researchers. These two groups differ significantly from each other. J. Michael Bailey (1996), referring to the research of Talamini (1982), points out that transvestites (those who cross-dress for sexual gratification) typically cross-dress in private and are usually married, heterosexual men. Transgender activists may not consider these individuals to be members of their community and may dislike the term because of its negative connotations, since in the DSM-IV the term used is "transvestic fetishism" and it is considered a psychiatric disorder. The often secretive nature of this behavior as well as the fact that these individuals are usually heterosexual males suggests that they may not consider themselves within the category of "transgender."

ANDROGYNE

Androgyne refers to individuals who assume or possess characteristics of both genders in order to feel emotionally complete. I am not aware of any other writers or researchers who include such individuals in the transgender category, although a generic interpretation of the term certainly would not prohibit such an inclusion. It is sometimes thought that people who can free themselves from gender stereotypes and fulfill all aspects of their human nature without concern about whether they are violating gender norms may be the most psychologically healthy people. This is obviously not a common viewpoint.

TRANSSEXUALS

Transsexuals are not psychologically comfortable with their gender. If they are male they may describe themselves as trapped in a female body and vice versa if they are female. In other words, their gender identity, that is, their sense of being male or female, does not match the physical body into which they were born. On an emotional and psychological level, their biological sex seems alien to who they are.

Transsexuals often seek to change their bodies to match their sense of identity and to change their physical appearance to be more like that of the opposite sex. Ryan and Futterman describe different ways of being transsexual. There are those who seek sex reassignment surgery to modify their genitals and those who do not. Hormonal treatment to change secondary sex characteristics as well as electrolysis to remove hair are also forms of treatment and may be used both by those who also plan to have surgery and those who do not. Sex reassignment treatments are generally carried out in gender identity clinics staffed with medical and mental health professionals. Reputable clinics and physicians usually recommend psychological evaluations and counseling prior to treatment and also recommend living full time as the opposite sex for at least a year before starting any surgical procedures.

Transsexuals who are transitioning from one gender to the other may be at various stages in their transformation and are referred to as pre- and postoperative. For those who go through hormonal treatment without the surgery, often the reason for not following through with surgery is the expense, and for the female-to-male transsexual (FTM) the results of surgery are not always satisfactory. Male-to-female transsexuals (MTF) are reportedly more likely to have genital surgery. However far along in the process, and despite the difficulties and the expense, the motivation for some is extremely strong to achieve the goal of living as the gender one believes he or she was meant to be. This will not always, however, involve genital surgery or even hormone therapy.

J. Michael Bailey's Definitions of Transsexuals

Bailey (1996) further defines two types of transsexuals. The classic transsexual is someone who, from a very early age, felt that he or she was born into the wrong body. The male-to-female transsexual was usually a very feminine boy and the female-to-male transsexual was usually a masculine girl. Cross-dressing is common, beginning in childhood and continuing in adolescence. Trying to pass as a member of the opposite sex is also common. Bailey describes a second type of transsexual, which he refers to, following Blanchard (1991), as autogynephilic. This is a completely different condition in which the beginning of wishing to change one's gender does not occur until later in adulthood. These individuals are usually in their thirties (Blanchard, Clemmensen, and Steiner, 1987) when this desire emerges, and they are almost always heterosexual males who have a history of transvestitism. Ryan and Futterman (1998) use a different terminology, referring instead to primary transsexualism, emerging in early childhood, and secondary transsexualism, emerging during or after puberty.

Gender Identity Disorder

In the American Psychiatric Association's *Diagnostic and Statistical Manual-IV,* the term transsexual has been dropped and the term "gender identity disorder" is now used both for children who show extreme gender dysphoria, meaning unhappiness with their gender, and for adults who wish to change their gender. Defining children and adolescents as having a gender identity disorder carries a host of ramifications. First of all, it has suggested to some that those children who display behaviors and mannerisms more like those normally associated with the opposite sex, for example, the so-called "sissy boys" in Green's (1987) study, are psychologically disturbed and in need of treatment to eliminate their "symptoms." This diagnosis may further suggest that these children will grow up to be transsexual. Actually, as noted already, the majority of the extremely feminine boys in Green's study grew up to be gay or bisexual, not transsexual men. In other words, these feminine boys were not destined to become transsexual men.

A close reading of the DSM-IV indicates that, according to the diagnostic criteria for gender identity disorder, children who simply fail to conform to stereotyped sex-role behavior, for example, those girls who are "tomboys" and those boys who are "sissys" should not be given the diagnosis. The DSM-IV clearly states that just because a child does not fit the cultural stereotype of masculinity or femininity is not a reason to say that she or he has a psychiatric disorder. In addition to being gender atypical, the child or adolescent must also openly express that he or she wants to be or actually believes he or she is the opposite sex and must show persistent discomfort with his or her gender. Many even extremely feminine boys do not exhibit these characteristics. Though they may exhibit feminine characteristics, they do not believe they are girls nor do they say they want to be girls. For the gender identity disorder diagnosis to be given, there must also be evidence of clinically significant distress or impairment in social or other important areas of functioning as a result of the dissatisfaction with gender. If these characteristics are not present the diagnosis should not be used.

Nevertheless, the diagnostic term gender identity disorder may lead some clinicians to conclude that children who are merely somewhat gender atypical have a disorder that needs to be corrected or treated. Instead it is society's lack of acceptance of cross-gender behavior that creates the problem, not the behavior itself. The gender stereotypes that define masculinity and femininity by certain rigid patterns of behavior and appearance and the insistence that children behave in ways that fit these stereotypes can seriously distort a child's social and emotional development. As noted earlier, several current writers (Pollock, 1998; Gabarino, 1999; and Real, 1997) have commented on how the imposition of rigid masculine stereotypes harms the emotional development of young boys, and contributes to male anger and violence in our society.

I have already referred to some of the difficulties faced by young children who do not fit into the stereotyped roles for their gender, especially when they are in unaccepting families and/or schools. Ryan and Futterman refer particularly to the difficulties faced by adolescents who believe they are transsexual, recommending counseling and support as well as help in clarifying any confusion about sexual identity. Some of the youth who are engaging in cross-dressing or other opposite-gender behavior may really be homosexual and under the mistaken impression that this is part of being gay. A therapist who is skilled in working with youth who have sexual identity issues can help in resolving conflicts about identity and in helping the youth become more self-accepting and hopeful about their futures, however their identity evolves.

Adolescents may sometimes want and seek sex reassignment surgery but this is not available until adulthood, given the assumption that identity in adolescence may still be fluid and sex reassignment surgery is necessarily final. Ongoing counseling will certainly be needed in these cases. Ryan and Futterman suggest that without emotional support and understanding a truly transsexual adolescent will be at high risk for depression, feelings of alienation and hopelessness, and even suicide.

In regard to whether a transsexual adult has a psychiatric disorder (i.e., gender identity disorder), even though the desire to be the opposite sex might not in itself be considered a disorder, the intense distress that the individual feels in being trapped in a body that does not represent his or her inner self is certainly sufficiently disabling in many people to be considered a mental disorder. Once a transformation to the opposite sex has been completed, presumably the individual should no longer be impaired in his or her psychological functioning. Little follow-up research exists, however, to verify this assumption.

INTERSEXED

Intersexed refers to individuals who are born with mixed sexual characteristics, that is, with some mixture of male and female characteristics. The percentage of male and female characteristics can vary considerably. The practice has long been to make a sexual assignment by surgery during infancy and then to raise the child as whichever gender was chosen. This is a practice that has become very controversial and adults who have had such surgery performed on them during their infancy have begun to raise the issue of whether this is a violation of one's body. These individuals are suggesting that the practice of surgery in infancy should be stopped and that the inter-sexual can choose or not choose surgery once he or she reaches adult-hood.

A study recently reported at a Lawson Wilkins Pediatric Endocrine Society meeting in Boston by Dr. William G. Reiner (2000) from the Johns Hopkins Children's Center, found that male children who were born without penises and raised as girls, nevertheless grew up consid-ering themselves to be boys. The study tracked the development of twenty-seven children who had no penises but had male genes and hormones. Twenty-five of these children were sex-reassigned and their parents raised them as girls. Nevertheless, all were more like boys as they grew up, engaging in the rough-and-tumble play typical of male children. Fourteen of them declared themselves to be boys, in one case as early as age five. The two who were not sex-reassigned and instead were raised as boys grew up fitting in well with their male peers and were better adjusted psychologically than the children who had sex-reassignment surgery. The conclusion of Dr. Reiner and his associates was that gender identity is determined before birth and that it is the effect of hormones on the brain that influenced gender identity.

NATURE VERSUS NURTURE REVISITED

The notion that medical science can determine or choose a particu-lar gender for a child in infancy and that raising the child in that gen-der role will be successful has been challenged in a recent book titled *As Nature Made Him: The Boy Who Was Raised As a Girl,* by John Colapinto (2000). This author recounts the story of identical twin brothers born in April 1966. At the age of eight months, both boys were taken to the hospital for circumcision. One of the twins' penises was accidentally sliced off during the surgery.

The parents were, of course, traumatized and sought medical ad-vice. According to the book they were advised by John Money, the sex researcher at Johns Hopkins University, that the child be cas-trated, given a cosmetic vagina, and raised as a girl. The assumption was that sexual identity was plastic or changeable and could be deter-mined by the environment. Despite being encouraged with dolls and doll houses and dressed as a girl throughout childhood, the child, pre-viously Bruce but renamed Brenda, seemingly never accepted being female. According to the author of the book, Brenda never felt or acted like a girl. He even insisted on standing up when he went to the bathroom. He stated that he had felt like a freak all during childhood and finally, at the age of fourteen learned about his past, and "reclaimed his male identity."

The book goes on to describe how Brenda became David, had a penis facsimile constructed through plastic surgery, and is happily married to a woman with three children, whom he has adopted. David does comment on what he learned as a result of living as a girl: he thinks that experience has made him more sympathetic to females than is the average man.

Comments

The influences of society told the children in Reiner's study and in the case of the boy in Colapinto's book that they were one gender, and yet they resisted those pressures. These stories make us think about the factors that lead transsexual individuals, whose outward and biological make-up suggest one gender identity, to develop an inner identity that is the opposite. All of the social influences on those children who are transsexual tell them that they are one gender and yet their identity resists these powerful influences and they proclaim themselves to be something different from what their bodies seemingly are. Does Reiner's conclusion that prenatal hormonal effects on the brain, no matter what social influences occur, indelibly determine one's gender identity, possibly apply also to transsexuals?

Chapter 17

Personal Stories of Transsexuals Growing Up

MICHAEL (ONCE MICHELLE)

Michael is a twenty-nine-year-old transsexual, a biological female who has partially made the transition to being male. He dresses as a male and is taking hormone treatment. He remembers that as early as four or five years of age, when his name was Michelle, he was dissatisfied with the gender he was taught to be. He didn't like girls' clothes or shoes and by age seven he demanded a boy's haircut. In regard to toys, he liked both Barbie dolls and G.I. Joe action figures. His tendency was to like the boys' toys somewhat more. He also felt more comfortable playing with boys and would have what seemed like crushes on girls. His drawings of people were neither male nor female but a combination. Looking back to his childhood he feels that he was fascinated with androgyny, the blending of the male and female genders. The times he was happiest during childhood were when he was included in activities with his father and brother, such as playing chess or going fishing. These times were like male bonding experiences, whereas his mother and sister bonded by going shopping, something Michael had no interest in.

In elementary school Michael felt like an outsider, felt that he never fit in with either the boys or the girls. He was teased for being boyish. By the seventh grade he started acting more feminine, thinking that he had to do this because he felt so alone and he wanted to have friends. His parents were really happy when he started taking care of his appearance and acting more "ladylike." He followed his older sister's example in the feminine role, but looking back he describes it as "like my drag days."

His first feeling that he actually wanted to change the ". . . gender I was assigned to" occurred at the onset of puberty. He was disturbed by the bodily changes of growing breasts and menstruation. He felt he must have done something wrong and when his older sister tried to explain it he couldn't relate to what she was telling him. He became anorexic and the thinness made him look more boyish. He tried to tell his parents that he wished he were a boy and they told him that was impossible and foolish. He was affected by having no role models, since he was like neither parent. The closest person to being a role model for him was a very masculine female mechanic that his Dad knew. In high school Michael started wearing dresses more and more and felt as if ". . . I had to overcompensate or everyone would find out something about me, would discover who I was. But wearing dresses made me feel like I was in drag, playing a part."

Gradually, by his senior year, Michael had gone back to his tomboy days. He started hanging out with a rough crowd of boys, drinking and partying. When he was asked about what he wanted to be when he was an adult and did he want to get married, Michael realized he had no answers. He felt he had no future. He had a sense of hopelessness about what his life would be and a feeling that "Nothing I can do will ever be all right. There's something wrong about me, something not quite right." It was a very sad time for Michael.

About this time, his senior year in high school, he developed a relationship with another girl. It began as a friendship but he began to dream about her. It wasn't really a sexual relationship but there was a strong emotional involvement and they were devoted to each other. He didn't label it at the time as sexual. Later, when he had sex with men, he did it because he thought that is what he should do. By around age twenty-two he began to identify as lesbian, and then by age twenty-four or twenty-five as a "butch lesbian." Once he was having a conversation with another lesbian and told her that he had always wished he did not have any breasts. She reacted very badly and that made Michael realize that his feelings were different from the lesbians he was associating with. He does not remember exactly when after that that he first discovered what transsexual meant. This discovery led him to start exploring and trying to find out more about drag queens, about what it meant to be transsexual, and about changing his gender.

When Michael started talking to his adult friends about changing his gender, only a few of his friends were supportive. Some of those who were critical suggested that his desire came from believing that because he was butch he must also be transsexual and they did not agree with this. Other friends told him they thought his desire to change his gender was the result of his having been sexually abused by his father when he was a child. Michael does not believe that his sexual abuse had anything to do with his need to change his gender. In fact, he thinks that the sexual abuse delayed the process of understanding his gender dysphoria and what it actually meant. Michael believes that the abuse led to his being so detached from himself and from his own body that sex just became something he had to do and do without thinking. Michael was very close to his father and never conceived of breaking his trust by telling about the abuse, as that would have been losing his world. Only much later did he realize how much his father had hurt him.

About three years ago, Michael made the decision to actually begin the transitional process of changing his gender. At this point he is receiving hormonal therapy and lives as a male. He thinks he might conceivably at some point have what is called "top surgery" or a mastectomy. In regard to actually going through genital or sex reassignment surgery, he is unsure about whether he would ever want to do that. The female-to-male surgical procedures are less successful and more complex than male to female. Michael added, "For me it's not really about having a penis."

Michael added some thoughts about the philosophy among transsexual people. Many do not choose to go so far in the transitional process as to have genital surgery, but there is some sense in the transsexual community that you are not quite where you should be unless you go all the way. He thinks there is danger in the view that the further along you are in the transitional process the more validated you are. This view may be changing, however, and there is the alternative view that maybe an individual does not have to be totally one or the other, totally male or totally female, in order to be accepted, to be validated. He explained by saying, "I look at sexuality as being more fluid and fluctuating. It's possible that twenty years from now I will still be preoperative."

Michael pointed out an additional complication from a legal standpoint—that it is sometimes difficult to legally change your gender unless the transition is complete. Also, medical care is complicated when a transsexual is in transition. It is important to identify physicians who are educated about transsexuality and to inform the transsexual community who these providers are so that they will not be humiliated by uninformed or unaccepting medical professionals.

Insofar as whether transsexuals are gay, straight, or bisexual, they can be any of these. Michael identifies as gay, being that he is currently in a relationship with another female-to-male transsexual. Though he is also attracted to women, he does not consider himself to be heterosexual. He jokes, "I was queer before transitioning and I still am, but actually I think maybe I am more bisexual." In describing how complex the whole process can be he describes the situation in which a heterosexual woman transitions to become male and then is sexually attracted to women and is thus still heterosexual.

Michael was asked about what we can do to help transsexual youth as they are growing up. He found this a difficult question to answer, commenting that so much of childhood is figuring out one's role. So even if you are raised in a family environment where you are allowed to express yourself and told you can be whatever you want, how can the family give you enough confidence and strength through support in the home to enable you to deal with rejection when you have to go out into the world? Nevertheless, it would probably be helpful for families to just say to a girl, for example, if you want to be a fireman, be a fireman. Don't shame your children or make them feel guilty because they do not act in gender appropriate ways.

Michael thinks that transsexuals should associate themselves with the gay rights groups and the gay activists in that they all have similar problems with prejudice and with the need for similar types of support and resources. Michael's final comment was, "Transgendered people are the monkey wrench in queer politics in a lot of ways."

ALEXANDER (ONCE VIRGINIA ALLEGRA)

Alexander is a thirty-nine-year-old African-American transsexual male who was born female and named Virginia Allegra. He was called Ginny while he was growing up. As early as five years of age he remembers being told about girl things and boy things. He realized that everyone thought he was a girl, that they were all telling him he was a girl, and that they were all wrong. He thought the basic concept of male and female was OK, but with him they just got it wrong. He was encouraged by his family toward female activities and clothing but he resisted. He would have tantrums if he had to wear a dress or if he was encouraged to play with dolls. At first his family seemed to think it was kind of cute, then it became irritating, and finally they just ignored it.

Alexander held onto being just a tomboy as long as possible. He was taunted and teased a lot at school and called a dyke. He could not be "girly-girly" and he thought the only alternative was to be an egg-head or nerd. So he applied himself to his studies, became one of the smart ones and got straight As. The most devastating thing in his childhood and adolescence was the onset of puberty, especially start-ing to menstruate. He felt that it was like a death. Menstruation was the symbol, the proof, that he was really a female and all his hopes that somehow "they" had gotten it wrong and that he would be able to be what he knew he was meant to be were dashed. Alexander had re-ally believed that his body would catch up to other males. Now he had to reconcile how he felt with what was happening to his body. He thinks he "went a little crazy." This was a confirmation that he would never fit in, that he would have a lifetime of pain and unhappiness.

At this time, even though his sexual attractions were more toward females, he started having sex with males. But then he began to think that maybe he was a lesbian and he had heard about "butch lesbians." He thought maybe this was about the closest he could be to what he felt and so when he was nineteen he began having sexual experiences with women.

Alexander's mother was not happy when he told her he (she) was a lesbian and she told him that it was hard enough to be black in this world, but to be both black and lesbian is too much. His mother's ma-jor concern was how society was going to treat him. Her concerns were not religiously based. Alexander admired his mother, who was a very strong, independent woman. She was a role model, a woman who could be strong and take care of herself. He had never been taught that girls were weak and could only do certain things. Alexan-der thinks that his experience goes against the theory that it is the op-pression of women in our society which causes some women to think that they want to transition to be men.

Even though Alexander, sometime around 1974 or 1975, heard about the transsexual male-to-female tennis player Renee Richards, who had had a sex change, it never occurred to him that the alternative female-to-male sex change was possible. When he was in his early twenties he met someone who knew someone else who had changed from female to male. This was the first time that he began to think a transition might be possible for him.

However, at the time Alexander was, in his own words, "screwed up." He described himself as a drunk and as severely depressed and suicidal. He was also very connected to the lesbian community and he thought he would lose their support if he came out as a transsexual. Some in the lesbian community fear that transsexuals threaten the gay community by influencing the straight community to believe that gays are the same as transsexuals, that all gay men want to be women and all lesbian women want to be men. Since Alexander's primary problems at this time were his addiction and his depression, he could not really deal with "trans" issues until these things got resolved. His depression became so severe that he almost died from a drug overdose. Going into a coma and being on life support after this suicide attempt left Alexander with some mild residual neurological problems.

When Alexander finally dealt with the addiction and depression through therapy and lifestyle changes he began to seriously think about sex-reassignment. His main reason for holding back was his mother. Their relationship was very strong and she had always stuck by him through everything. He was afraid of losing her. He was thinking he would wait until his Mom died. However, he realized that she was very healthy and not likely to die soon. So he made the decision, despite his reservations, to begin the transition by starting hormonal therapy.

Around this time he met D., his current partner. They met as lesbians and each did not know the other was transsexual until later. Alexander's mother was not upset about D.'s being transsexual because it made her think that the two of them could be a heterosexual couple. However, her pleasure about his new relationship told him how difficult it would be for her to know that her "daughter" was transsexual. When Alexander's voice started to change as a result of the hormone treatment, he thought maybe she was starting to figure out what was happening, but when she questioned him he brushed it off. Eventually Alexander decided to write his mother a letter, telling her the truth, and then just accept whatever happened. After the letter she phoned him and told him that she did not understand but that she loved him and would support him. Some of his other family members have been less positive. His stepfather and one of his brothers will not speak to him. One of his sisters refused to call him Alexander for a long time.

At this point Alexander has been on hormones for an extended period of time and has had a mastectomy. He has a very masculine appearance. He does not necessarily plan on genital surgery. From Alexander's viewpoint, the quality of the outcome of the female-to-male genital surgery is very poor. If the quality were the same as the male-to-female surgery he would probably proceed. Alexander feels he can be a man without a penis, although he recognizes that not all female-to-male transsexuals feel the way he does. Alexander believes that some female-to-male transsexuals will be miserable until they have a penis. Alexander is more concerned about his particular relationship with D., a relationship that is not based on whether either one has a penis or not, but that is based on mutual love and respect.

Alexander was asked about what childhood experiences might be helpful or not helpful to those children growing up feeling that psychologically they do not belong to the gender they were born with. In his own case he said that his mom did not really force him to be "girly" or to act in a certain way. He feels that would have been very damaging. Also his mother did not use religion to cast judgment upon his gender-atypical behavior. He thinks that for children having difficulty with accepting their biological gender, the opportunity to talk to a nonjudgmental therapist who could be understanding would be extremely valuable. It would have to be someone with whom the child feels safe and with whom he or she can be open. He or she should be able to say, I think I'm a girl or I think I'm a boy.

Should transsexuals and transgender persons join the gay rights and gay advocacy groups and organizations or should they have their own? How are their issues similar to or different from those of gays and lesbians? In Alexander's opinion the struggles of the two groups are linked. He believes it is the same fight, the fight against sexual oppression. He believes that the "trans" community wants to be linked to the gay community. However, he believes that the gay/lesbian/bisexual community resents the fact that it has been building an infrastructure and is enjoying a measure of power and success and that the "trans" community is trying to ride on its coattails. Gays also complain that the media tend to focus on transgendered people and the "drag queens" and that this links them to the gay community, suggesting that all gays are really transsexuals, people who want to be the opposite sex. But Alexander believes that it will demean gays if they refuse to accept the transgender population because it suggests a pattern of an oppressed group oppressing another oppressed group.

Alexander's opinion about the DSM-IV diagnosis of gender identity disorder is that it should not be eliminated, but should be applied very carefully in a way that is not transphobic or homophobic. In Alexander's words, "Being 'trans' is a psychological state, it is not an abnormal condition that needs to be corrected." But the decision to actually go through sex-reassignment surgery is one that often needs the assistance of mental health professionals. He does not think that the decision to change one's gender should, however, be left solely in the hands of mental health professionals; the decision-making should be a shared process. He feels that there is an assumption among some professionals that if you are a woman who wants to become a man you will then want to sleep with women after the change (i.e., become a "nice heterosexual"). But if you are just going to end up being a gay man, then some professionals seem to wonder, what is the point of going through all of this? Alexander disagrees with this assumption, as he assumes do most transsexuals.

MARK (ONCE VIVIAN)

Mark (then Vivian) was born a biological female and is currently living as a male, following hormonal treatment and a mastectomy. He realized by age four or five that there was a difference between boys and girls and at about the same time he knew that he disagreed when his parents would say that he was a girl. He thought that his parents were just wrong and that eventually they would realize that he had been a boy all along. He did not argue with them so much as just repetitively question them. When they began to be exasperated with his questions he began to look for other ways to bolster his argument, looking for clues that he really was a boy.

Mark had an older and a younger brother and he was much more interested in sports than they were. He was also interested in climbing trees, playing cowboys and Indians, and so forth. He had no interest in dolls or girls' toys. He never became interested in makeup or clothes or hair styles. Although at the time he was going to school all the girls had to wear dresses and so he did also, the moment he got home from school he would put on his older brother's jeans and T-shirts. In his family Mark was accepted as different but OK. He was never made fun of or shamed for being so gender atypical. However, when his older brother beat up a friend who was calling Mark a lesbian, he learned that homosexuals were considered bad people.

The big shock came to Mark when he started developing breasts and having menstrual periods. These changes were just so contrary to what he had believed about himself. For awhile he still tried to hold on to the conviction that everyone was just wrong in defining him as a girl but it became harder and harder to maintain that belief. Finally he just started using the word person and refused to use the word girl in referring to himself. He did not mind being called a tomboy; that was much better than being called a girl.

During high school Mark enjoyed fantasizing about being a boy. He would pretend he was a boy disguised as a girl. In his fantasies he could be whatever he wanted to be. Mark did not know the word transgender or transsexual then, but he had heard about sex change operations (i.e., Christine Jorgenson and Renee Richards), and he began to think that was what he needed, but he could not figure out how he would ever be able to afford it or even how to go about it.

During his late adolescence, Mark began to realize he was attracted to gay men, but he remained somewhat sexually uninvolved until his early twenties when he began to identify as a lesbian. He had begun to meet lesbian women who were much more masculine than he and so he began to think, "I must be one of these people." He had several relationships with lesbians, mostly fleeting but several longer term. However, his feelings were still that he should be a man. He began to think more about actually changing his gender but he was sure that this would really upset his mother and would break her heart. He made the decision that he should wait until his mother died to change, wait until she died to be happy.

Through his early twenties, Mark's unhappiness with trying to be what he was not led to a period of alcohol and drug abuse. These were ways of medicating himself for his depression and for the psychological trauma of his constant dissatisfaction with his physical body. He had dropped out of college at age twenty, but later went back, got a degree in biology and worked in a medical laboratory. This led to an interest in becoming a physician and he applied to medical school. In medical school as a lesbian he joined a gay support group and experienced very little overt prejudice. He completed medical school and a residency, but still had never, as one supervisor later described him during those days, "seemed comfortable in his skin."

In 1997, Mark became increasingly troubled about living as a woman. By then he was a practicing physician and in his medical practice he sometimes treated transsexuals. He found that he was having feelings of resentment toward them. He started to analyze these feelings and he was led to the realization that what he resented was that these individuals had the courage to do something he wanted to do but was afraid to do, that is, change his gender. He began to think that the only way he could save himself, resolve his grief, and have a life that was meaningful was to become a man. Vivian would become Mark. He realized that in trying to suppress who he really was he had almost destroyed his life. He could not wait until his mother died in order to be himself. When his decision was made he experienced an inner peace he had never known in his life.

Mark began to tell his friends one by one what he had decided to do, found a therapist, found a physician, and began the process of changing his gender. At the hospital where he worked he wrote a letter to his immediate supervisor telling him what he planned to do and then told the other people he worked with. There were minimal repercussions and everyone seemed to accept his decision. In the process Mark has had hormonal therapy and a mastectomy. He has not experienced any difficulty in obtaining any of the treatment he has had. His physician did not require a seal of approval from a mental health professional, which apparently many clinics do. Mark may at some point have genital surgery or he may not. He does not feel the need for such surgery to feel comfortable and happy with himself just the way he is now. He dresses as a man and looks like a man. He feels that he is a man.

Mark did not tell his mother immediately after he had made the decision to change his gender, but he did tell her within a couple of months. Right at first she seemed sympathetic, but within a week or two she became angry. She would not address him by his new name and she would not address her letters to him with his new name. Mark never reacted with anger toward his mother, but with love and understanding, and it was not long before she came to accept that she could lose her child or she could embrace him as her third son. The latter is what she chose to do.

Mark thinks that one way to help children who are experiencing extreme gender dissatisfaction is to expand their options. He suggests letting them choose what they will be called and asking them what they want to wear. He recommends that there be more opportunities to participate in athletics without the restrictions imposed by gender stereotypes. He also thinks that teachers and school administrators need to have more understanding of transgender identity. Mark also suggests that transgendered adolescents and adults as well as children could be helped by increasing the penalties for hate crimes and educating the public about transgendered people.

Mark was asked about whether he knows of any data that show what percentage of transsexuals actually go through sex-reassignment surgery. He thinks these figures are unknown. It also depends upon who is defined as transgender. Some people who do not fit the standard stereotypes for their gender are not really interested in going through any type of medical or surgical procedures.

Mark was asked whether he considered himself straight, homosexual, bisexual, or none of these. Mark does not like any of these terms particularly. He prefers the word queer. It is a broader term and includes all those who are a little different, who do not fit the standard gender. If he is really pushed to identify himself he will say he is a gay man. However, he believes that inherently, he could be labeled as bisexual.

Mark supports the concept of transgendered persons being included within the overall gay rights movement. Many of the battles all of these individuals fight are against gender stereotyping. He also notes that many transsexuals have already been involved in gay rights causes. He thinks all sexual minorities are seeking human rights and fighting the same battle. Mark also thinks that he understands female oppression in a way most men do not, because he has experienced it himself.

JEFFREY/ADRIANNA

Jeffrey/Adrianna, forty-three years old at the time of this interview, was born a biological male and is in the process of transitioning to female. I use both names because Jeffrey is not completely "out" as a woman and I will refer to him, therefore, throughout this narrative as a male. For various financial and business reasons he is unable at this point to live fully as a woman. He has been receiving estrogen treatment for approximately eight months and is androgynous in his appearance. When he is dressed in male clothing he might be mistaken for a somewhat feminine gay man, but when dressed in female clothing he is probably able to pass relatively well as an attractive female. When I interviewed him he was dressed as a male and was in his business attire.

As a young child, Jeffrey had much less clear-cut unhappiness with his gender than did the previous three individuals whose stories you have just read. Also, his interests as a child were not stereotypically masculine or feminine but a bit of both. He always felt like somewhat of an outsider during childhood. He remembers being a little withdrawn, shy, and reserved. He always felt as if something in himself was missing. He had some physical problems related to a kidney ailment which for awhile interfered with his growth, so he was smaller than most other boys. By the age of seven or eight he remembers looking at his body, seeing his penis and wondering why he had this. It just seemed odd to him; his body didn't seem exactly right, but he could not figure out why he felt this way.

Jeffrey's family life was relatively happy. He had a very loving, intelligent, caring mother whom he still loves very much. His father was a career military man and somewhat distant and uninvolved. Overall, Jeffrey's childhood was relatively free of trauma or conflict. He was troubled, however, about vague feelings of something being wrong with his body and with feelings of emptiness and dissatisfaction. He was small and thin as a young boy and did not get chosen much for sports. He sometimes felt like an outsider and that something was missing, some missing ingredient, but he had no idea what it might be. He was not singled out by other children as so different that he was teased or shamed.

Jeffrey remembers that between age twelve and thirteen, as he was entering puberty and having sexual feelings, he began to visualize himself as a female in his sexual fantasies and when he masturbated. He felt confused about these feelings and he could not understand what these fantasies meant. During his childhood and adolescence Jeffrey does not remember ever having that strong feeling that many transsexuals describe, that he was really meant to be the opposite sex or that he wanted to be the opposite sex. His sense of gender identity seemed then to be male.

As an adolescent, Jeffrey considered himself heterosexual. He was not at all sexually attracted to males, but to females. Jeffrey was interested in looking at girls, was interested in what they wore, in their hair, their skin. The fantasies of himself as female continued throughout adolescence and young adulthood. At some point, in his early thirties, Jeffrey began buying women's clothes and wearing them in the privacy of his own home. His sexual fantasies were best realized while he was dressed as a female and imagined himself as being a female.

Jeffrey's sexual life was not extensive during this time. He liked women and had emotional relationships with them but was not very active sexually. Finally, at age thirty-five, he married a woman he had known only a few months. The two were not compatible in many ways and the sexual relationship was somewhat unsatisfying. Jeffrey was able to perform sexually but did not enjoy sex that much and seemed to find the whole notion of the male/female sex act somewhat unsatisfying. Sex was not frequent enough to please his wife. The two divorced after three years.

In his late thirties Jeffrey, for the first time, went out in public dressed as a woman. He went to a Halloween party, which perhaps gave him permission to act out his desires. This experience was so profound that he finally "came to grips" with his cross-dressing and came to realize that what he really wanted was to become a woman. He realized he was ". . . coming to the end of my emotional well-being and I couldn't live any longer as a man. Cross-dressing part-time was just not enough."

Jeffrey sought out psychotherapy with a psychologist who had expertise in working with transsexuals and he found a physician who, with the approval of the psychologist, agreed to prescribe estrogen. He began taking estrogen and the effect has been to transform him psychologically. He expected the physical changes but he was totally unprepared for what happened to him emotionally and mentally. Jeffrey feels that his entire sense of himself, of his identity, has changed. Acknowledging his femaleness and taking estrogen has affected his taste in music, has elevated his mood, has given him confidence in himself, has made him feel more whole and complete, less tense, and less impulsive. Jeffrey never felt sure of his masculinity and he feels much more self assured as a female. Jeffrey feels as though a miracle has happened. He believes his life would end if he had to stop taking estrogen. "My life would be over."

What is most difficult for Jeffrey right now is the necessity for going back and forth between male and female. Because of some business plans he is involved in currently, it is not possible for him to reveal his transsexuality to most people. It is very difficult for him to go back and forth in his mind and very disappointing because he cannot allow himself to totally be his female self. Jeffrey sees himself now as a "mixed recipe."

Jeffrey thinks he will be on estrogen for probably two years before the full effects are realized. He definitely plans then to have sex-reassignment surgery. He said that he knows some transsexuals do not feel the need for this final transformation, but he does. He does not think that he can ever be happy unless he has the physical body of a female. Insofar as whether he will then consider himself to be heterosexual and want to have sex with men, he is unsure. He thinks that until he has fully transformed himself into a woman he cannot predict what his sexual orientation will be. The idea of sex with another man has always repelled him. He thinks it would remind him that his body is not the way he wants it to be. Once his transformation to female is complete however, he thinks he may want to experiment with having sex with a man. He may, though, find that he still prefers sex with women and he guesses this would make him a lesbian. Jeffrey thinks that being a lesbian would be OK. What is most important to him is to be emotionally attached.

How can people like Jeffrey be helped as they are growing up? Jeffrey says that understanding parents are needed because they control so much of a child's life. Nurturance and love are important in childhood and he feels that he received these, more perhaps from his mother than from his father. Society should accept "shades of gray." He worries that most people do not understand transsexuality or a gender identity that does not conform to the norm because these differences are not what society expects.

When Jeffrey was asked about the DSM-IV diagnosis of gender identity disorder, he said that he thinks it is needed because it is very emotionally disturbing to have these feelings of wanting to change your gender. He knows that he is dissatisfied with his gender and he thinks that people like himself should have professional help to adjust to their troubling experiences.

Jeffrey agrees with Michael, Alexander, and Mark that trans-gendered persons should be included in the gay movement. Many of their issues, especially having to deal with prejudice toward those who do not exactly fit the mold, are similar.

COMMENTS

Certain themes stand out in these personal stories of individuals who define themselves as transsexuals. I cannot claim that these are universal truths or even substantive findings, as they are based on a very small sample. Nevertheless, it is striking how similar were many of the childhood experiences of Michael, Alexander, and Mark, all female-to-male transsexuals. All three at a very early age identified strongly with the gender that did not match their physical bodies. These individuals were not just flirting with the notion that they would like to be the opposite gender. Their convictions seemed to go far beyond just having mild preferences for certain types of clothing or activities. In fact, having to dress in girls' clothing for Michael felt so foreign that it was like being "in drag." In every way that could be imagined these three seemed to feel they were not the gender their bodies told them they were.

Alexander and Mark were even convinced that everyone around them telling them they were girls, not boys, was wrong. They felt that a terrible mistake was being made when they were treated as the gender opposite to the gender they felt themselves to be and that the mistake would soon be rectified. Then they would be recognized for who they really were, who they believed themselves to be.

On the other hand, Jeffrey, growing up as a male, did not have an unusual gender identity during childhood. He had some interests that were perhaps less stereotypically masculine, but not unusually so. He did have vague feelings of his body not being quite right, but none of the intense early identification with the opposite gender and no desire that he remembers to be a girl, at least not until later puberty. A recognition of his transsexuality came only when he was in his thirties, although cross-dressing and taking the female role in sexual fantasies occurred much earlier. These transsexuals have been referred to by

Bailey (1996) and Blanchard (1991) as autogynephilic transsexuals, and they are almost exclusively heterosexual men before the onset of their wish to change their gender. Jeffrey appears to be a classic example of this type of transsexual.

The personal stories of Michael, Alexander, and Mark were notable in the intensity of the emotional pain and confusion they experienced during childhood as a result of their extreme discomfort with their biological sex. The pain became even more severe as the bodily changes of puberty emerged and forced each of them to confront the reality of the mismatch between their bodies and their inner identity. Developing breasts and starting to menstruate were described by Alexander as "like death." As the reality of their lives grew in their consciousness they all experienced periods of either serious depression or feelings of hopelessness and used drugs or alcohol to escape the pain. There also was no one with whom they could discuss their feelings, no one to whom they could say "I don't feel like I'm a girl." Being so gender atypical while they were growing up, especially for Michael and Alexander, presented its own problems and probably would have even if they had not turned out to truly be transsexual.

Jeffrey's emotional pain emerged more gradually as he realized the significance and meaning his cross-dressing had acquired and realized that his emotional well-being was at stake. The compulsion to become a woman became paramount and he now feels that if he were unable to do so he would just as soon be dead.

Sexual orientation is a confusing issue in all of these individuals. Michael, Alexander, and Mark have had sexual experiences with both genders in their attempts to understand themselves and make sense of their gender identity. Each of them lived as lesbians for part of the time prior to their decision to change their gender. Michael and Alexander both identified for a period of time with "butch" lesbians but soon discovered that they did not really fit into this category either. Indeed, some of their other lesbian friends were horrified at the notion that anyone would want to get rid of their breasts or change their gender.

Michael, Alexander, and Mark seemed to be much less fixated on gender per se in their sexual orientation than they were on the strength and closeness of their relationships. Sexual orientation appeared to be more flexible and fluid than among many gays or heterosexuals. Two of the female-to-male individuals have partners who are also in the process of changing their genders from female to male. Does this make these couples heterosexual or homosexual or neither? They all had difficulty answering the question regarding their sexual orientation. On the other hand, Jeffrey was for most of his adult life a heterosexual male who did not come to the realization that his cross-dressing was anything more than part of his sexual fantasies until he was in his thirties. At this point, however, he is not sure what his orientation will be once his transformation to female is complete. Maybe he could enjoy sex with a man but maybe he will, in effect, be a lesbian.

Another interesting point is that there seems to be no compelling need in these particular female to male individuals to complete the entire sex-reassignment procedure to the point of genital surgery. Hormonal therapy to masculinize their appearance and physical bodies and getting rid of their breasts seem to be sufficient to allow them to feel as though their bodies match their inner identity. Only Jeffrey is convinced that he must go the full route of sex-reassignment surgery in order to feel complete.

Each of these individuals supported the notion of transsexuals joining with gays, lesbians, and bisexuals in their political and social aims since they view the issues and the battles as similar. All these groups are seeking equal human rights and hoping that sexual oppression can eventually be eliminated.

These stories remind us of how "gender straightjacketing" (Pollock, 1998) and gender stereotyping may not only restrict and inhibit the development of ordinary heterosexual individuals and more so the development of gay and lesbian children, but may have even more devastating and traumatic effects on those children whose gender identities do not match their bodies. These stories also remind us that we have a group of children growing up who may be in even greater need of understanding and support for who they are than do the gay, lesbian, and bisexual children. The prejudice and stigma attached to the transgender population is so much greater than that attached to the gay population and there is even less understanding of their particular needs. And the suicidal risk for this population is believed to be even higher than it is for gays and lesbians. Ryan and Futterman (1998) in particular have noted the high suicide risk for transsexual teens due to lack of social and emotional support and feelings of hopelessness. The small size of the transgender population is probably a factor that contributes to prejudice. So many people have never had contact with a person they know to be transsexual, whereas almost everyone now personally knows someone who is an open homosexual.

Many of the recommendations that have been made in this book may also apply to the transgender population, but there is so little research to guide us that it is uncertain what additional or different strategies will be needed to help these children as they grow up. However, the recommendations for social acceptance and protection in homes, schools, and churches can certainly do no harm and are likely to be of at least some benefit.

Chapter 18

The Tipping Point

Malcolm Gladwell has written a popular book titled *The Tipping Point: How Little Things Can Make a Big Difference* (2000) in which he theorizes why major changes in our society often seem to happen suddenly and unexpectedly. He proposes that ideas are like infectious diseases and that they can spread in the same way as viruses through a few individuals, even a single person. He uses the term social epidemics to describe this phenomenon. Gladwell describes these social epidemics as follows:

> . . . the best way to understand the emergence of fashion trends, the ebb and flow of crime waves, or for that matter, the transformation of unknown books into bestsellers, or the rise of teenage smoking, or the phenomena of word of mouth, or any number of the other mysterious changes that mark everyday life is to think of them as epidemics. Ideas and products and messages and behaviors spread just like viruses do. (p. 7)

The "Tipping Point" of the book title is the point at which there is no going back. The epidemic, whatever it may be, is in full swing. A critical mass has been reached and the epidemic takes off and cannot be stopped. "The name given to that one dramatic moment in an epidemic when everything can change all at once is the Tipping Point" (p. 9).

You are probably wondering what these esoteric ideas have to do with gay children, with homophobia, and with what this book is supposed to be about. If we consider that homophobia is an attitude or viewpoint that should be subject to change through the spread of more positive views about homosexuals, then Gladwell's theories have relevance for our present purposes. I believe that Gladwell's concepts are also relevant in the sense that there may be a tipping point, a point at which the public attitude about homosexuals may reach that place where suddenly it is no longer acceptable to belittle them, where there is a sudden shift of opinion that makes a homophobic remark totally off limits, a point where the efforts of certain influential gay activists, the influence of people like yourselves who are reading this book, and the emergence of more and more individuals coming out as gay will have brought about a major shift in public opinion. Just as a virus spreads to the point where there is an epidemic of illness, so could the virus of acceptance spread so widely that some single event or some charismatic individual could capture the public attention and bring about a tipping point, after which homophobia would no longer be a socially acceptable prejudice.

So, to proceed with more details about Gladwell's theories, he proposes that our view of the world would be radically different if we were to follow the rules of epidemics in thinking about the way trends emerge, whether these trends be crime rates, fashion, smoking habits, or simply beliefs. Gladwell suggests that, although ideas and messages can spread like viruses, the spreading occurs by word of mouth, rather than by physical contact with the infectious agent. Certain types of individuals can play a big part in the spread of social ideas or messages, people who, by virtue of their expansive social networks or special ability to influence others, can help turn a minor trend into an epidemic. Social epidemics can be epidemics of self-destructive behavior, for example, the rise in teenage smoking, but can also be epidemics of constructive behavior change, for example, the decrease in smoking by adults.

The first principle in epidemics is the concept of contagiousness. To apply this word to a social epidemic we must think in terms of ideas and behaviors as spreading through a population in a way similar to the spread of an infectious disease. Even a behavior as innocuous as yawning can be contagious. If one person yawns another person nearby is likely to yawn also.

Gladwell says that another principle of epidemics is that little changes can have big effects and that social change, rather than being gradual and incremental, is often dramatically sudden. Gladwell explains that the concept of a tipping point came into being in the 1970s as an explanation by sociologists of the consequences of whites deserting city neighborhoods and fleeing to the suburbs. It was noted that whenever a certain percentage of the white community had left a neighborhood, perhaps 20 percent, the community would "tip" and all the remaining white families would suddenly move out.

Gladwell describes another example of this phenomenon in a study by a sociologist, Jonathan Crane, one of the sociologists who has written about the tipping point model. Crane (1989) learned that when high-status role models (i.e., professionals, managers, and teachers) move out of a neighborhood, the general well-being of those remaining in the neighborhood declines. It appears that measures of well-being among youth, such as teenage pregnancy rates and school drop-out rates, do not differ when there is between 5 and 40 percent of high-status workers living in a neighborhood. But when the percentage of high-status workers drops to 3.4 percent or below, suddenly school drop-out rates and teenage pregnancy rates nearly double. The disappearance of a certain bare minimum of positive role models can have a major impact on the social behavior of the youth population, the small change being the difference between 5 percent of positive role models and 3.4 percent, with the consequences being sudden and dramatic.

Another example of small changes producing major effects on certain kinds of behavior has been noted in the decrease in the New York City crime rate beginning in the 1980s and continuing into 2000. Gladwell attributes this reduction, at least in part, to the implementation of the "broken windows" theory as an approach to fighting crime. This theory was the brainchild of criminologists James Q. Wilson and George Kelling (1982), who proposed that crime spreads as a result of disorder in the social environment. When a broken window, for example, is ignored and not repaired, the people in the neighborhood begin to think that no one cares and that there is no mechanism for monitoring such things. More windows begin to be broken, sending a signal that this is an area of chaos and lawlessness. The theory suggests that many other relatively small problems such as graffiti and panhandling are like broken windows and that they can lead to more serious crime.

Gladwell writes that when William Bratton was hired in 1990 to head the transit police in New York City he subscribed to the broken windows theory and proceeded to attack crime on the subways with an approach some thought was dealing only with the trivial. The plan was to put a stop to people who were managing to avoid paying the subway fares by jumping over turnstiles or forcing their way through.

Though there were many more serious crimes occurring on the subways, Bratton decided to put the police to work stopping this seemingly minor crime. Offenders were immediately arrested, taken to the police station, fingerprinted, and checked for previous arrests. As it turned out, many of those arrests for minor offenses resulted in the discovery that the individual arrested had an outstanding warrant or was carrying a weapon. As a result of the police attention to the minor misdemeanor of fare beating, overall crime in the subways began to fall suddenly and dramatically.

When Rudolph Giuliani was elected mayor of New York, he appointed Bratton as the head of the New York City Police, where Bratton promptly applied the broken windows theory to police work throughout the city. No longer were offenses such as urinating in public, public drunkenness, or minor property damage ignored. Arrests were prompt and crime began to fall suddenly and dramatically. A tipping point in the incidence of violent crime was seemingly brought about by police attention to the small, "insignificant" crimes that had contributed to an atmosphere of disorder and to a pervasive feeling that no one was in charge. Just as broken windows may contribute to lawlessness, so might antigay remarks, seemingly insignificant in themselves, contribute to antigay hate crimes.

Getting back to homophobia and gay children, what we have discussed throughout this book is that the small daily incidents that gay children face, the things they hear, the things they see, the remarks that are made or not made in their presence, the messages in the media, all contribute to the way they feel about themselves. We have urged everyone who has a connection to children to recognize how little things can make a huge difference in the lives of gay children. Perhaps there is a tipping point for such a child, the moment at which, upon hearing a respected adult say something positive about gays, or upon realizing that someone he or she knows and admires is also gay, or upon viewing a TV show in which a character with whom he or she can identify is openly gay, the child suddenly realizes that he or she is not alone, that perhaps there is hope for the future. Just as broken windows may seem unimportant until we realize how they contribute to lawlessness, so too may the little antigay remarks seem trivial unless we recognize how they might affect the well-being of an individual gay child or adolescent.

I am also concerned with a tipping point, a turning point, not just for individual gay children, but in public attitudes, the point at which homophobic expressions and behavior suddenly become socially unacceptable. Every one of us who stands up for and is openly supportive of a gay friend, a gay son or daughter, or a gay parent, and every one of us who makes the casual affirming remark about gays in the presence of a child who might turn out to be gay, or makes these remarks to adult friends, family members, or co-workers, can be a part of a social epidemic, an epidemic that spreads an affirmation of homosexuals as bona fide members of society.

Some have suggested that the Matthew Shepard incident was a turning point which might lead to a monumental change in public attitudes about homosexuality. However, I suspect the tipping point has not yet come, but that slowly, through word of mouth, through the courageous openness of many of our gay youth, through the willingness of more and more gay adults to be open about their orientation, through the openness of famous or influential gay people (for example, the actress Ellen de Generes or U.S. Congressman Barney Franks), and through the small things each of us says and does, the virus of acceptance is being spread and will help to precipitate a real tipping point for our gay children and for all sexual minorities. We can sway opinions, perhaps even eliminate antigay prejudice and gender stereotyping, and change the world for children growing up gay, lesbian, bisexual, or transgendered and also for their families. We do not know when the moment might come when a threshold will be crossed, when perhaps one single small event or even one single individual will suddenly be the catalyst for monumental social change.

Comments

We are unable to predict exactly what the long-term consequences of antigay prejudice may be for any individual child who is growing up gay; whether there will be enduring scars or glowing success. The circumstances and influences are multiple, and are both benign and pernicious. As I have suggested throughout this book, among the factors that will influence the way a child adjusts to his or her different sexual orientation are the parenting abilities of his or her parents, the experiences he or she has with peers, the number of unrelated stresses he or she experiences during childhood and adolescence, the schools he or she attends, the influential adults in his or her life, personal, in-born strengths and weaknesses, and the many other helpful or harm-ful influences of the schools, the neighborhood, the community, and the society in which he or she grows up. Will gays always be outsid-ers to some extent? Or can we, with our increasing knowledge and understanding, reach out to include them and to take advantage of the special perspectives and insights they may have to offer society as a whole?

References

Aarons, L. (1995). *Prayers for Bobby: A mother's coming to terms with the suicide of her gay son.* New York: Harper Collins.

Allen, L. (1991). Sex differences in the corpus callosum of the living human being. *Journal of Neuroscience,* 11, 933-942.

Allen, L. S. and Gorski, R. A. (1992). Sexual orientation and the size of the anterior commissure in the human brain. *Proceedings of the National Academy of Science U.S.A.,* 89, (No. 7199).

American Association of University Women. (1993). *Hostile hallways: The AAUW survey on sexual harassment in America's schools.* Washington, DC.

American Psychiatric Association. (1994). *Diagnostic and Statistical Manual of Mental Disorders* (Fourth edition). Washington, DC: Author.

American Psychological Association. (1998). *Answers to your questions about sexual orientation and homosexuality.* Washington, DC: APA Public Interest Directorate.

American Psychological Association. (1999). *Just the facts about sexual orientation and youth: A primer for principals, educators, and school personnel.* Washington, DC: Public Interest Directorate.

Asidao, C. S., Vion, S., and Espelage, D. L. (1999). *Interviews with middle school students: Bullying, victimization, and contextual factors.* Poster session presented at the 107th Annual Convention of the American Psychological Association, Boston, MA.

Bailey, J. M. (1996). Gender identity. In R.C. Savin-Williams and K.M. Cohen (Eds.), *The lives of lesbians, gays, and bisexuals: Children to adults.* Fort Worth, TX: Harcourt Brace and Company.

Bailey, J. M. and Pillard, R. C. (1991). A genetic study of male sexual orientation. *Archives of General Psychiatry,* 48, 1089-1096.

Bailey, J. M. and Zucker, K. J. (1995). Childhood sex-typed behavior and sexual orientation: A conceptual analysis and quantitative review. *Developmental Psychology,* 31, 43-55.

Baker, J. M. (1998). *Family secrets: Gay sons—A mother's story.* Binghamton, NY: The Haworth Press, Inc.

Bell, A. P., Weinberg, M. S., and Hammersmith, S. K. (1981). *Sexual preference: Its development in men and women.* Bloomington: Indiana University Press.

Bem, D. J. (1996). Exotic becomes erotic: A developmental theory of sexual orientation. *Psychological Review,* 103(2), 320-335.

Blanchard, R. (1991). Clinical observations and systematic study of autogynephilia. *Journal of Sex and Marital Therapy,* 17, 235-251.

Blanchard, R., Clemmensen, L. H., and Steiner, B. W. (1987). Heterosexual and homosexual gender dysphoria. *Archives of Sexual Behavior,* 16, 139-152.

Bontempo, D. E. (1999). *At-school victimization of LGBQ Youths.* Paper presented at the 107th Annual Convention of the American Psychological Association, Boston, MA.

Borhek, M. V. (1979). *My son Eric: A mother struggles to accept her gay son and discovers herself.* Cleveland, Ohio: The Pilgrim Press.

Bowlby, J. (1969). *Attachment.* Volume 1. London: Hogarth Press and The Institute of Psychoanalysis.

Bowlby, J. (1973). *Separation.* Volume 2. London: Hogarth Press and The Institute of Psychoanalysis.

Boynton, R. S. (1996). God and Harvard. *The New Yorker,* November 11, pp. 64-73.

Browning, C. (1987). Therapeutic issues and intervention strategies with young adult lesbian clients: A developmental approach. *Journal of Homosexuality,* 14(1/2), 45-52.

Burgess, A. W., Groth, A. N., Holmstrom, L. L., and Sgroi, S. M. (1978). *Sexual assault of children and adolescents.* Lexington, MA: D. C. Heath.

Casper, V. and Schultz, S. (1996). Lesbian and gay parents encounter educators: Initiating conversations. In R. C. Savin-Williams and K. M. Cohen (Eds.), *The lives of lesbians, gays, and bisexuals: Children to adults* (pp. 305-330). Fort Worth, TX: Harcourt Brace College Publishers.

Cass, V. (1979). Homosexual identity formation: A theoretical model. *Journal of Homosexuality,* 4, 219-235.

Cass, V. (1984). Homosexual identity formation: Testing a theoretical model. *The Journal of Sex Research,* 20, 143-167.

Colapinto, J. (2000). *As nature made him: The boy who was raised as a girl.* New York: Harper Collins.

Coleman, E. (1982). Developmental stages of the coming out process. In J. Gonsiorek (Ed.), *Homosexuality and psychotherapy: A practitioner's handbook of affirmative models* (pp. 31-44). Binghamton, NY: The Haworth Press, Inc.

Coleman, E. and Remafedi, G. (1989). Gay, lesbian, and bisexual adolescents: A critical challenge to counselors. *Journal of Homosexuality,* 18(3/4), 70-81.

Collins, W. A., Maccoby, E. E., Steinberg, L., Hetherington, E. M., and Bornstein, M. H. (2000). Contemporary research on parenting: The case for nature and nurture. *American Psychologist,* 55(2), 218-232.

Crane, J. (1989). The epidemic theory of ghettos and neighborhood effects on dropping out and teenage childbearing. *American Journal of Sociology,* 95(5), 1226-1259.

D'Augelli, A. R. (1994). Lesbian and gay male development: Steps toward an analysis of lesbians' and gay mens' lives. In B. Greene and G. M. Herek (Eds.), *Psychological perspectives on lesbian and gay issues: Volume 1. Lesbian and gay psychology: Theory, research, and clinical applications* (pp. 118-132). Thousand Oaks, CA: Sage.

D'Augelli, A. R. (1996). *Victimization of lesbian, gay, and bisexual youths in community settings.* Paper presented at the 104th Annual Convention of the American Psychological Association, Toronto, Canada, August.

D'Augelli, A. R. (1998a). Developmental implications of victimization of lesbian, gay and bisexual youths. In G. M. Herek (Ed.), *Psychological perspectives on lesbian and gay issues: Volume 4. Stigma and sexual orientation: Understanding prejudice against lesbians, gay men, and bisexuals* (pp. 187-210). Thousand Oaks, CA: Sage.

D'Augelli, A. R. (August, 1998b). *Victimization of lesbian, gay, and bisexual youths: A community psychology perspective.* Paper presented at the 106th Annual Convention of the American Psychological Association, San Francisco, CA.

D'Augelli, A. R. (August, 1999). *Consequences of lesbian, gay, and bisexual youth victimization in schools.* Symposium presented at the 107th Annual Convention of the American Psychological Association, Boston, MA.

D'Augelli, A. R., and Rose, M. L. (1990). Homophobia in a university community: Attitudes and experience of white heterosexual freshmen. *Journal of College Student Development, 31,* 484-491.

Dew, R. F. (1994). *The family heart: A memoir of when our son came out.* New York: Addison-Wesley.

Diener, E., Suh, E. M., Lucas, R. E., and Smith, H. L. (1999). Subjective well-being: Three decades of progress. *Psychological Bulletin, 125,* 276-302.

Division 44/Committee on Lesbian, Gay, and Bisexual Concerns Joint Task Force (2000). Guidelines for psychotherapy with lesbian, gay, and bisexual clients. *American Psychologist, 55*(December), 1440-1451.

Duberman, M. (1991). *Cures: A gay man's odyssey.* New York: Dutton.

Erikson, E. (1950). *Childhood and society.* New York: Norton.

Fairchild, B. and Hayward, N. (1989). *Now that you know: What every parent should know about homosexuality.* San Diego: Harcourt, Brace, Jovanovich.

Franklin, K. (1998). *Psychosocial motivations of hate crimes perpetrators: Implications for educational intervention.* Paper presented at the 106th Annual Convention of the American Psychological Association, San Francisco, CA.

Gabarino, J. (1999). *Lost boys: Why our sons turn violent and how we can save them.* New York: The Free Press, Simon and Schuster, Inc.

Gibbs, N. and Roche, T. (1999). "The Columbine tapes." *Time Magazine.* December 20, pp. 40-51.

Gibson, P. (1989). Gay male and lesbian youth suicide. In M. R. Feinleib (Ed.), *Report of the secretary's task force on youth suicide. Volume 3: Preventions and interventions in youth suicide* (pp. 110-142). Rockville, MD: U. S. Department of Health and Human Services.

Gladwell, M. (2000). *The tipping point: How little things can make a big difference.* Boston, MA: Little, Brown and Company.

Gonsiorek, J. C. (1982). Results of psychological testing on homosexual populations. In W. Paul, J. D. Weinrich, J. C. Gonsiorek, and M. E. Hotvedt (Eds.), *Homosexuality: Social, psychological and biological issues* (pp. 71-88). Beverly Hills, CA: Sage.

Gonsiorek, J. C. (1988). Mental health issues of gay and lesbian adolescents. *Journal of Adolescent Health Care,* 9(2), 114-121.

Gonsiorek, J. C. (1991). The empirical basis for the demise of the illness model of homosexuality. In J. C. Gonsiorek and J. D. Weinrich (Eds.), *Homosexuality: Research implications for public policy* (pp. 115-136). Newbury Park, CA: Sage.

Gonsiorek, J. C. and Rudolph, J. R. (1991). Homosexual identity: Coming out and other developmental events. In J. C. Gonsiorek and J. D. Weinrich (Eds.), *Homosexuality: Research implications for public policy* (pp. 161-176). Newbury Park, CA: Sage.

Goode, E. (1999). "Group sends book on gay tolerance to schools." *The New York Times,* November 23.

Goodenow, C. and Hack, T. (August, 1998). *Risks facing gay, lesbian, and bisexual high school adolescents: The Massachusetts Youth Risk Behavior Survey.* Paper presented at the 106th Annual Convention of the American Psychological Association, San Francisco, CA.

Gottlieb, A. R. (2000). *Out of the twilight: Fathers of gay men speak.* Binghamton, NY: The Haworth Press, Inc.

Governor's Commission on Gay and Lesbian Youth. (1993). *Making schools safe for gay and lesbian youth: Breaking the silence in schools and in families.* Publication No. 17296-60-500-2/93-C.R. Boston, MA: State House.

Green, R. (1987). *The "sissy" boy syndrome and the development of homosexuality.* New Haven, CT: Yale Univerity Press.

Greenhouse, L. (2000). "Considering gay-scout case, Justices explore implications." *The New York Times,* April 16, p. A-1.

Greenhouse, L. (2000). "Considering gay-scout case, Justices explore implications." *The New York Times,* April 27, p. A-20.

Griffin, C. W., Wirth, J. J., and Wirth, A. G. (1986). *Beyond acceptance: Parents of lesbians and gays talk about their experiences.* New York: St. Martin's Press.

Groth, A. N. and Birnbaum, H. J. (1978). *Men who rape: The psychology of the offender.* New York: Plenum.

Haldeman, D. C. (1991). Sexual orientation conversion therapy for gay men and lesbians: A scientific examination. In J. C. Gonsiorek and J. D. Weinrich (Eds.), *Homosexuality: Research implications for public policy* (pp. 149-160). Newbury Park, CA: Sage.

Haldeman, D.C. (1994). The practice and ethics of sexual orientation conversion therapy. *Journal of Consulting and Clinical Psychology,* 62, 221-227.

Hamer, D. H. and Copeland, P. (1994). *The science of desire: The search for the gay gene and the biology of behavior.* New York: Simon and Schuster.

Hamer, D. H., Hu, S., Magnuson, V. L., Hu, N., and Pattatucci, A. (1993). A linkage between DNA markers on the X chromosome and male sexual orientation. *Science*, 261, 321-327.

Harris, J. R. (1998). *The nurture assumption: Why children turn out the way they do.* New York: Free Press.

Harry, J. (1982). *Gay children grown up.* New York: Praeger.

Herek, G. M. (1988). Heterosexuals' attitudes toward lesbians and gay men: Correlates and gender differences. *Journal of Sex Research,* 25, 451-477.

Herek, G. M. (1989). Hate crimes against lesbians and gay men: Issues for research and policy. *American Psychologist,* 44(6), 948-955.

Herek, G. M. (1994). Assessing heterosexuals' attitudes toward lesbians and gay men: A review of empirical research with the ATLG scale. In B. Greene and G. M. Herek (Eds.), *Lesbian and gay psychology: Theory, research, and clinical applications* (pp. 206-228), Thousand Oaks, CA: Sage.

Hershberger, S. L. and D'Augelli, A. R. (1995). The impact of victimization on the mental health and suicidality of lesbian, gay, and bisexual youths. *Developmental Psychology,* 31, 65-74.

Hetrick, E. S. and Martin, A. D. (1984). Ego dystonic homosexuality: A developmental view. In E. S Hetrick and T. S. Stein (Eds.), *Innovations in psychotherapy with homosexuals* (pp. 2-21). Washington, DC: American Psychiatric Association Press.

Hetrick, E. S. and Martin, A. D. (1988). The stigmatization of the gay and lesbian adolescent. *Journal of Homosexuality,* 15, 163-183.

Hooker, E. A. (1957). The adjustment of the overt male homosexual. *Journal of Projective Techniques,* 21, 17-31.

Hunter, J. (1990). Violence against lesbian and gay male youths. *Journal of Interpersonal Violence,* 5, 295-300.

Isay, R. A. (1989). *Being homosexual: Gay men and their development.* New York: Farrar, Straus, Giroux.

James, S. E. (August, 1996). Gays and lesbians in the family and the schools. In B. W. Litzenberger and M. Buttenheim, Chairs, *Symposium: Sexual orientation and family development.* Presented at the 104th Annual Convention of the American Psychogical Association, Toronto, Canada.

Jay, K. and Young. A. (1979). *The gay report: Lesbians and gay men speak out about sexual experiences and lifestyles.* New York: Summit.

Jenny, C., Roesler, T. A., and Poyer, K. L. (1992). *Assessing the risk that sexually abused children have been molested by recognizably adult homosexuals.* Unpublished paper. Denver, CO: The Children's Hospital.

Jenny, C., Roesler, T. A., and Poyer, K. L. (1994). Are children at risk for sexual abuse by homosexuals? *Pediatrics,* 94 (1), 41-44.

Just the Facts About Sexual Orientation and Youth: A Primer for Principals, Educators, and School Personnel. (1999). <www.apa.org/pi/lgbc/publications/just the facts.html>.

Lacayo, R. (1998). "The new gay struggle." *Time,* October 26, pp. 32-36.

Lambda Legal Defense and Education Fund (November 1, 1999). *National overview: The fight to win the freedom to marry.* Marriage Project Fact Sheet. New York: Author.

Leland, J. and Miller, M. (1998). "Can gays convert?" *Newsweek,* August 17, pp. 47-50.

LeVay, S. (1994). *The sexual brain.* Cambridge, MA: Massachusetts Institute of Technology Press.

Lipsyte, R. (2000). "An icon recast: Support for gay athlete." *The New York Times,* April 30, pp. A1 and A18.

Logue, P. M. and Buckel, D. (1996). Lambda success in Jamie Nabozny's case is victory against anti-gay student violence. *The Lambda Update: The Newsletter of Lambda Legal Defense and Education Fund,* 13(3), 1 and 6.

Marsiglio, W. (1993). Attitudes toward homosexual activity and gays as friends: A national survey of heterosexual 15- to 19-year-old males. *The Journal of Sex Research,* 30, 12-17.

Money, J. (1988). *Gay, straight, and in between: The sexology of erotic orientation.* New York: Oxford University Press.

Muller, A. (1987). *Parents matter: Parents' relationships with lesbian daughters and gay sons.* Talahassee, FL: Naiad Press.

National Commission on Acquired Immune Deficiency Syndrome. (1991). *America living with AIDS.* Washington, DC: U.S. Government Printing Office.

Patterson, C. J. (1994). Children of the lesbian baby boom: Behavioral adjustment, self-concepts, and sex-role identity. In B. Greene and G. Herek (Eds.), *Contemporary perspectives on lesbian and gay psychology: Theory, research, and applications* (pp. 156-175). Beverly Hills, CA: Sage.

Patterson, C. J. (1996). Lesbian and gay parents and their children. In R. C. Savin-Williams and K. M. Cohen (Eds.), *The lives of lesbians, gays, and bisexuals: Children to adults* (pp. 274-304). Fort Worth, TX: Harcourt Brace College Publishers.

Pollock, W. (1998). *Real boys: Rescuing our sons from the myths of boyhood.* New York: Henry Holt and Company, Inc.

Real, T. (1997). *I don't want to talk about it: Overcoming the secret legacy of male depression.* New York: Simon and Shuster.

Reiner, W. G. (2000). "Sexual identity study says womb is source." *Arizona Daily Star,* May 13, p. A-4.

Remafedi, G. (1987). Adolescent homosexuality: Psychosocial and medical implications. *Pediatrics,* 79, 331-337.

Remafedi, G. (1988). Homosexual youth: A challenge to contemporary society. *Journal of the American Medical Association,* 258, 222-225.

Remafedi, G., Farrow, J. A., and Deisher, R. W. (1991). Risk factors for attempted suicide in gay and bisexual youth. *Pediatrics,* 87, 869-875.

Remafedi, G., French, S., Story, M., Resnick, M., Michael, D., and Blum, R. (1998). The relationship between suicide risk and sexual orientation: Results of a population-based study. *American Journal of Public Health,* 88 (1), 57-60.

Roesler, T. and Deisher, R. (1972). Youthful male homosexuality: Homosexual experience and the process of developing homosexual identity in males aged 16 to 22 years. *Journal of the American Medical Association,* 219, 1018-1023.

Rutenberg, J. and Elliott, S. (2000). "Advertisers shun talk show as gay protest gains power." *The New York Times,* May 19, pp. A-22.

Ryan, C. and Futterman, D. (1998). *Lesbian and gay youth: Care and counseling: The first comprehensive guide to health and mental health care.* New York: Columbia University Press.

Sack, K. (1998). "Gay rights movement meets big resistance in S. Carolina." *The New York Times,* July 7, pp. A-1 and A-12.

Savin-Williams, R. C. (1990). *Gay and lesbian youth: Expressions of identity.* New York: Hemisphere.

Savin-Williams, R. C. (1996). Memories of childhood and early adolescent sexual feelings among gay and bisexual boys: A narrative approach. In R. C. Savin-Williams and K. M. Cohen (Eds.), *The lives of lesbians, gays, and bisexuals: Children to adults* (pp. 94-109). Fort Worth, TX: Harcourt Brace and Company.

Savin-Williams, R. C. (1998). *Suicide among sexual minority youths reconsidered: Methodological alert.* Paper presented at the 106th Annual Convention of the American Psychological Association, San Francisco, CA, August.

Savin-Williams, R. C. and Dube, E.M. (1996). Parental reactions to disclosure of their child's same-sex attraction. In B. W, Litzenberger and M. Buttenheim, Chairs, *Symposium: Sexual orientation and family development.* Presented at the 104th Annual Convention of the American Psychological Association, Toronto, Canada, August.

Schemo, D. J. (2000). "Survey finds parents favor more detailed sex education." *The New York Times,* October 4, pp. A1 and A23.

Schlant, E. (1999). *The language of silence: West German literature and the holocaust.* New York: Routledge Press.

Scripps Howard News Service (1993). "Court is told homosexuality may be inherited trait." *The Arizona Daily Star,* October 16, P. A-10.

Steckel, A. (1987). Psychosocial development of children of lesbian mothers. In F. W. Bozett (Ed.), *Gay and lesbian parents* (pp. 75-85). New York: Praeger.

Sullivan, A. (1998). *Love undetectable: Notes on friendship, sex, and survival.* New York: Alfred A. Knopf.

Sullivan, A. (1999). "What's so bad about hate? An unsentimental reflection on schoolyard shootings, Matthew Shepard, genocide, and the easy consensus on hate crimes." *The New York Times Magazine,* September 26, pp. 50-57, 88, 104, 112-113.

Talamini, J. T. (1982). *Boys will be girls: The hidden world of the heterosexual male transvestite.* Washington, DC: University Press of America.

Troiden, R. R. (1979). Becoming a homosexual: A model of gay identity acquisition. *Psychiatry,* 42, 362-373.

Troiden, R. R. (1988). Homosexual identity development. *Journal of Adolescent Health Care,* 9, 105-113.

Troiden, R. R. (1989). The formation of homosexual identities. In G. Herdt (Ed.), *Gay and lesbian youth* (pp. 43-73). Binghamton, NY: The Haworth Press, Inc.

Vistica, G. (2000). "Gay today: The military: One, two three, out." *Newsweek,* March 20, pp. 57-58.

Werner, E. E. (1982). *Vulnerable but invincible: A longitudinal study of resilient children and youth.* New York: McGraw-Hill.

Wilcox, B. L. and Tharinger, D. J. (1996). Discussants for Public Interest Miniconvention Symposium: *Lesbian, gay, bisexual development in adolescence—building resiliency.* Chair, Clinton Anderson. Presented at the American Psychological Association 104th Annual Convention, Toronto, Canada, August.

Williams, P. (1998). *Seeing a Color-Blind Future: The Paradox of Race.* New York: The Noonday Press/Farrar, Straus and Giroux.

Wilson, J. Q. and Kelling, G. (1982). "Broken Windows." *The Atlantic Monthly,* 249, pp. 29-36.

Zucker, K. J. (1990). Gender identity disorders in children: Clinical descriptions and natural history. In R. Blanchard and B. W. Steiner (Eds.), *Clinical management of gender identity disorders in children and adults* (pp. 1-23). Washington, DC: American Psychiatric Association Press.

Index

Order Your Own Copy of
This Important Book for Your Personal Library!

HOW HOMOPHOBIA HURTS CHILDREN
Nurturing Diversity at Home, at School, and in the Community

_____ in hardbound at $49.95 (ISBN: 1-56023-163-7)
_____ in softbound at $24.95 (ISBN: 1-56023-164-5)

COST OF BOOKS_____

OUTSIDE USA/CANADA/
MEXICO: ADD 20%_____

POSTAGE & HANDLING_____
(US: $4.00 for first book & $1.50
for each additional book)
Outside US: $5.00 for first book
& $2.00 for each additional book)

SUBTOTAL_____

in Canada: add 7% GST_____

STATE TAX_____
(NY, OH & MIN residents, please
add appropriate local sales tax)

FINAL TOTAL_____
(If paying in Canadian funds,
convert using the current
exchange rate, UNESCO
coupons welcome.)

❏ **BILL ME LATER:** ($5 service charge will be added)
(Bill-me option is good on US/Canada/Mexico orders only;
not good to jobbers, wholesalers, or subscription agencies.)

❏ Check here if billing address is different from
shipping address and attach purchase order and
billing address information.

Signature_____

❏ **PAYMENT ENCLOSED: $**_____

❏ **PLEASE CHARGE TO MY CREDIT CARD.**

❏ Visa ❏ MasterCard ❏ AmEx ❏ Discover
❏ Diner's Club ❏ Eurocard ❏ JCB

Account # _____

Exp. Date_____

Signature_____

Prices in US dollars and subject to change without notice.

NAME_____

INSTITUTION_____

ADDRESS_____

CITY_____

STATE/ZIP_____

COUNTRY_____ COUNTY (NY residents only)_____

TEL_____ FAX_____

E-MAIL_____

May we use your e-mail address for confirmations and other types of information? ❏ Yes ❏ No
We appreciate receiving your e-mail address and fax number. Haworth would like to e-mail or fax special
discount offers to you, as a preferred customer. **We will never share, rent, or exchange your e-mail address
or fax number.** We regard such actions as an invasion of your privacy.

Order From Your Local Bookstore or Directly From
The Haworth Press, Inc.
10 Alice Street, Binghamton, New York 13904-1580 • USA
TELEPHONE: 1-800-HAWORTH (1-800-429-6784) / Outside US/Canada: (607) 722-5857
FAX: 1-800-895-0582 / Outside US/Canada: (607) 722-6362
E-mail: getinfo@haworthpressinc.com
PLEASE PHOTOCOPY THIS FORM FOR YOUR PERSONAL USE.
www.HaworthPress.com

BOF00

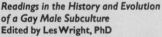

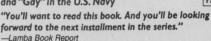